God and the Crisis of Freedom

God and the
Crisis of Freedom

Biblical and Contemporary Perspectives

RICHARD BAUCKHAM

Westminster John Knox Press
LOUISVILLE • LONDON

Scripture quotations, unless otherwise indicated, are from the New Revised Standard Version of the Bible, copyright © 1989 by the Division of Christian Education of the National Council of the Churches of Christ in the U.S.A., and are used by permission.

Grateful acknowledgment is made to SPCK Publishing for permission to reprint excerpts from chapter 7 of *The Bible in Politics* by Richard Bauckham. Copyright © 1989 by SPCK Publishing. Reprinted by permission.

Grateful acknowledgment is made to The Continuum International Publishing Group Ltd. for permission to reprint excerpts from the following material: (A revised version of) R. Bauckham, "Tradition in Relation to Scripture and Reason," in R. Bauckham and B. Drewery, eds., Scripture, Tradition and Reason: A Study in the Criteria of Christian Doctrine (Edinburgh: T & T Clark, 1988), pp. 117–145. Reprinted by permission. Excerpts from (a shorter version of) R. Bauckham, "Freedom in the Crisis of Modernity," which is to be published in W. F. Storrar and A. R. Morton, eds., *Public Theology in the Twenty-First Century* (Edinburgh: T & T Clark, 2002). Reprinted by permission.

Grateful acknowledgment is made to IVP Books for permission to reprint excerpts from R. Bauckham, "Egalitarianism and Hierarchy in the Biblical Traditions," in A.N.S. Lane, ed., The Interpretation of the Bible (Leicester: Apollos, 1997), pp. 259–273. Reprinted by permission.

Grateful acknowledgment is made to Grove Books Ltd. for permission to reprint revised versions of *Freedom to Choose* and "Scripture and Authority Today." Reprinted by permission.

Book design by Sharon Adams
Cover design by Eric Walljasper
Cover Art: Alberto Ruggieri/Getty Images

First edition
Published by Westminster John Knox Press
Louisville, Kentucky

This book is printed on acid-free paper that meets the American National Standards Institute Z39.48 standard. ♾

PRINTED IN THE UNITED STATES OF AMERICA

02 03 04 05 06 07 08 09 10 11 — 10 9 8 7 6 5 4 3 2 1

Library of Congress Cataloging-in-Publication Data

Bauckham, Richard.
    God and the Crisis of Freedom : Biblical and Contemporary Perspectives / Richard Bauckham.— 1st ed.
        p. cm.
    Includes bibliographical references and index.
    ISBN 0-664-22479-2 (pbk. : alk. paper)
    1. Liberty—Religious aspects—Christianity. 2. Liberty—Biblical teaching. 3. Christianity and politics. I. Title.

    BT810.3 .B38 2002
    233'.7—dc21

                                                                2002071341

To Graeme Rutherford

Contents

Preface

The essays collected in this book have a variety of origins, over a dozen or so years. The idea of collecting them, along with new material, as a book came to me in the summer of 2000, when I was giving a lecture on "Authority in a Postmodern Church and World" at the Spirituality Centre of St. John's Anglican Church, Camberwell, Victoria, Australia. Graeme Rutherford, then vicar of St. John's (now bishop of Newcastle, New South Wales), had invited me to give this and other lectures. Without his invitation I would probably not have had the idea of the book, and in gratitude for this, as well as his faithful interest in my theological endeavors, I am dedicating this book to him.

Others played a part in the origins of other chapters. It was Tim Dean who invited me to write a book on *The Bible in Politics* for the series of Third Way books that were published in the late 1980s. Chapter 1 had its first form as a chapter of that book. The late Michael Vasey, when we were both members of the Grove Spirituality Series group, suggested I write a short book on freedom for that series. It appears here in revised form as chapter 2. Chris Sugden invited me to speak on "Scripture and Authority" to a conference of Anglican bishops in Dallas, and Ian Paul asked me to expand the material to make a volume in the Grove Biblical Studies Series; these were the origins of chapter 3. Chapter 4 was originally one of a group of responses by members of the Doctrine Committee of the Scottish Episcopal Church to Richard Holloway's book *Godless Morality*.

Three other chapters originated as contributions to *Festschriften*, and I should like to mention here the scholars they were written to honor. Chapter 5 was written for the late Richard Hanson, chapter 6 for David Wright, and chapter 8 for Duncan Forrester. All have made their own distinguished contributions to aspects of the themes of this book.

These personal connections are only some of the many that work of this kind reflects. That true freedom only exists in dependence and relationship is surely validated in the experience of everyone who writes a book.

Richard Bauckham

Introduction

God and the Crisis of Freedom

I am writing five weeks after the terrorist "attack on America" of September 11, 2001. One of the first things President George W. Bush said about it was to call it an "attack on freedom." There is, of course, a simple and minimal sense in which a terrorist act of such horrifying scale is an attack on freedom: it attacks people's freedom to go about their daily lives in reasonable security. But much more than this was undoubtedly meant. Bush continued, "America was targeted because we are the brightest beacon for freedom and opportunity in the world." The freedom that had been attacked was the freedom for which the United States and her Western allies had stood throughout the period of the Cold War. In the days immediately after the catastrophe, we heard again about "the free world," a term that had been largely redundant since the "collapse of communism," and the military operation in Afghanistan was eventually entitled "Enduring Freedom." The freedom to which Americans rallied with patriotic fervor in September 2001 was the freedom of representative democracy, freedom of speech and worship, and the free market economy. But from the viewpoint of their attackers, the targets were plainly chosen for their symbolic meaning as symbols of oppression rather than freedom. The Pentagon and the World Trade Center stood for American military and economic domination of the rest of the world. In the eyes of the terrorists, American "freedom" might be freedom for Americans, but not for those for whom they imagined themselves to be fighting. There are certainly many people in the world to whom the massacre of thousands on September 11 was abhorrent, but who do not experience American power as an unmixed blessing.

It is clear that the term *freedom* is fraught with ideology. It is one of the keywords of the myth by which the modern age has lived. This is not at all to say

1

that the term has no reference to real aspects of life that people experience and value. But the word also has mythic power. Its transcendent resonances exalt it as the one thing that must at all costs be achieved and defended. Not only is it, in the rhetoric of war, the defining feature of Western civilization under attack; it is also, for the typical individual of Western culture, the most essential and the most alluring of individual needs and aspirations. Its power lies partly in its comprehensive and ambiguous character. As Isaiah Berlin, like many others, observed, the meaning of freedom "is so porous that there is little interpretation that it seems able to resist."[1] A glance through the quotations gathered in the epilogue to the present book will illustrate the point. Freedom has all the power and all the danger of a radically under-determined notion. Left to function at the level of habitual associations and unexamined assumptions, it becomes a serious obstacle to understanding, manipulable by all kinds of political and commercial interests, sheltering desires that would seem much less admirable without its cover, enticing rather than convincing us, offering in cut-price versions what can be truly had only at considerable cost. Moreover, the meaning of freedom is unstable, because it necessarily varies with the context of world-interpreting or life-directing meaning to which, in any instance, it belongs. Its meaning relates to that of other big and malleable terms, such as goodness, justice, equality, rights, truth, progress, authority, and God. Contemporary rhetoric of freedom requires some demythologizing or deconstruction if we are to get beyond rhetoric to the issues that are really at stake at the present juncture of political, social, cultural, and religious history in the West.

The "crisis of freedom" in my title is not the one evoked by the war against terrorism, but the crisis within Western societies, for which freedom is becoming almost the only common value. To many it appears that the emphasis on individual freedom in our culture has led to the breakdown of community and of family structures, the increasingly isolated lives that many people lead, the decay of traditional values, and the competitive acquisitiveness and commercially driven hedonism that have taken their place. Key symptoms that there is a problem can be observed in the way that freedom has come to seem opposed to other values with which it used to seem much more at home: faithfulness, commitment, neighborliness, self-discipline, responsibility. Above all, in contemporary Western society freedom threatens community and entails rejection of authority.

We cannot address this situation adequately by seeking, as some do, merely a balance between values that must be held in tension. It is likely that all societies experience some tension between the human need to be independent and

---

[1]Quoted in J. Webster, *Barth's Moral Theology* (Edinburgh: T. & T. Clark, 1998), 100.

the human need to belong, as also between the need for autonomy and the need to be guided by authority. But in our society such tensions are in danger of becoming sheer contradiction. Freedom seems to lead inevitably to the atomization of society. And while freedom is one of the most popular of all concepts, authority has become one of the most unpopular, virtually defined as the enemy of freedom, synonymous with authoritarianism and coercion. If this is problematic, the problem lies in the kind of freedom, the particular understanding of freedom that has become culturally dominant: freedom conceived exclusively as the emancipation of the individual from all constraints and as unlimited freedom of choice. This is also a freedom constructed as the only absolute in a radically relativistic culture. In our increasingly postmodern culture, all other values become matters of individual preference. It is dubious how freedom can survive at all in such splendid isolation.

An argument of this book is that we need to recover a richer understanding of freedom that is possible only by restoring it to a context of other values and beliefs. Such a freedom is not threatened but formed and nurtured by dependence, belonging, relationship, community, and—importantly and most controversially—authority. Of course, these other factors must themselves be understood as hospitable to freedom and productive of freedom if they are to function in positive synergy with an appropriate form of freedom. Such an understanding of freedom, drawn primarily from the resources of the Bible and the Christian tradition, is developed in chapters 1, 2, and 8 of this book. But because this understanding of freedom is drawn from the resources of the Bible and the Christian tradition, it also requires reference to God. Implicitly all along but explicitly in chapter 8, we shall argue that only in a context of values and practices of life in which human life is related to God can such freedom be adequately sustained. Outside such a context, reduced to the absolute right of the individual to self-determination, freedom degenerates into the banal pursuit of self-gratification or the cynical pursuit of power.

God is undoubtedly implicated in the contemporary crisis of freedom. In the present cultural climate, belief in God—or, at least, in a God to any extent resembling the Christian God—seems to many incompatible with human autonomy. The modern process of emancipation of life from traditional authorities has also been a process of liberation from God. Can we think and speak about the authority of God in such a way as to affirm human freedom, as given and nurtured by God? Are there Christian understandings of both freedom and authority that avoid the dilemmas of contemporary culture and point to a positive interaction of the two? Can we find God to be the ground of true human freedom and the one who liberates from compulsions that go deeper than the restraints contemporary people are concerned to throw off? This book offers reasons for answering these questions in the affirmative.

If the crisis of freedom is the context in which Christians in the contemporary West must think again about the meaning of human freedom and of the authority of God, it also sets some very old and long-running Christian debates about authority in a fresh context. Christians have attributed authority to the Bible as the norm for true belief and practice and also, less unanimously, to the tradition of the church. Much Christian thought in the past has been expended on the relationship between these authorities, as also between those of the church and of human reason. Such debates have not lost their relevance, but they need now to be set within the broader cultural questioning of authority as such, from which the church can hardly escape influence. As we shall see especially in chapters 3 and 5, the challenges of a new context can be met in positive and fruitful ways of affirming authority as liberating rather than repressive.

It may not be obvious that the world ecological crisis, with which we have now become rather too complacently familiar, is closely connected with the contemporary crisis of freedom. It is the direct result of the modern age's great project of achieving and enhancing human freedom through technological domination and exploitation of nature. Modern humanity understood itself to be freeing itself from nature, taking its destiny into its own hands, achieving godlike mastery over nature and godlike creativity to refashion nature for its own purposes. This is the same kind of correlation between freedom and domination that can also be seen in the history of imperialism, and it is no accident that the first phase of the modern technological project coincided with the age of the great empires. But is the Christian understanding of God, humanity, and the natural world not complicit in the attitudes and practices that have led to ecological crisis? Many in the green and new-age movements have held Christianity directly responsible, referring especially to the "dominion" over other creatures given by God to humans at the time of their creation, according to the Genesis creation account. It is an important question for Christians whether this human dominion, as a God-given authority within creation, can be distinguished from the exploitative domination that has characterized the modern project of technological mastery. The issue is tackled in chapter 7.

Each of the chapters in this book is a self-contained essay, but readers will readily identify the themes and forms of argument that tie the essays together and make them a complementary set of explorations of various different aspects of the topic. Chapter 1, "Freedom in the Bible: Exodus and Service," draws out the various dimensions of the biblical portrayal of freedom, stressing the multidimensional character of freedom and showing how the Bible offers a rich understanding of human freedom that should not be reduced to only one of these dimensions. Chapter 2, "Freedom in Contemporary Context," proceeds by way of a critical analysis of political, social, and cultural ideas of freedom in contemporary Western society to construct the outlines of a Christian understanding of freedom relevant to the aporias of freedom today. Chapter 3, "Authority and Scripture," explores the rejection of authority in modern and post-modern contexts and offers an understanding of the authority of Scripture that meets these challenges to authority. In chapter 4, "Authority and Morality," the authority of Christian ethics is discussed by way of a critique of Richard Holloway's recent claim that even Christians should keep God out of morality, since religious morality is irredeemably authoritarian and coercive. Chapter 5, "Authority and Tradition," takes up the question of the nature and authority of Christian tradition, in relation to Scripture and in relation to the depreciation of tradition in Western thought since the Enlightenment. Chapter 6, "Egalitarianism and Hierarchy in the Bible," takes up the claim that the Bible provides ideological support for structures of patriarchal and oppressive hierarchy, and argues that the direction of biblical thought is towards a fully egalitarian vision of human society. Chapter 7, "Human Authority in Creation," confronts the charge that the Genesis idea of human dominion over nature is the ideological root of the ecological crisis, investigates the history of this idea in relation to the beginning of the modern technological project, shows how it has been co-opted to alien ends, and concludes by restoring it to its biblical context as the key to its properly Christian meaning. Finally, chapter 8, "Freedom in the Crisis of Modernity," takes up the ideas of recent thinkers who identify a crisis of values in the contemporary West, recognizes the positive achievements of the pursuit of freedom in the modern age, but also identifies the fatal flaw in this modern pursuit of freedom, as its consequences now face us. The argument of the book comes to a head in the final section of this chapter with the thesis that true freedom is grounded and formed in relationship with the triune God of Christian faith.

Details of previous publication

Chapter 1 is a revised and expanded version of chapter 7 of *The Bible in Politics: How to Read the Bible Politically* (London: SPCK, 1989/Philadelphia: Westminster Press, 1990).

Chapter 2 is a revised version of *Freedom to Choose*, Grove Spirituality Series 39 (Bramcote, Nottingham: Grove Books, 1991).

Chapter 3 is a much expanded version of material that appeared in "Scripture and Authority," *Transformation* 15/2 (1998) 5–11; and *Scripture and Authority Today*, Grove Biblical Studies Series 12 (Cambridge: Grove Books, 1999).

Chapter 4 is a revised version of "Richard Holloway in the Moral Maze: The Lost Leading the Lost," *Scottish Episcopal Church Review* 8/2 (2001): 26–36.

Chapter 5 is a revised version of "Tradition in Relation to Scripture and Reason," in R. Bauckham and B. Drewery, eds., *Scripture, Tradition and Reason: A Study in the Criteria of Christian Doctrine: Essays in Honour of Richard P. C. Hanson* (Edinburgh: T. & T. Clark, 1988), 117–45.

Chapter 6 was first published as "Egalitarianism and Hierarchy in the Biblical Traditions," in A. N. S. Lane, ed., *The Interpretation of the Bible: Historical and Theological Studies in Honour of David F. Wright* (Leicester: Apollos, 1997), 259–73.

Chapter 7 has not been previously published.

Chapter 8 is a longer version of a chapter that will appear in the Festschrift for Duncan Forrester: *Public Theology in the Twenty-First Century*, ed. W. F. Storrar and A. R. Morton (Edinburgh: T. & T. Clark, 2003).

1

Freedom in the Bible: Exodus and Service

The Bible is a collection of very different types of writings written over a very long period by a large number of authors and editors. So in the nature of the case we cannot expect it to provide us with ready-made summaries of its own teaching in all its component parts. For the most part, the task of discerning the general thrust and major components of the Bible's treatment of a topic is a difficult task of creative interpretation. It requires much more than the gathering of relevant information from all parts of Scripture. The appropriate categories for a synthesis may not be handed on a plate to the interpreter by Scripture itself; he or she may need to search for the most appropriate categories or to invent new ones. Without discounting any part of the scriptural witness, the interpreter will have to make judgments about what is central and what is peripheral, what is relative and what is absolute, or what is provisional and what is enduring. In some cases it will be important, not only to report the actual positions reached by particular biblical writings, but to also discern the direction in which biblical thinking is moving. For the Bible contains the records of a dynamic, developing tradition of thought, and the aim of interpretation should be to let Scripture involve its reader in its own process of thought, so that the reader's own thinking may continue in the direction it sets. In this chapter, we shall be attempting a synthesis of the theme of freedom in the Bible.

Introduction

"The bigger the words, the more easily alien elements are able to hide in them. This is particularly the case with freedom," observed Ernst Bloch.[1] Because freedom is

---

[1]E. Bloch, *The Principle of Hope* (Oxford: Basil Blackwell, 1986), 258.

such a "big" word, appealing to such fundamental human aspirations and therefore so politically potent, it is easily abused. The defense or promotion of one form of freedom is frequently used as a political excuse for suppressing other forms of freedom. As often as the word seems to open unlimited horizons of human self-fulfillment for those who aspire to freedom, so often its real meaning is reduced to a minimum by those who use it to acquire or maintain political power. Because all too often the selective use of the Bible has been used to justify the restriction of freedom—in the claim that the Bible endorses only *this* kind of freedom and *not that*—we must try to be open to the actual dimensions of freedom in Scripture. And because the ambiguity of the notion of freedom makes it all too easy to cloak our own concept in biblical rhetoric, we need to work hard at discerning the central thrust of the Bible's understanding of freedom.

We are not looking in the Bible for some kind of blueprint for a free society today. Just as forms of human society have necessarily changed and developed—especially in complexity—since biblical times, so political liberties have developed and continue to develop. Specific freedoms that need to be embodied and safeguarded politically are historical in character, however much they may be rooted in fundamental human nature. We cannot expect to find them ready-made in Scripture, which can tell us nothing directly about, for example, the freedom of the press or even freedom of religious worship. What we are looking for is the direction in which the Bible points, the fundamental nature of God's will for human freedom. This is what we need in order to follow that direction into the dimensions of liberation that are required in our contemporary world.

Relevant material in the Bible is plentiful, but will not be found merely or even mainly by looking for the word *freedom*, which the Old Testament almost never uses and which is not at all common in the New Testament, or for related words that are rather more common but still do not indicate the scope of the theme.[2] The notion of freedom is much more central to the biblical message than words alone would suggest. For example, the exodus, which throughout both testaments is frequently recalled as an event and used as a model or metaphor for later events and experiences, always carried powerful connotations of liberation from oppression.[3] The Old Testament constantly identifies

---

[2]For a brief survey of relevant New Testament words, see R. T. France, "Liberation in the New Testament," *Evangelical Quarterly* 58 (1986): 9–12.

[3]S. Croatto, "The Socio-historical and Hermeneutical Relevance of the Exodus," in *Exodus—A Lasting Paradigm*, ed. B. van Iersel and A. Weiler (Edinburgh: T. & T. Clark, 1987) = Concilium 189 (1/1987): 126–29. For a contrary view, see J. Barr, "The Bible as a Political Document," *Bulletin of the John Rylands University Library of Manchester* 62 (1980): 286–87.

God from this event as "the LORD your God, who brought you out of . . . the house of slavery" (Exod. 20:2, etc.). "This is the Old Testament definition of God: God the liberator."[4] A somewhat similar significance attaches to the fact that, in Luke's Gospel, Jesus' mission is programmatically described at the outset of his ministry as a mission of liberation: "To proclaim release to the captives . . . to let the oppressed go free" (Luke 4:18). We can expect the theme of freedom to encompass a rather large area of biblical concerns.

God's freed slaves

The Old Testament has no abstract definition of freedom but conceives of freedom in quite concrete terms. Obviously, enslavement means subjection to the will of another, and freedom is freedom from constraint or coercion. But in the paradigmatic case of Israel's enslavement in Egypt, for example, it is not the abstract status of subjection but the concrete evils of oppression—intolerably hard labor, enforced infanticide (Exod. 1:11–16)—that distress the people and evoke God's concern and redemptive action (Exod. 2:23–25; 3:7–10; 6:5–7). This is not to say that Old Testament people did not value freedom in itself, but simply that its value was felt, as it is for most people, in its concrete benefits: freedom to supply one's basic needs and to enjoy the ordinary pleasures of life without being exploited by others.

Of course, the Exodus did not simply liberate Israel from any kind of lordship, but freed Israel from her Egyptian oppressors so that she could serve God. God's insistent challenge to the pharaoh was not simply, "Let my people go," but "Let my people go, that they may serve me" (Exod. 7:16; 8:1, 20; 9:1, 13; 10:3 RSV). Jon Levenson comments: "The emphasis, I think, falls on that last word: that they may serve *Me* and no one else. The point of the exodus is not freedom in the sense of self-determination, but *service*, the service of the loving, redeeming, and delivering God of Israel, rather than the state and its proud king."[5]

But for this very reason, to exchange the lordship of the Egyptians for the lordship of God was not really to move from one slavery to another, since God was dedicated to the interests of God's people, and God's lordship was experienced as liberation from all human lordship. As Jürgen Moltmann comments on this divine lordship, "The expression 'the Lord' is none other than the assurance of freedom for the enslaved people. It has nothing to do with the

---

[4]J. Moltmann, in E. Moltmann-Wendel and J. Moltmann, *Humanity in God* (London: SCM Press, 1983), 57; cf. Croatto, "The Socio-historical and Hermeneutical Relevance," 127: "the very name of the God of Israel is indissolubly bound up with the exodus experience of oppression-liberation."
[5]J. D. Levenson, "Exodus and Liberation," *Horizons in Biblical Theology* 13 (1991): 152.

lords who are enslaving them."[6] From Israel's sense of being a nation of freed slaves, with only a divine master, Israel acquired an unusual (in the ancient Near Eastern context) sense of the equal right to freedom of all Israelites. The principle that Leviticus 25:42 expresses by means of the actual institution of slavery militated against all relationships of subjection among Israelites: "they are *my* slaves, whom I brought out of the land of Egypt; they shall not be sold as slaves." A similar consideration is at work in 1 Samuel 8, in which the people are not content with having God as their king, but want a human king "like other nations." Samuel's argument is that they will be subjecting themselves to the kind of oppressive despotism that much contemporary monarchy amounted to, and his catalogue of the evils of monarchy is summed up: "you shall be his slaves" (1 Sam. 8:17). A political relationship of subjection was inappropriate in the nation God had redeemed from slavery (see also Judg. 8:22–23).

All over the ancient world (and not only the ancient world), freedom for some meant subjection for others. To be free meant to be a master and, therefore, to have slaves. So rulers were free at the expense of their subjects, masters at the expense of their slaves, the rich and powerful at the expense of the poor and vulnerable, men at the expense of women. In Israel this correlation between freedom and subjection was broken through *in principle*, because Israel—and thus all Israelites—had been liberated by God and were his slaves alone. Hence, in Israel freedom entailed not inequality, but equality. That this *principle* of freedom was not carried through with complete consistency—in relation, for example, to the status of women or the institution of slavery (to which we shall return below)—should not obscure the enormous significance of the breakthrough in principle.

Economic independence

Much of the Old Testament law, and many of the denunciations of the prophets, are concerned with the danger of exploitation (loss of freedom) arising from social and economic inequalities. This not only required impartiality in the administration of laws that enshrined every Israelite's right to freedom from harm to his or her life and livelihood. It also meant that the law and the prophets were positively concerned with maintaining the economic independence of Israelite families, consisting in their inalienable right to a share in the land that God had given to all Israel. The loss of economic independence made people vulnerable to exploitation by others and often led to

---

[6]J. Moltmann, *Experiences in Theology*, trans. M. Kohl (London: SCM Press, 2000), 34. With reference to contemporary criticism of the use of the term "Lord" for God, the sentence continues: "and nothing to do with male domination either."

actual enslavement. Hence the prophets denounced those who accumulated property, "who add house to house and join field to field, until not an acre remains, and you are left to dwell alone in the land" (Isa. 5:8 NEB). Hence also the constant concern to protect those who did not have economic independence: resident aliens, orphans, widows. No one in Israel, not even resident aliens, should be exploited, since it was precisely from oppression as landless aliens in Egypt that God redeemed Israel (Exod. 23:9; Lev. 19:33, 34; Deut. 24:18).

Thus the ideal of freedom in Israel took the concrete forms of economic independence and freedom from fear of harm. This imposed, it should be noticed, not only the kinds of restraints that all legal systems impose—against obvious kinds of harm to the persons and property of others—but also economic restraints, since only a relative equality of economic resources could prevent the effective oppression of the poor by wealthier classes. In practice, social and economic equality was very much eroded during the monarchical period, but this was the burden of many of the prophets' complaints, and the eschatological hope that recurs throughout the prophets expressed the ideal of economic independence and freedom from fear of harm for all: "they shall all sit under their own vines and under their own fig trees, and no one shall make them afraid" (Mic. 4:4).[7]

A final observation may be needed to correct any impression that freedom in Israel was understood purely as freedom for the individual (or family) *from* oppression by others. Such an individualistic understanding of freedom is easily projected back from modern times. If we think of freedom as lordship in correlation with subjection, then freedom for all means that each is his or her own master, and each experiences others as limits on his or her freedom, in competition with him or her. This is modern liberal individualism. That it was not the ancient Israelite's experience of freedom was in part because the Israelite was not his or her own master, but God's slave. Acknowledgment of the divine lordship gave each Israelite responsibilities to one's fellow Israelites. Thus, while it is a fundamental feature of the Old Testament law—as it must be of all realistic attempts to safeguard freedom—that it embodies many restraints on antisocial abuse of freedom, it is equally characteristic of Old Testament law that it enjoins positive caring helpfulness for others. My neighbor is not simply a restraint on my freedom, but one whom I am to love as myself (Lev. 19:18). The New Testament's understanding of freedom, as not so much *from* others as *for* others, is already implicit in the Old Testament sense of social responsibility.

---

[7]Cf. Isaiah 32:18; Jeremiah 30:10; Ezekiel 34:25–9; Zephaniah 3:13.

Slavery in the Old Testament

The institution of slavery, of course, existed in Old Testament Israel, and Old Testament law contains a good many laws intended to regulate it.[8] In accordance with common practice in the ancient Near East, slaves were both foreigners, captured as prisoners of war, and Israelites, who had fallen disastrously into debt and had to sell themselves into slavery. Slavery meant that the master had very considerable rights over his slave and the rights of the slave, though not abolished altogether, were very restricted.

However, it is important to notice, first of all, that the Old Testament fully recognizes the inconsistency of the enslavement of Israelites with the fundamental freedom and equality of all God's people, whom God redeemed from slavery in Egypt. The legislation accepts the fact of slavery but treats it as an abnormality to be minimized as far as possible. It therefore gives slaves the opportunity of release, after six years, without payment for their release (Exod. 21:2) and, in fact, with provisions to tide them over a period of unemployment (Deut. 15:13–14). Only by free choice could a slave opt, instead of release after six years, to remain permanently in his or her master's service (Exod. 21:5–6); Deut. 15:16–17). These laws attempt, in the face of economic realities that produced slavery, to give some continued substance to the fundamental right of Israelites to freedom. It is because "you were a slave in the land of Egypt, and the LORD your God redeemed you" (Deut. 15:15), that the master is to liberate his slaves after six years of service.

The law in Leviticus 25:39–43 goes further. While allowing Israelites to possess foreign slaves (25:44–46), it prohibits the actual enslavement of fellow Israelites, who may be forced by poverty only into a kind of semislave status. This is probably an attempt to deprive the existing practice of slavery of the legal status of slavery, though some scholars have argued that all the other laws on slavery refer only to non-Israelite slaves.[9] In any case, the theological reason given for not enslaving fellow Israelites is noteworthy: "they are my slaves, whom I brought out of the land of Egypt; they shall not be sold as slaves" (Lev. 25:42).

In addition to recognizing the fundamental right of all Israelites to freedom, some of the laws also have the effect of considerably mitigating and humanizing the institution of slavery, in ways that are not paralleled in other ancient

---

[8]See, generally, H. W. Wolff, *Anthropology of the Old Testament* (London: SCM Press, 1974), 199–205; C. J. H. Wright, *Living as the People of God: The Relevance of Old Testament Ethics* (Leicester: Inter-Varsity Press, 1983), 178–82.

[9]So C. J. H. Wright, "What Happened Every Seven Years in Israel? Part 2," *Evangelical Quarterly* 56 (1984): 193–201; but against this view, see, e.g., A. Phillips, "The Laws of Slavery: Exodus 21.2–11," *Journal for the Study of the Old Testament* 30 (1984): 51–66.

societies. The laws protecting slaves against their masters (Exod. 21:20–21, 26–27) are unique in their contemporary context and represent a step beyond the legal treatment of slaves as no more than chattels; as mere property they could have no rights to protect them from harm by their owners, but as human beings they do. The laws on release and on runaway slaves (Exod. 21:2–6; Deut. 15:12–18; 23:15–16) must, if effective, have ensured that slavery was not oppressive in practice, since a harsh master would not have been able to keep his slave. Since an obligation to return runaway slaves to their masters was taken for granted in ancient society (cf. 1 Sam. 30:15), the law commanding Israelites on the contrary to harbor runaway slaves (Deut. 23:15–16) is again quite remarkable. Though the motivation is not stated, Israelites would remember, readily enough, that Israel originated as a nation of runaway slaves. The sympathies of such people should therefore belong with the runaway slave rather than with the master.[10] Thus, while not actually abolishing an institution that was universal in the ancient world, the Old Testament law did considerably humanize and even, we might say, undermine it, as a result of Israel's experience of liberation from Egypt. Even concubines captured in war were human beings with rights to be respected (Deut. 21:10–14).

If the law and the prophets (cf. Jer. 34) based their attitude to slavery on the salvation-historical ground of the exodus liberation, it is typical of the Wisdom literature that it reaches the same conclusion on creation-theological grounds: that the same God created both master and slave (Job 31:13–15). In the end, both kinds of argument require the abolition of slavery, and it is perfectly proper that we should follow the *direction* of these Old Testament principles as far as they point, even beyond Old Testament practice and, for that matter, even beyond New Testament practice. Indeed, they carry us further than the abolition of slavery defined in a narrow sense. All relationships of subjection that permit the exploitation of one human being by another are contrary to the fundamental will of God as the Old Testament reveals it. They have no basis in the created status of human beings, who are all equally subject to God, and the historical purpose of God is for the abolition of all such relationships. God's liberation of Israel from slavery cannot, in the end, be an exclusive privilege for Israel alone, but is prototypical of God's will that all humanity should similarly come under God's liberating lordship.

Freedom in the New Testament

The concept of freedom undergoes major development in the New Testament. In attempting to delineate this briefly, we shall focus on four aspects.

---

[10]Wolff, *Anthropology*, 202.

In the first place, the New Testament *deepens and extends* the whole issue of freedom and subjection, taking it into areas beyond the reach of politics and law. Thus Jesus' ministry freed no slaves of humans, but liberated slaves of guilt and sin, those held captive by demons, oppressed by disease and handicaps, imprisoned by themselves, and subject to death. The exodus liberation thus becomes in the New Testament a type of Christ's liberation of those enslaved to sin and death (e.g., Rev. 1:5–6). But this is precisely an extension and deepening of the Old Testament concept of freedom, not a replacement of it. A liberation from all oppression cannot exclude the political sphere, even while it goes much further than the political.

Second, the implications of freedom in Christ certainly affected the social life of the church, the new people of God liberated by the new exodus. Christian freedom, in the New Testament, is certainly not purely inward and individual, but concerns the outward, social relationships of Christians in the church. In principle, there can be no relationships of subjection among Christians, "no longer slave or free" (Gal. 3:28). Some New Testament advice to masters and slaves could be understood as merely ameliorating the situation, without changing the fundamental relationship, but Philemon 16 carries through the basic Christian principle more consistently. Philemon is to receive back his runaway slave Onesimus *"no longer as a slave,* but more than a slave, a beloved brother." The legal form of slavery is retained, but master and slave are to relate no longer as master and slave, but as brothers.

Perhaps even more remarkable is Ephesians 5:21–6:9, which deals with three types of authority relationship (wives and husbands, children and parents, slaves and masters). Here the asymmetrical advice given to the respective parties in the first two relationships must be balanced by the fact that all three relationships come under the rubric in 5:21, which is fully reciprocal: "Be subject to one another out of reverence for Christ." The principle of freedom in mutual service underlies the more socially determined elements of authority in the discussion of family relationships. But lest the point of the rubric had been forgotten by the time the reader reached the third relationship (slaves and masters), it is reiterated there in a quite startling form. When the masters are told to "do the same" to their slaves (6:9), the reference can only be to rendering service as a slave (6:7). In other words, if the slaves are told to be good slaves to their masters, "as to the Master" (6:7 RSV), the masters are also told *to be slaves* to their slaves, "as to the Master." Presumably they are to exercise their authority in a way that is just as much a service to their slaves as the slaves' work is service to them. Such advice taken seriously would mean that the continuing outward order of freedom and subjection would be inwardly transformed by the new Christian principle of freedom in mutual service (see the fourth point below). It should also be noticed that the way the master-slave relationship is here transcended is not by making everyone masters.

The revolutionary potential of this New Testament principle is recognized, in a social context closer than ours to that of the early Christians, by Dostoevsky's character Father Zosima, in his discourse on "whether it is possible for masters and servants to be brothers in spirit":

> One cannot survive without servants in this world, but you should arrange things in such a way that your servant is freer in spirit than if he were not a servant. For why should I not be a servant to my servant, and why, for that matter, should he not be aware of it, and without any self-righteousness on my part or mistrust on his? Why should I not treat my servant as a relative and accept him finally into my family, and do so with joy? Even now, this could still come about and serve as the basis for the future, glorious union of people, when man will not, as now, be looking for servants, and will not, as now, be making servants of his own kind, but on the contrary will himself wish, from the bottom of his heart to become a servant to everyone, as is laid down in the Gospels.[11]

Third, the New Testament gives a quite new emphasis to freedom as voluntary service. Although the New Testament continues to use the somewhat paradoxical language that equates subjection to God's lordship with freedom (e.g., 1 Pet. 2:16), the heart of its understanding of freedom is that, through Jesus the Son of God, Christians are free *sons and daughters* of God their Father (John 8:32; Gal. 4:7; Rom. 3:14–17). The point is that, while a child fulfills himself or herself in dedicated obedience to his or her parent's will, as Jesus did, this is not the involuntary subjection of a slave, but the glad and willing service of a child. Voluntary service to God means also, again on the model of Jesus, voluntary service of others. Instead of replacing a model of society in which there are masters and slaves with a model in which everyone is his or her own master, Jesus and the early church replaced it with a model in which everyone is the slave of others—with, of course, the understanding that this "slavery" is entirely willing (Luke 22:26–27; John 13:14; Gal. 5:13). In other words, freedom is the freedom to love: "you were called to freedom, brothers and sisters; only do not use your freedom as an opportunity for self-indulgence, but through love become slaves to one another" (Gal. 5:13).[12] If the Old Testament emphasis is on God's people as *freed* slaves, the New Testament emphasis in on God's people as free *slaves*.

---

[11]F. Dostoevsky, *The Karamazov Brothers*, trans. I. Avsey (Oxford: Oxford University Press, 1994), 398.
[12]My translation.

Authority in the church is no exception to this principle. It exists only in the form of service ("ourselves as your slaves for Jesus' sake," 2 Cor. 4:5 RSV marg.; cf. Mark 10:43–44; Matt. 23:10–11), and therefore as part of a pattern of mutual submission and service by all to all.[13] Hence, freedom in this form, as the spirit of glad and loving service, creates not a collection of independent and competitive individuals, but a real *community* of mutual dependence. Exploitative relationships are replaced by liberating relationships.

Fourth, this to some extent explains the early church's attitude to the existing structures of political and social subjection in their contemporary society. They did not attempt to abolish them in the name of freedom, but they did attempt to transform them from within by turning them into relationships of *voluntary* and (where possible) *mutual* subjection. This is most evident in Ephesians 5:21–6:9, with regard to marriage, parenthood, and slavery, as we have already noticed, and in 1 Peter 2:13–17, with regard to political structures. In this latter case, while government remained wholly outside the church's influence, it could not enjoin *mutual* subjection, but Christians' acknowledgment of the authority of the state is notably linked with the freedom of God's slaves (v. 16).

Arguably, this strategy of Christian transformation of authoritarian structures from within was both more practicable than and, in its own way, as effective as any attempt to set up new egalitarian structures. In the end, egalitarian structures are also required, but in themselves they cannot produce freedom in its fullest sense. They may be vehicles for the competitive liberty that is still enslaved to self-service, rather than the true freedom that creates community.

In the following four short sections we shall comment on particular aspects (by no means an exhaustive analysis) of the New Testament's account of human freedom in their relevance for contemporary society.

Liberation from the compulsions of sin

> Do you not know that if you present yourselves to anyone as obedient slaves, you are slaves of the one whom you obey, either of sin, which leads to death, or of obedience, which leads to righteousness? But thanks be to God that you, having once been slaves of sin, have become obedient from the heart to the form of teaching to which you were entrusted, and that you, having been set free from sin, have become slaves of righteousness. I am speaking in human terms because of your natural limitations. (Rom. 6:16–19a)

---

[13]Cf. already in the Old Testament, 1 Kings 12:7.

Western Christianity has tended to think of salvation primarily as forgiveness and correspondingly of sin as guilt. This undoubtedly reflects one aspect of the human plight: that as sinners we stand guilty before the judgment of God. But another aspect of the human plight, according to both the New Testament and the Christian tradition, is subjection to the power of sin. This is one of the kinds of context in which Paul speaks of salvation as liberation or freedom. We are sin's slaves until God liberates us into God's own service, which is freedom.

This is a point at which, if articulated well, the gospel might speak particularly relevantly to many contemporary people. If we wish to put it concretely in terms of some of the prime realities of our culture, we should think of the compulsions of sin, from whose grip we cannot get free by ourselves, as not just the inner compulsion to sin in fallen human nature, but also the forces outside individual persons, such as consumerism, which appeal to the base desires of human nature and exploit people by latching onto the human tendencies to greed, lust, envy and excess. The grip in which many contemporary people are held is an alliance between the worst of the forces that control our society and the worst aspects of their own inner selves. This is a different kind of oppression requiring a different kind of exodus.

Part of what we are given in that new exodus is a new kind of loyalty or commitment. It becomes possible to resist the otherwise irresistible pressures because we have something above and beyond them that enables us to see through and to resist them. Loving obedience to God is not, as so many see it today, an alienating loss of personal freedom but liberation from all the compulsions to which would-be independent selves so often find themselves subject. For Christians to behave as truly free people in the midst of the compelling desires and addictions of contemporary life may be what can best give tangible substance to Christian faith and life in Western society today.

Liberation by the truth and by the Son

> "If you continue in my word, you are truly my disciples;
> and you will know the truth, and the truth will make you free. . . .
> Very truly, I tell you, everyone who commits sin is a slave to sin.
> The slave does not have a permanent place in the household; the son has a
>   place there forever.
> So if the Son makes you free, you will be free indeed."
> (John 8:31–32, 34–36)

The force of the word "truth" in John's Gospel is often conveyed better by the word "reality." Truth is the reality we see when all the illusions and delusions of sin are dispelled by the word of God. To get past all the seductive images of the good life that contemporary society constructs for us with such consummate expertise, to see beyond them to the real truth of things, is liberation. Not to construct a world of our own, to our own taste, but to discern reality is liberation. But that reality should not be misunderstood as authoritarian imposition of dogma. Reality is more than a creed, however useful creeds may be in pointing us to reality. In John's Gospel, Jesus himself is the truth of God and humanity. Truth is personal, and what liberates is the encounter with the reality of things in the person of Jesus who reflects his Father's divinity and models true humanity.

The rebellious son comes home

The tension between independence and belonging is something inherent in the human situation which manifests itself in a particularly problematic cultural form in the problem of freedom today. Humans need both independence and belonging to some degree and in a working relationship between the two. The contemporary problem is that desire for autonomy threatens to rob us of any belonging to others or taking responsibility for others. Committed relationships are felt as restrictions to which we must sit loose in order to be ourselves in freedom.

What follows is certainly not an adequate reading of the parable of the prodigal son (Luke 15:11–32), but an attempt to let one dimension of the parable speak to the cultural context just mentioned. The younger son in the parable demands his independence of father, family, and familial home in order not just to enjoy himself, but surely, more profoundly, in order to be himself. It is a form of adolescent rebellion. In the necessary process of moving from a childish to an adult relationship to parents, there is often a stage of asserting independence in which young people feel the need to demand and to grasp their independence from their parents. The son in the parable cannot bear to wait for his father to die before stepping into the father's shoes. He wants independence but therefore also tastes its bitterness and comes home to be a son again, belonging to his father and his family. But this belonging will not be just the same as it was before he left. Now he has learned about independence and has freely chosen the freedom he will find in an adult way of belonging to father and home.

In the relentless pursuit of autonomy, at the cost of community and belonging, contemporary Western society is living out an exaggerated and prolonged adolescence. The isolation, the loneliness, and the emptiness are the prodigal son's pig-swill. The fullest freedom is not to be found in being as free from others as possible, but in the freedom we give each other when we belong to each other in loving relationships. Coming home to the father's embrace is an apt image of what it is like for many contemporary people to find God and at the same time to find others with whom they can begin to be truly themselves.

A real home and a father's loving embrace are sadly outside the firsthand experience of many contemporary people, but the desire to return home hides somewhere in every psyche and is perhaps all the more potent in some who have never had a home to leave.

Being ourselves in one another

> "I ask not only on behalf of these, but also on behalf of those who will believe in me through their word, that they may all be one. As you, Father, are in me and I am in you, may they also be in us, so that the world may believe that you have sent me. The glory that you have given me I have given them, so that they may be one, as we are one, I in them and you in me, that they may become completely one, so that the world may know that you have sent me and have loved them even as you have loved me." (John 17:20–23)

A strong trend in recent systematic theology has been to contrast and counter modern Western individualism with a model of persons in community that reflects the Trinitarian personhood of God, the Father, the Son, and the Holy Spirit.[14] The Christian understanding of God is said to require a relational understanding of being a person, such that we cannot be truly ourselves in freedom from others but only in free relationship with others. This theological trend is sometimes reduced (though not by its major exponents) to the rather unsatisfactory form that the Trinity provides humans with an external model to which to conform. The passage in Jesus' prayer in John (above) that comes closest, among biblical texts, to that notion also suggests something more. Certainly Jesus prays that his disciples may be one, as he and the Father are one. The oneness is that in-one-anotherness that is John's distinctive way of expressing the intimacy of the divine persons, described in later theology as perichoresis. But the passage portrays not only an analogy between the Trinity and human community. It portrays the Trinity (in this case the relationship of the Father and the Son) as the active source of human community. The in-one-anotherness of the Father and the Son is shared by them with those who know God the Father in Jesus. It is in intimacy with God that the disciples discover also the in-one-anotherness of their own community with each other.

Some people who have forgotten or never known how to relate to others in the genuine openness of love may discover it in getting to know God, just as others may discover intimate relationship with God through experiencing the love of other people.

---

[14]A recent example is D. S. Cunningham, *These Three Are One: The Practice of Trinitarian Theology* (Oxford: Blackwell, 1998), chapter 5.

Jesus the free person

In the Gospels Jesus acts and speaks with the freedom not to be controlled by
the structures and ideologies of his social context. Quite clearly he also acts in
total obedience to his Father. Jesus delights to do his Father's will, which is his
food and drink. Thus he models the free and glad obedience of love.

In his relationship to other people, Jesus expressed his freedom nowhere
more remarkably than in depicting himself as the slave who serves others
(Luke 22:27) and in performing the act that was most distinctively the slave's:
washing the feet of others (John 13:3–15). In this act Jesus did what no one
else in his position would have done, something that everyone else would have
felt constrained by established values and social conventions not to do. In this
act Jesus was free in regarding nothing as beneath him. Whatever others might
think, Jesus saw nothing as degrading if he did it for those he loved. In the act
of washing feet he prefigured the shameful, slave's death he was very soon to
die. Thus he models the cost of being free for others.

Concepts of freedom

All too often in church history God has been misrepresented as suppressing
rather than promoting freedom. He has been the heavenly despot who is the
model and sanction for oppressive regimes on earth: divine right monarchies
in the state, clerical rule in the church, patriarchal domination in the family.
It is clear that this is not the biblical God. His lordship liberates from all
human lordship. His slaves may not be slaves of any human master (Lev.
25:42). Those who call God their Father and Christ their Master may call no
man either (Matt. 23:9–10). This is because the divine Master himself fulfills
his lordship not in domination but in the service of a slave (Phil. 2:6–11).

But what kind of freedom is it that the biblical God promotes? According
to liberal individualism, highly influential in Western democracies, "the only
freedom which deserves the name, is that of pursuing our own good in our
own way, so long as we do not attempt to deprive others of theirs, or impede
their efforts to attain it" (John Stuart Mill).[15] Perhaps a definition of the biblical understanding of freedom might be formulated in parallel to Mill's definition: the only freedom that deserves the name is that of freely pursuing
the good of others, not by depriving them of liberty, but by promoting their
liberty.

Mill's definition creates a tension between freedom, so defined, and equality. The state's positive activities toward the common good seem to conflict

---

[15]Quoted in A. Passerin d'Entrèves, *The Notion of the State* (Oxford: Clarendon Press,
1967), 204–5.

with the individual's liberty to pursue his or her own good. The tension between individual freedom and social justice pervades contemporary politics. For example, governments attempt to maximize freedom of consumer choice, but this is a kind of freedom that too easily benefits the affluent at the expense of the inability of the poor to choose anything other than poverty.

Our definition of freedom, according to which the individual is most free not in self-fulfillment for his or her own sake but in self-giving for others, escapes the tension between freedom and social justice; but as soon as it is applied to the political sphere, it creates a different tension: between freedom and coercion. Government is characteristically, though by no means exclusively, the exercise of coercive authority, and even in a democracy that means coercing people to contribute to the common good. Of course, the good citizens, truly free people in our sense, will welcome the laws that, for example, oblige them to pay taxes to support welfare provisions and medical services for all, and they will gladly and willingly obey them. But the unwilling taxpayer is not, as Jean-Jacques Rousseau maintained, being "forced to be free": he is simply not, in this respect, free. If Rousseau were right, a totalitarian state would be the political structure most closely corresponding to our definition of freedom. But he is wrong, because it is a contradiction in terms to think that freedom can be created by coercion. This being so, a democratic system provides the only adequate structural context for freedom in the political sphere. It reduces the tension between freedom and coercion as far as possible, but the tension remains. Political education, within a democratic system, reduces it somewhat further but cannot eliminate it.

It becomes evident, as so often when we relate the New Testament to politics, that the political sphere, important as it is, is neither all-embracing nor self-sufficient. The freedom that creates a real and healthy political community can only to a limited extent be created by political means. It arises from those deeper dimensions of enslavement and liberty to which Jesus' liberating mission was directed.

The Dimensions of Freedom

Freedom in the Bible is a broad and complex notion. It extends, for example, from the freedom from Egyptian oppression that the Israelites were given at the exodus to the freedom of Jesus' acceptance of suffering and death out of love for humanity and faithfulness to his Father's will. It embraces freedoms *from* (exploitation, for example), freedoms *of* (choice, for example), freedoms *for* (service of others, for example), freedoms *to* (hope, for example). It is as complex as human life, and no one model can adequately categorize it. But a model that can help to counter the frequent tendency to reduce freedom to certain types of freedom is that of *multidimensional* freedom corresponding to a multidimensional model of human life and experience.[16]

Human life can be understood as having a variety of dimensions, such as the psychological, the physical (relating to the body), the immediate social (person-to-person relations), the economic, the cultural, the political, and the environmental (human society's relation to nature). Any such list of dimensions is flexible; others could be added and distinctions made in different ways, because these are not absolute distinctions inherent in human experience but convenient categories for thinking about a complex whole. The dimensions are distinguishable but *interrelated*. Action or experience in one dimension has effects in others. Unemployment, for example, which belongs in the economic dimension, has drastic psychological and social effects, may make people physically ill, and calls for political action. We should resist attempts to see one dimension as uniquely determinative of the others, as though, for example, economic conditions determine (as distinct from merely affecting) all other dimensions. No one dimension determines unilaterally the others. Rather, the dimensions interrelate in very varied and complex ways.

The political dimension—meaning ordering of human life for and by government—is one dimension, not, as totalitarian claims would have it, the all-encompassing dimension that includes all the others, but one dimension that can *affect* all the others and in turn be affected by them. The religious dimension can in one sense—as the sphere of specifically religious activities—be treated as one of the many dimensions, but, as the dimension of relationship to God, it is more adequately understood as the one *really* all-encompassing dimension. God is the Creator, Lord, and Savior of human life in all of its dimensions. To know God is to relate to God in all dimensions of life.

Multidimensional thinking enables us to think more flexibly about freedom and liberty. It is not simply that enslavement and oppression occur in many different dimensions of life—economic exploitation, psychological oppression, and so on. It is also that most forms of oppression affect several dimensions and can be attacked by liberating activity in more than one dimension. Thus, for example, physical disability may look like an issue in one dimension (the physical) that should be tackled in that dimension. If we cannot remove the disability itself, we might think liberation from the handicap impossible. But in fact the physical disability in itself may be the least of the disabled person's problems, since it is compounded by the attitudes of people who treat the disabled as another species and by the organization of society and the design

---

[16]For the notion of multidimensional liberation, see J. Moltmann, *The Crucified God* (London: SCM Press, 1973), 329–35.

of buildings, which exclude the disabled from much of normal society. Freedom for the disabled can be achieved through action in these other dimensions of the matter, as also, of course, through a kind of psychological liberation in the disabled person's own attitude to his or her situation.

With this perspective it is useful to look again at the early church's treatment of slavery. This was a form of oppression affecting virtually every dimension of life for both slaves and their masters. It could have been abolished as an institution only by strong political action accompanied by radical restructuring of society and the economy and requiring widespread public support. Because early Christians could not and did not attempt this, they could be accused of tolerating slavery. But what they really did was to promote liberation from slavery in *those dimensions* where it was possible: in the psychological and immediate social dimensions. Even the slaves of pagan masters found a kind of liberation from the psychological dehumanization of the slave condition: they recovered the dignity of human equality in a community where they were treated as Christian brothers and sisters. This was not everything, but it was worth having. Where the church failed was in remaining content with this at a later period, when it gained both the political influence and the power to mold public opinion which would have made the abolition of slavery as an institution at least something that should have been attempted. At this point—and until the nineteenth century—the church called an artificial halt to the biblical dynamic of freedom that belongs not to one dimension but flows through all.[17] Liberation from slavery within the sphere of the church's own social relationships could have been the yeast that eventually leavened the whole lump.

The interrelation between the dimensions of freedom is most frequently posed in terms of the relation between inner and outer freedom, "spiritual" and "secular" freedom, or existential and structural freedom.[18] These pairs are not stable or easily delimited, but it is possible to distinguish broadly between, on the one hand, the economic, political, and social structures of freedom, and, on the other hand, the kind of personal freedom that is possible even *despite* oppressive structures.[19] That the latter kind of freedom is real and important can be seen, for example, in such extreme cases as dissidents in the gulag in the days of the Soviet empire, remaining free, in their thinking, of the system that

[17]For a brief account of the church's later attitudes to slavery, see R. N. Longenecker, *New Testament Social Ethics for Today* (Grand Rapids: Eerdmans, 1984), 60–66.

[18]On such distinctions, see A. O. Dyson, "Freedom in Christ and Contemporary Concepts of Freedom," *Studia Theologica* 39 (1985): 55–72.

[19]For this kind of freedom in Paul, see B. Gerhardsson, *The Ethos of the Bible* (London: Darton, Longman & Todd, 1982), 76–78.

oppressed them unbearably, or in the Christian martyrs under the Roman Empire, who could be regarded as the most truly free people of their time, in their refusal to let even the threat of death cow them into submission. Such freedom in and despite oppressive structures is not only real but essential to the cause of liberation *from* oppressive structures. It was only out of their liberation from the system that Russian dissidents could publicly protest against and hope to change the system. Or to take the American example that Leander Keck gives: "Had Rosa Parks not had a measure of inner freedom she would never have refused to sit at the back of the bus in Montgomery, Alabama, and thus trigger the movement that brought Martin Luther King to prominence."[20] In the same way it needed a Moses liberated by God from resignation to the irresistible power of Pharaoh to lead the people out of Egypt, and it needed the gradual psychological liberation of the people themselves to free them from Egypt even after their escape from Pharaoh's army.

Real freedom cannot be confined to one dimension. Inner freedom cannot rest content with outer unfreedom, though it may have to suffer the contradiction in circumstances where outer freedom is unattainable. Where the experience of existential freedom happily coexists with structural oppression, merely compensating for it rather than reacting against it, it is to that extent inauthentic. Admittedly, one should not press the point where, for example, the churches of the oppressed make life bearable in otherwise unbearable circumstances. But the more impressive example is that of American black slaves, who, while experiencing the liberation of the gospel, which gave them inner freedom from the dehumanizing effects of enslavement ("I'm a chile of God wid my soul set free / For Christ hab bought my liberty"), were certainly not reconciled to their chains. On the contrary, their experience of the liberating God sustained a longing for outward freedom ("My Lord delivered Daniel / Why can't he deliver me?") that was both eschatological ("Children, we shall be free / When the Lord shall appear") and realistic ("Pharaoh's army got drownded / Oh Mary, don't you weep").[21]

The contribution of the New Testament's insights into the nature of real freedom as liberation from enslavement to self-interest and freedom to give oneself for others is also important in this context. The oppressed who long for freedom are not truly liberated from the system that oppresses them so

---

[20]L. Keck, "The Son Who Creates Freedom," in E. Schillebeeckx and B. van Iersel, eds., *Jesus Christ and Human Freedom* (*Concilium* 3/10, 1974), 71–82.
[21]On inner and outer freedom in the spirituals, see J. H. Cone, *The Spirituals and the Blues* (New York: Seabury Press, 1972), chapter 3; idem, *God of the Oppressed* (London: SPCK, 1977), chapter 7; idem, *Speaking the Truth: Ecumenism, Liberation and Black Theology* (Grand Rapids: Eerdmans, 1986), 31–34.

long as the freedom they desire is only the freedom their oppressors have: freedom for themselves, no matter what this entails for others. In such circumstances the struggle for liberation is simply a mirror image of the system it opposes: it becomes ruthless in its self-interest, creates as many victims as it liberates, and produces a new kind of tyranny in place of the old. Outward liberation worthy of the name requires people who have been freed to live for others, and for all others, even for their oppressors.[22]

---

[22]In this respect, the Old Testament paradigm of liberation through the exodus, which ended in the subjection and elimination of the Canaanites, is transcended in the New Testament understanding of liberation.

2

Freedom in
Contemporary Context

Introduction

Freedom is one of the most potent words in the modern age. Perhaps it is the most potent word of all—or rivaled only by *love*. Other words used to be more powerful: *truth, goodness, beauty*. Of course, they can still move hearts and minds, inspire dedication and sacrifice. But *freedom* has stolen much of their magic. Like them, it is one of the big words that refuse to be tied down to a definition. Too many human aspirations have gathered around it. Too many and various evils have been resisted with its aid. At its most potent it is a word that seems to open a limitless prospect. It beckons humanity into a better future, the better for being undefined. Its meaning is always yet to be fully discovered.

Of course, like the other big words, it can be abused. Its very potency makes it irresistible to every politician and opinion maker. The political rhetoric of freedom may cover a multitude of evils. It may be no more than a slogan among the empty claims and counterclaims of those who compete for power. One kind of freedom may be used to justify suppression of other kinds. Securing the freedom of some people may excuse the oppression of others. In the modern age, governments and revolutionary movements have inflicted untold human suffering in the name of freedom. But also ordinary individuals, claiming personal freedom as a right, find themselves able to disregard the interests of others with a clear conscience. *Freedom* is a word that can express the highest idealism and the crassest selfishness. But it has not been totally tarnished by abuse. It still points to something infinitely desirable. As George Steiner evocatively puts it, "[T]he indistinct intimation of a lost freedom, or of a freedom to be regained—Arcadia behind us, Utopia before—hammers at the far

26

threshold of the human psyche. This shadowy pulsebeat lies at the heart of our mythologies and of our politics. We are creatures at once vexed and consoled by summons of a freedom just out of reach."[1]

If the phrase "something infinitely desirable" is an appropriate description of the contemporary perception of freedom, it tells us something important about the appeal of freedom in the modern world. It used to be God who was infinitely desirable. God and freedom have much in common, not only for liberation theologians. For freedom has the lure of transcendence. It represents the openness of life to new and different possibilities. Thus, for oppressed people who believe in God as the source of freedom, struggle for liberation and faith in God go hand in hand. But also for those who understand God as a symbol of oppression and precisely for the sake of freedom reject God, freedom wears a halo. It is liberating transcendence in place of the oppressive divine transcendence.

But freedom has particular resonances in the contemporary West. What form does the lure of transcendence take in our context? Here we shall give some particular attention to the ideas of freedom that have influenced contemporary Britain, which has its own traditions of political and cultural freedom but can also stand in many ways as representative of the problems of freedom in Western societies today. After an analysis and assessment of these ideas, we will take up the issues they raise in an outline of a Christian understanding of freedom.

Freedom in Contemporary Britain

The libertarian tradition

To understand the ideas of freedom current in contemporary Britain, we need first to take account of the two major traditions of political philosophy that still influence British political thinking and attitudes. The one that enjoyed a major revival during the decade of Margaret Thatcher's rule, a revival that has left a considerable permanent impact on British political and economic life, is the libertarian tradition. Its understanding of freedom is neatly encapsulated in the definition of John Stuart Mill:

> The only freedom which deserves the name is that of pursuing our own good in our own way, so long as we do not attempt to deprive others of theirs, or impede their efforts to attain it.[2]

---

[1]G. Steiner, *Real Presences* (Chicago: University of Chicago Press, 1991), 153.
[2]Quoted in A. Passerin d'Entrèves, *The Notion of the State* (Oxford: Clarendon Press, 1967), 204–5.

This understanding of freedom is highly individualistic. The much-quoted dictum of Margaret Thatcher that there is no such thing as society was a polemical overstatement, no doubt, but wholly intelligible as an implication of this tradition of thought. The point is not simply that freedom is attributed to the individual, but that the individual, with a right to his or her freedom, logically precedes society. Society is the result of the free choice of individuals who voluntarily associate together. Society does not enter into the definition of freedom except in the minimal sense that Mill indicates: each must recognize that others have the same right to freedom as oneself. This definition gives the state only the minimal function of preventing any one individual's pursuit of his or her good from impairing the liberty of others. Since in fact the modern state has exceeded this function, the Thatcherite ideal was to restore the freedom of the individual by rolling back the frontiers of the state. Any idea that the state can positively promote freedom—for example, by funding public transport—is strictly incompatible with this fundamental notion of freedom. (This is not, of course, to say that the Thatcher government was always consistent in following the logic of libertarian ideology.) Subsidizing public transport infringes the liberty of taxpayers by obliging them to contribute to services they may not wish to use. It may help some who would not otherwise be able to travel, but only by infringing the liberty of others. The state's role is to prevent such infringements of liberty, not to perpetrate them. This basic concept of liberty should be distinguished from the economic argument that privatized transport services are more efficient because exposed to competition. The latter was more prominent in political discussions of public services in the Thatcher period, but the importance of the underlying notion of freedom should not be underestimated.

This concept of liberty is not, of course, unconnected with the liberal commitment to the unrestricted operation of the free market economy. In itself, Mill's definition of freedom has political implications in many areas of life other than the economic. It requires, for example, liberal laws on sexual behavior, on censorship, on freedom to practice religious faith (allowing, of course, scope for disagreement in all these areas about the point at which one individual's freedom restricts that of others). But on these matters libertarian assumptions are the political consensus. This fact, combined with the fact that economic questions have long dominated British politics, mean that it has been primarily in the economic sphere that the libertarian idea of freedom has enjoyed a new ascendancy in recent decades. The individual's right to private property is seen as fundamental to his or her freedom. Because taxation infringes the rights of individuals to do as they wish with their own money, it should be minimized. The property-owning democracy was a Thatcherite ideal because those who have an interest in protecting their own rights to their own property will be less likely to vote for political policies that infringe property rights. Furthermore, Thatcherism tended to assume that pursuit of one's own (or one's family's) economic betterment will be the dominant means by which individuals will choose to pursue their own good in their own way. This assumption is by no means required by Mill's definition of freedom, but when combined with Mill's definition of freedom it produces that idealization of the free market economy that has been so influential throughout the Western world in the recent period. For this kind of libertarianism, support for the free market is not just a pragmatic economic judgment that it works. More than that, it is commitment to an ideal of economic freedom for the individual. This is why consistent Thatcherism is extreme in its commitment to the free market. The market must be freed from restrictions because this is the way to maximize individual liberty.

The libertarian tradition has major strengths and major political achievements to its credit. Its firm hold on the intrinsic value and dignity of the individual is basic to these. In focusing on the right of the individual to free choice, it highlights something essential to human freedom. Human beings can find genuine fulfillment only as a result of their own free choices, only as self-determining beings. In its insistence on this point, the libertarian tradition has secured and protects from totalitarian tyranny important individual rights, such as freedom of opinion and expression, freedom of association, freedom of worship. It protects the individual from any tendency towards the totalitarian principle that individuals must be sacrificed for the good of the collectivity. Of course, democratic socialism also endorses this aspect of the libertarian tradition. The special value of the libertarian tradition is perhaps that it stands for the individual's freedom of choice, not only vis-à-vis undemocratic political systems, but also vis-à-vis the democratic danger of a tyranny of the majority over minorities.

The contemporary appeal of the libertarian tradition also has something to do with its apparent suitability to a pluralistic society. If a pluralistic society is one that no longer has common values, because it contains a variety of cultural and religious traditions, no one of which has a privileged role in public society, then there seems great advantage in a political philosophy that affirms only one public value: the freedom of all individuals to choose and to follow their own values. However, it could also be said that such a political philosophy, by renouncing all public values except individual freedom of choice, aggravates the difficulties of a pluralistic society. It contributes to the decay of public values and discourages the emergence of public values. Only on the assumption that there is no such thing as society can this be a good thing.

The central difficulty in the libertarian concept of freedom is that it has no concept of the common good, and it defines the freedom of the individual in such a way that it has no necessary relation to the common good. If the individual's choice benefits others, this is accidental. This disjunction, in the libertarian tradition, between liberty and any notion of the common good explains why even Thatcherism was never entirely consistently libertarian. But it also explains why the most widespread popular dissent from libertarian policies—for example, on the health service, which from the Thatcher period onwards has become a sacrosanct area of public funding in Britain—has taken the form of supporting concepts of the common good which the general public perceived to be threatened by the Thatcherite commitment to extending the liberty of the individual.

Libertarianism has two ways of resolving the tension between individual freedom and the common good. The first is a belief so extraordinary that it is astonishing how widely it seems to have been accepted: the contention that the pursuit of individual self-interest automatically ensures the common good. This is usually applied to the economic sphere, where it means that the free market makes everyone better off. This seems to be empirically false. While Thatcherite policies in Britain contributed, no doubt, to making most people better off, they did not benefit the poorest. The dominance of free-market economics globally has similarly only widened the gap between the affluent and the poor. The conviction that libertarian economic policies must in the end benefit everyone seems suspiciously more like an article of faith than a sober empirical conclusion. As an article of faith, it expresses an odd kind of theology. It combines an excessively pessimistic view of human nature (most human beings must be expected to act largely from self-interest) with an excessively optimistic view of the world (self-interest coincides with the good of all). It seems to require us to believe that God has so written the laws of economics that the most determined pursuit of one's own economic gain is the best way to provide for the poor. Put like that, it surely appears as ideologically suspect as the prosperity gospel.

The second way in which libertarianism reconciles individual freedom and the common good is to leave the common good to private charity. Unlike, for example, funding public services from taxation, private charity does not infringe the freedom of individuals to do as they wish with their own money. They are free to choose to contribute to charity or not. But, leaving aside other issues, this exposes the fundamental weakness in the libertarian notion of freedom. If freedom is defined simply as freedom to choose, no matter what choice is made, then promoting the common good is just one possible way of exercising freedom. Those who care about the common good may regard it as a better use of freedom than a wholly selfish way of life, but it is not, on this view, greater freedom. The good person is no freer than the bad.

The socialist tradition

In this tradition, the individual cannot be considered in abstraction from society. Social and economic relationships—the distribution of power and economic resources in society—both give freedom and deprive of freedom. Where economic structures benefit one class at the expense of another, the freedom of the latter is reduced. Workers whose lives are determined by the economic interests of their employers are to that extent not free. Therefore social and economic justice is the condition for the full distribution of resources. Such measures as the redistribution of wealth by taxation and the public provision of free health care and education on an equal basis for all are therefore not infringements of individual freedom but the way to enhance the freedom of all.

Especially following "the fall of communism," there is not much vestige to be found in Western political opinion of the full-blooded Marxist hope that, with a change of economic system, human beings will cease to be dominated by the pursuit of economic self-interest and become free for each other: free to work for the benefit of others as well as of themselves. Only in a very subdued way—in its continued espousal of more communitarian policies much tempered by "economic reality" and in its occasional appeal to the more altruistic motives of the electorate—does contemporary mainstream socialism offer an understanding of freedom as freedom from self-interest and freedom for others.

This means that the socialist understanding of freedom has just one principal—and very important—advantage over the libertarian: it recognizes that social and economic structures not only infringe freedom, but also grant freedom. Freedom must be fostered and extended, not only by protecting the individual's rights against infringement by society, but also by creating an equitable social order as the social and economic condition for freedom.

If the classic problem for libertarianism is a tension between freedom and the common good, the classic problem for socialism is a tension between freedom and coercion. Those who desire the common good, as embodied in government policy, willingly support the measures designed to ensure it, but others are coerced into contributing to the common good. Of course, some degree of tension of this kind is inevitable in political society and is far more tolerable in a democracy than in other political structures. But it is important that the tension be fully recognized, in order to prevent the dangerous utopian illusion that people can be forced to be free.

The myth of self-creation

The interaction of these two traditions of political thought about freedom only partly accounts for current ideas of freedom in our society. We need to grasp the force of the root concept of freedom that has characterized the whole modern age, and we need to recognize the particular cultural forms it takes in our technological and consumerist society.

Much of the modern age, with its distinctive aspirations and achievements, has been inspired by a vision of human beings as the sovereign subjects of history, capable of transcending all limits and mastering all the conditions of their life. Freedom is conceived as radical independence. Nothing is received, all is to be freely chosen. Freedom is the freedom to make of oneself what one chooses. Human beings aspire to be, in effect, their own creators.

The origins of this vision of freedom lie in the Renaissance. The fifteenth-century Florentine philosopher Pico della Mirandola, in a justly famous passage, imagined God addressing the newly created Adam:

> "The nature of other creatures, which has been determined, is confined within the bounds prescribed by us. You, who are confined by no limits, shall determine for yourself your own nature, in accordance with your own free will, in whose hand I have placed you. . . .
> We have made you neither heavenly nor earthly, neither mortal nor immortal, so that, more freely and more honorably the moulder and maker of yourself, you may fashion yourself in whatever form you shall prefer. . . ."
> O sublime generosity of God the Father! [Pico continues] O Highest and most wonderful felicity of man! To him it was granted to have what he chooses, to be what he wills.[3]

This extraordinary vision of human nature, as consisting precisely in the absence of determination, in freedom from the given limits that characterize every other creature, and therefore as free to create itself as it chooses, did not, as one might have expected, follow the development of modern science and technology but preceded it. It had, of course, some basis in fifteenth-century European people's actual abilities to choose and to implement ways of being human, which certainly marked out humanity as unique among animals. But the vision had far more basis in human imagination and human aspiration to be godlike. What is attributed to humanity is little short of the freedom of God. Only the traditional concept of God as the absolutely self-determining reality could have inspired this vision of humanity. It comes as close as a theist like Pico could to the denial of human creatureliness.

For Pico, humans are still creatures, because their godlike ability to create themselves is derived from God. But it is a short step to the even greater fan-

---

[3]Quoted in D. Brown, *To Set at Liberty: Christian Faith and Human Freedom* (Maryknoll, N. Y.: Orbis, 1981), 16.

tasy that human beings are in the fullest sense self-created. Karl Marx put it as bluntly as any:

> A being only considers himself independent when he stands on his own feet; and he only stands on his own feet when he owes his existence to himself. A man who lives by the grace of another regards himself as a dependent being. But I live completely by the grace of another if I owe him not only the maintenance of my life but if he has, moreover, created my life. . . . When it is not of my own creation, my life has necessarily a cause of this kind outside of it. The Creation is therefore an idea very difficult to dislodge from popular consciousness. But since for the socialist man the entire so-called history of the world is nothing but the creation of man through human labour, nothing but the emergence of nature for man, so he has the visible, irrefutable proof of his birth through himself, of the process of his creation.[4]

Integral to this line of thought is the concept of the world as the material with which human beings can construct their freely chosen future. The world is not, as traditional societies always supposed, a given context for human life, setting limits to human freedom. Rather, it is entirely subject to human will. Pico, like many Renaissance intellectuals, sought this expanded control over nature, which his vision of humanity demanded, in magic. But in this respect modern science is the heir of Renaissance magic. What was sought in magic was achieved to a remarkable degree through science and technology. The extraordinary achievements of science have given substance and credibility to a myth that would surely not otherwise have survived so long: the myth of humanity's freedom to transcend all limits. Even now the prospect of human genetic engineering appeals to those who have lived by this myth, for it brings us closer than ever to Pico's vision of an Adam able to determine his own nature for himself. But the myth remains a myth. One need not denigrate the real achievements of modern science in order to read its history differently.

Freedom of opportunity and freedom of consumer choice

In its sublimest form the modern myth of humanity's godlike freedom is perhaps rather remote from the everyday concerns of the average person in the contemporary West. But it forms the background to virtually all concrete thinking about freedom. It means that freedom is felt to be opposed to all limits. Freedom means the ability to determine oneself however one wishes by making any choices without restriction. In contemporary Britain this kind of

---

[4]Quoted in J. Macken, *The Autonomy Theme in the Church Dogmatics: Karl Barth and His Critics* (Cambridge: Cambridge University Press, 1990), 19–20.

freedom is thought to be available in two major forms: freedom of opportunity and freedom of consumer choice.

Freedom of opportunity is, of course, the libertarian alternative to social justice, and it has proved a peculiarly appealing one. It says a lot about contemporary British cultural attitudes that Margaret Thatcher's successor as (Conservative) prime minister, John Major, was able to establish his reputation as a man of the people by speaking of the classless society, and meaning not at all what that potent phrase had previously meant in political rhetoric. He was able, in effect, to hijack the Marxist phrase in order to rename a libertarian ideal. His classless society was not one in which there are no longer capitalists and workers, rich and poor, but one in which everyone has the opportunity, should they be enterprising enough, to become rich. It is not the Marxist but the American dream, and it has all the resonances of legendary America as a land of wide-open opportunities. It reflects a widespread desire for freedom to do what I want with my life, unrestricted by social expectations, responsibilities to others, class structures, and economic pressures.

Of course, it is true that, for a variety of social and economic reasons, freedom to choose both work and lifestyle is now for many people greater than it ever has been. But the myth of unrestricted freedom of opportunity goes far beyond the empirical facts. It neglects the concrete limitations of freedom in people's actual circumstances. It denies the essential conditionedness of all freedom. As political rhetoric it covers up the unpleasant realities. As popular dream it seduces people into fantasy and irresponsibility. It promotes the belief that what I really want in life must be within my grasp if only I can break free of the restrictions that impede my freedom. The myth of unrestricted freedom of opportunity has much to do with the divorce statistics, which include a high percentage of subsequent regret. It is the dream which tragically leads many young people to find that the streets of the capital are not paved with gold but frequented by drug-dealers and pimps. It is also the dream behind the equally tragic get-rich-quick mentality of many other young people, who see that freedom of opportunity in contemporary Britain is largely purchased and enter a career with the sole object of purchasing as much of it as soon as possible.

Freedom of opportunity in fact comes down, more than anything else, to consumer choice, the freedom to take advantage of endlessly increasing opportunities to spend money. Levels of spending in the shops are apparently the measure of a country's economic health and a government's overall success. The freedom we are all encouraged to want is the freedom to have more and more of what can be bought, to enjoy more and more of what can be bought. Banal as this seems alongside Pico's vision of Adam confined by no limits, determining his own nature, it is not unconnected. It is Pico's vision packaged by commercial interests for popular consumption. If it seems banal from an intellectual distance, at close range it has all the addictive glamour of the American (and now also British) shopping mall. It offers transcendence of limits. Opportunities to spend are limitless, and the novel experiences that can be purchased are endless. All the felt restrictions of life can be transcended by purchasing something. Even satiety with what can be bought is not easily reached; in the consumer culture it is most readily understood simply as satiety with what I have bought so far. The remedy is to look for some new experience to buy. The seemingly endless novelty available to modern consumer choice is the key to its illusion of freedom.

The transcending of limits is largely an illusion, though a powerful one. It has been often enough pointed out that the choices available to consumers are often trivial and the novelty quite spurious. Most purchases consist in replacing what people already have with something they consider better not out of free preference but constrained by what is now fashionable or said to be technologically improved (whether or not the consumers are likely actually to benefit from the improvement). Their desire for endless novelty is stimulated and manipulated by commercial forces for commercial ends. Even the freedom to prefer what one really likes to what commerce decrees that everyone now wants is hard to retain. Even harder is the greater freedom of Socrates, who when he walked through the Athenian market would say to himself, "Who would have thought there could be so many things that I can do without!"[5] Socrates did not have to contend with the virtually unchallenged dominance of commercial forces that we do. But he would certainly not have mistaken their tyranny for freedom.

The way in which contemporary libertarianism most betrays real freedom is probably in its attitude to consumerism. By glorifying consumer choice and not recognizing the vast power of commercial forces to exploit people by molding attitudes, it ignores one of the greatest threats to freedom in our society. Moreover, there is a further evil: the process of commercialization of the whole of life, which has accelerated under the impact of the enterprise culture. For example, in public services such as education, qualities and motivations such as pride in professional excellence, desire to help people, and simple enjoyment of work have been steadily eroded. What replaces them are the quantification of commercial value and purely monetary incentives. In ordinary life, all kinds of things that people once did for one another out of neighborliness, friendship, and family duty are becoming professional services to be mediated by money. This is a reduction of freedom. The freedom of really human relationships is reduced to the freedom to purchase. But if freedom is

---

[5]Diogenes Laertes, *Lives of the Eminent Philosophers* 2.25, quoted in V. K. Robbins, ed., *Ancient Quotes and Anecdotes* (Sonoma, Calif.: Polebridge Press, 1989), 159.

defined as consumer choice, the reduction is not noticed; it looks like an extension of freedom.

So in consumerism and commercialization we see a particular form of the modern age's understanding of freedom as mastering the world and transcending all limits. The consumer is persuaded to see himself or herself as an autonomous individual mastering the world by money, transcending limits by achieving an ever higher standard of living and enjoying endless novelty. But this freedom, such as it is, is bought at a very high price. It is made possible by modern technological society's ruthless and destructive exploitation of the earth's resources; it is my freedom at the expense of nature and of future generations. It is also made possible by the dominance of the world's affluent elite over the rest of the world; it is my freedom at the expense of the poor. This is the nature of the kind of freedom that means the rejection of all limits. However much it may be dangled before all as a tantalizing carrot, it is grasped by only some at the expense of others, by the powerful few at the expense of the powerless many.

The car as symbol of freedom

The modern dream of freeing humanity to be whatever we choose to be by transcending all limits has, of course, produced the ecological crisis. This has exposed the myth as a dangerous fantasy. The attempt to transcend all limits has brought us up against the undeniable finitude of the creation to which we belong. We cannot reject limits without destroying the creation on which we depend. We cannot make ourselves gods, independent of the rest of nature, supreme over it, molding it into whatever future we choose. But the habit of trying is not easy to break. Modern humanity is addicted to the freedom that rejects all limits.

There is no more pervasive symbol of this freedom and its destructive futility than the car. Cars are the modern sacrament of freedom; they symbolize it and promise actually to give it. We can glimpse the kind of freedom they promise in the typical television advertisement: an individual driving through open countryside, mountain ranges, and deserts with the widest possible horizons. Some also navigate nimbly through picturesquely narrow streets. Cars offer individuals the freedom to go wherever they wish, whenever they like, as fast as possible. They give independence, freedom to be entirely one's own master, not dependent on others, not even accompanied by others. They suggest the freedom of escape from any situation and of new opportunities and experiences always to be found along a new road. They give the feeling of control over one's destiny. This is why most car owners cannot imagine living without one. But, as always, this kind of freedom restricts the freedom of others. The more people have cars, the more difficult life becomes for those who cannot afford them or are too old or too young to drive; public transport decays, and shops and community facilities are no longer within walking distances. But the more people have cars, the less the car owners themselves enjoy the freedom they value. Commuters spend highly stressful hours in bumper-to-bumper, slow moving traffic. Motorways become car parks. Roads destroy the countryside the car owner wants the freedom to enjoy at the weekends. Moreover, since car ownership has become common, cities and most aspects of life in cities have developed in such a way that normal life requires constant long journeys. The freedom to travel has incurred the necessity to travel. Again typically of this kind of freedom, cars increase personal independence at the expense of the community. Many a vast residential area is for many residents no more than a place through which they drive on the way from their houses to other destinations.

All this would be true even without the ecological disaster. But we must add that cars are the single largest drain on the earth's resources and major polluters of the environment. Most cars still belong to the affluent West. As they spread inexorably to the rest of the world, the environmental consequences will be dire. What applies to the differential between car owners and others in our society applies to a much greater degree on a world scale. The planet can support the kind of freedom the car gives only for an elite. The more car owners there are, the more the freedom of others suffers. The more car owners there are, the more the quality of their own life suffers. There is no way out of this trap except by reevaluating freedom.

Outline of a Christian Understanding of Freedom

Freedom as given and appropriated

We human beings, like all other finite beings, come into existence. We do not come to be by our own choice. We do not make ourselves. We are given existence. Moreover, throughout our lives we remain utterly dependent on the conditions that make life possible at all and on the conditions that make possible the particular lives we lead. In the last resort, everything we are and have is *given* us—by nature and history, by culture and society, by parents, friends, teachers, relatives, lovers, and so on. Ultimately, everything we are and have is given us by God, who is the source of all finite existence. Except for this reference to God, the point is entirely obvious and indisputable. But modern people so rarely reflect on it that it needs to be stressed. We cannot begin to understand ourselves and to live rightly until we accept ourselves as a gift. If we try to reject our finitude and dependence, we deny our own real being as creatures and live a destructive fantasy.

However, it is equally important to observe that we human beings, unlike many other finite beings, are given *freedom*. Along with existence and everything else, we are given a significant degree of freedom to choose what to make of ourselves and our lives. This freedom is *given*. In an important sense it is given by the particular circumstances of our lives: social conditions, personal relationships, and so on. External possibilities of choice obviously vary enormously for these reasons, but it is also true that a person's internal capacity to make free choices can be fostered or hindered, developed or stifled by those who play a part in his or her development as a person. Freedom is not simply something we possess in an absolute and self-sufficient way. Its concrete possibilities are given us by the contexts and relationships in which we become ourselves. Dietrich Bonhoeffer's poem "The Friend" speaks of friendship not only as a relationship initiated in freedom but also as a relationship that enables and fosters freedom: "each in the other/ sees his true helper/ to brotherly freedom."[6]

In addition to the way in which particular people, circumstances, and events confer freedom on us, we should also acknowledge a more fundamental sense in which freedom is inherent in being human, and therefore given us simply as human creatures. This is why freedom can be claimed and asserted in spite of the most oppressive circumstances. There do not seem to be any circumstances—psychological, social, economic, political—that can wholly prevent either the experience of freedom in spite of them or the desire for greater freedom than they allow.

Whether we think of this fundamental freedom that is inherent in our human personhood or of the concrete possibilities of being free that are dependent on our actual circumstances, freedom is given us. But the freedom that is given us has also to be appropriated. By its very nature, freedom cannot be passively received; it must be actively appropriated in the actual exercise of freedom. And in the way we exercise it, by the choices we make, we become more free or less free. We may make choices by which we enslave ourselves (not only in obvious ways, such as drug addiction, but also in subtler psychological ways, which the New Testament sums up as slavery to sin). But we may also make choices through which our freedom matures by responsible use. Freedom may be lost or developed, but in any case it must be appropriated. It is not freedom unless we make it our own by exercising it. This is partly why in the experience of freedom it is all too easy to forget—as the whole modern age has tended to do—that human freedom is not the absolute self-

---

[6]D. Bonhoeffer, *Letters and Papers from Prison*, ed. E. Bethge, trans. R. H. Fuller, F. Clarke et al., 3d ed. (London: SCM Press, 1967), 390.

determination of God but the freedom of finite creatures, given us to be exercised within limits. Against this temptation we must maintain both aspects of *finite freedom*. It would not be *freedom* if we did not appropriate it, but it would not be *finite* if it were not given us.

In order to see the error in the typically modern human aspiration to the limitless freedom of God, it is essential to realize that finiteness is not an evil. To be limited is the good of the creature. As John Webster puts it, "limitation *specifies* rather than *hems in* the creature."[7] It defines the specific, God-given good of being the creatures we are. To deny our finitude is to refuse to be who we are, an impossible attempt to be something else. Our specifically human, creaturely freedom is not, therefore, opposed to finiteness, but is specified as our own, properly human form of freedom by its finiteness. To appropriate it without spoiling it, without distorting it into some form of enslavement, we must *receive* it gladly as *given* to us.

All we are and have is given us. Along with all we are and have, we are given some freedom to choose what to make of ourselves. This is the very limited sense in which we may be said to create ourselves. But to say that we create ourselves, though rather common today, is really dangerously misleading. It is true that what we are is not something static; we are the selves we become. And it is true that we have limited freedom to become what we choose. But this is no more than making something of what we are given. It is a freedom wholly dependent on gift. If I make myself, for example, into a brilliant musician, then certainly I am exercising a real freedom to make all the choices, some no doubt very hard, that lead to this. But this freedom is entirely dependent, not only, immediately and obviously, on being born with musical talent and having the opportunities to develop it (which have to be available even if one has to struggle to avail oneself of them). It is also dependent on a whole range of other facts about my circumstances that one would normally take for granted (but precisely for *granted*, that is, given!), for example, that there is music and that my culture has a musical tradition in which I can learn to love and to play music. Becoming a brilliant musician is therefore much more fundamentally gift than it is achievement. The same would be true of becoming a good parent, or a good friend, or just a good person. This is not to denigrate the achievement. But it is to recognize the priority of grace (to use the theological word for gift) to all human achievement. Pride and joy in the achievement are not in the least diminished by recognizing, with thankfulness and joy, the grace that made it possible.

---

[7] J. Webster, *Barth's Moral Theology* (Edinburgh: T. & T. Clark, 1998), 115. Webster is expounding Karl Barth's treatment of "freedom in limitation" in *CD* III/4.

I have labored this point, obvious as it may seem, because it is so important to resist the persistent tendency of the modern age to think of freedom as though it were the absolute freedom to create ourselves. An interesting illustration is the language that feminist theologian Susan Nelson Dunfee uses when she wishes to speak of women's freedom to define themselves, not to be defined by others. She says, "Women experience our liberation as a call to selfhood, to self-affirmation—the call *to give birth to ourselves, to name ourselves and to grow into our fullness.*"[8] The imagery seems deliberately and explicitly drawn from the facts of giving birth to and naming a child. But giving birth to oneself is precisely what no one can do. The imagery is scarcely intelligible except exactly as an attempt to *replace* the experience of birth—in which it is so obvious that we do not create but are given ourselves—by an act of self-creation. Of course, the attempt is absurd. But even more interesting is the image of naming. A name symbolizes identity. That children are given names by their parents is a kind of recognition that who they are is fundamentally *given* to them, before they are able to choose it. It is, of course, possible for adults to rename themselves. But few actually do what Dunfee uses as a metaphor for self-definition. Most people do not seem to find it restrictive or oppressive to be identified by names they did not choose. (Even feminists who, quite reasonably, object to being known by their husbands' names do not usually replace the names they have borne since birth.) Most people seem content with the names they were given.

The way we unquestioningly own the names we have been given is significant. To be properly human, we have similarly to own the selves we have been given. The freedom we have is not freedom to start from scratch in creating whatever self we choose. One may want to change oneself and can, to an important extent, change oneself. But one cannot exchange oneself for another.

Not even Christian conversion is such a change, though it may feel like it. It is, metaphorically, a new birth (John 3:3–7), but a new birth for the old self, not the birth of a new self. Moreover, it is not a giving birth to oneself, but a being born of the Spirit. In Christ God gives us back ourselves, redeemed, renewed, liberated from sin. As the New Testament portrays salvation in the image of new birth (being given oneself), so it also portrays it in the image of liberation (being given one's freedom) (e.g., Gal. 5:1). If it is clear in creation that we are not free to create ourselves, it is even clearer in redemption. We are given ourselves and we are given freedom.

---

[8]S. Nelson Dunfee, *Beyond Servanthood: Christianity and the Liberation of Women* (Lanham/London: University Press of America, 1989), 25 (my italics).

To live in an authentically human way, we need not just to acknowledge in theory that our freedom and its concrete possibilities are given us. We need to realize this in our actual experience and exercise of freedom. This is best done through the practice of prayer, in which we acknowledge, with thankfulness, our dependence on the God to whom we owe everything. This is not some kind of slavish subjection of ourselves to divine despotism, which is how some modern writers misunderstand the Christian devotional tradition. It is not denial of freedom but the realization of the givenness of freedom. It delivers us from the illusory desire to absolutize our freedom by becoming our own creators—a desire that in the end is dehumanizing. It enables us to exercise freedom in a properly human way—with trust, love, courage, and responsibility.

Independence and belonging

The modern myth of freedom tends to set freedom in absolute contrast to dependence, relationship, community, belonging. The truly free person is imagined as the sovereign individual, free of all dependence, relating to the world only by way of mastery and control, steadfastly refusing to be "tied down" by any relationships or social involvements that entail enduring commitment, always retaining the option to "take off" again in pursuit of freely chosen goals. Steve Holmes suggests that the "iconic figures" of this modern ideal of freedom are "the cowboy, riding the empty plains with no history to enslave him, who involves himself for a few days in a situation and then leaves it and its ties behind; the long distance lorry driver, or solo pilot, whose existence is separated from any society by the nature of the role."[9] We may add that the economically induced mobility of contemporary Western society offers many more people the opportunity to act out these iconic roles in their own lives. Instead of experiencing the impossibility of putting down roots as a diminishment of human experience, people are seduced by the myth of freedom into celebrating it. Once again, as with consumerism, we can see the promotion of a form of freedom as an ideology serving commercial interests. The characteristically late modern or post-modern fear of commitment is, to some degree at least, an internalization of the imperious needs of the market.

This modern myth of freedom as untrammeled independence is the myth that destroys community, inhibits commitments in relationships, exploits the natural world, and can envisage God only as a restriction on freedom. But once we recognize the givenness of freedom, we can see that dependence and

---

[9]S. Holmes, "Edwards on the Will," *International Journal of Systematic Theology* 1 (1999): 269.

independence, belonging and freedom are not exclusive opposites but reciprocal factors. There is no human independence that is not rooted in a deeper
dependence—on nature, on other people, and on God. From the utterly help-
less dependence of a newborn infant, a human being is not simply able but
enabled to develop the independence of a mature adult. This development is
enabled by relationships, just as it can also be inhibited by relationships. The
freedom thus given and appropriated is not a freedom from relationship but a
freedom in relationship. It is continually enabled and fostered by liberating
relationships, just as it continually enables and fosters liberating relationships.

Thus the two fundamental human needs for freedom and belonging are not
in contradiction but reciprocal. Belonging is necessary to true freedom, and
freedom is necessary to true belonging. Grace Jantzen makes a helpful distinction between belonging and being owned.[10] People may belong to each
other, but a person may not be owned by another. The latter is slavery and
contradicts freedom. The outlawing of slavery is a great achievement of the
modern recognition of the right of every human being to freedom. It has
rightly led to the rejection of old legal concepts that gave parents rights of
ownership over children, husbands rights of ownership over wives, and
employers rights of ownership over employees. But freedom is misunderstood
when it is opposed not only to ownership but also to belonging. One interesting difference between owning and belonging is that only the latter is mutual.
A slaveowner owns his slave, but the slave does not own his master. By contrast, spouses belong together—each to the other. This is true even of relationships that cannot be fully symmetrical, like that between a small child and
its parents. The child is radically dependent on its parents, as the parents are
not on the child. The parents have responsibilities for the child that the child
does not have for its parents. But belonging is mutual: the child belongs to its
parents and the parents to their child. Within such mutual belonging a relationship can develop that fosters the child's growing freedom, instead of
inhibiting and suppressing it.

This example may help us to understand the freedom of human beings in
relationship with God. The biblical concept of the covenant between God and
God's people is one of mutual belonging: "I . . . will be your God, and you shall
be my people" (Lev. 26:12, and often). The relationship is not symmetrical.
We are radically dependent on God, as God is not on us. We pledge obedience to God, as God does not to us. God has responsibilities for us that we do
not have for God. God and God's people are not related as equals. But it is a

---

[10]G. Jantzen, "Human Autonomy in the Body of God," in A. Kee and E. T. Long, eds.,
Being and Truth: Essays in Honour of John Macquarrie (London: SCM Press, 1986), 188.

relationship of mutual belonging. God, in the freedom of God's love, commits God's self to being our God, as we freely commit ourselves to God as God's people. Such a relationship can enable our freedom, instead of stifling it.

The difference between mutual belonging and unilateral owning also illuminates one of the very rare passages in which the word *free* is used in the Gospels. Jesus says, "Very truly, I tell you, everyone who commits sin is a slave to sin. The slave does not have a permanent place in the household; the son has a place there forever. So if the Son makes you free, you will be free indeed" (John 8:34–36). Here the contrast is between slavery, on the one hand, and both freedom and belonging on the other. The slave, because he or she is owned, can also be disowned. He or she does not belong in the master's house in the way that the son belongs in his father's house. What the slave lacks is not only freedom from bondage but also belonging. So when Jesus makes people free, he not only liberates them from bondage to sin; he also makes them children of God his Father. He gives them freedom in relationship. He gives them the freedom of his Father's house. He shares with them the mutuality of belonging to each other that he and his Father have from eternity in the loving freedom of the Trinitarian relationships. Paul also contrasts slavery with the freedom of being children of God (Rom. 8:15, 21). In the light of these passages, we can see that the idea of freedom in a relationship of belonging is implicit whenever the New Testament uses the image of believers as sons and daughters of God.

The alternative image of friendship (John 15:14–15) puts perhaps an even stronger emphasis on freedom, since friendship (unlike the relationship of children and parents) is a relationship created by mutual choice. But it is no less a relationship of committed belonging. The freedom of friends is not simply their free choice to be friends but the freedom they find themselves given and giving in belonging to each other. Only through this reciprocity of freedom and belonging can we begin to understand freedom as not only freedom from others (from being owned or dominated by others) but also, just as importantly, freedom for others.

Of course, in human development there have to be phases of maturing freedom in which the balance shifts from dependence on others to greater freedom in relation to others. Such phases may require a deliberate, even painful assertion of freedom from others. This is good so long as this relative freedom from others is not absolutized but is allowed to contribute to a maturer form of freedom in belonging and a greater freedom for others. The classic case, of course, is adolescence. The adolescent has to break free of childish dependence and assert independence. The break may even feel like a complete repudiation of belonging. But in fact the independence is rooted in dependence. It is the adolescent's parents, among others, who, if they have been good parents, have enabled him or her to grow into the independence he or she can now assert. Once secure in mature adult independence, the son or daughter has no difficulty acknowledging what they owe to their parents. The relationship has changed. But mutual belonging can be reaffirmed in a new form of freedom in relationship.

The image of adolescence or "coming of age" (the phrase popularized by Dietrich Bonhoeffer) has been frequently used for the whole human project of the modern age, which began with the Enlightenment. This was conceived as breaking free from dependence on nature through technological mastery of the natural world and as self-liberation from religious domination by assertion of independence from God. This account of the modern project has its limitations. But we could give it the most generous Christian interpretation if we saw it in terms of an adolescent assertion of independence that has so far failed to mature into an adult reappropriation of the relationships that have been repudiated. In appropriating freedom, modern humanity has not yet recognized that this very freedom is rooted in dependence on God and on nature. With the immaturity of the adolescent, modern humanity has absolutized its independence. Confusing belonging with domination or ownership, it has failed to integrate the freedom it has asserted into new forms of belonging to nature and belonging to God. As Nicholas Lash puts it, "It is surely time to learn the discipline of adulthood, the transcending of autonomy in community and finitude."[11]

Limits and transcendence

Freedom is about transcending limits. This is both its authentic appeal and its inauthentic allure. The question is how limits are to be transcended.

We must first acknowledge fully that there are oppressive conditions and repressive relationships that contradict the freedom for which human beings are made. Liberation theologies of all kinds (including feminist theologies) have been rightly concerned with the liberation of human beings from all kinds of oppression. Here we take their main concerns for granted. It is not because they are not of great importance that they are not repeated here, but because contemporary Western society also raises other issues about freedom that have not received so much Christian attention.

The need for liberation from oppressive conditions should not be confused with the quite different notion of liberation from all limits. The latter is the modern Western myth of godlike freedom. Its dominance explains both the

---

[11]N. Lash, *The Beginning and the End of "Religion"* (Cambridge: Cambridge University Press, 1996), 244.

great achievements of modern Western culture in the sphere of freedom (democracy, human rights, the success of medicine in freeing us from many diseases and disabilities) and also its failure to deliver freedom in the fullest and deepest sense. For the sake of the latter we must renounce the dream of abolishing all limits. We must accept our finitude as the condition for properly human freedom. The lesson of the ecological crisis is unmistakably the need to live within limits. But does this simply mean that we must restrict our freedom within certain limits? In that case, we still have the same concept of freedom but concede that we cannot have as much of such freedom as we may hitherto have thought. This is an unsatisfactory conclusion, because it leaves us feeling that what would still really be desirable would be the abolition of all limits, even though unfortunately this is not possible. In that case, the dream of godlike freedom retains its dangerous allure.

What we need to grasp is that limits need not be opposed to freedom.[12] They need not restrict freedom but can enable true freedom, when they are accepted in love. Love is a way of transcending limits by accepting them, not trying to abolish them. Consider, first, freedom in relation to other people. If my freedom consists in abolishing all limits to what I may do and have, then other people are bound to appear as limits to my freedom. My freedom competes with theirs, and so I can extend it only at their expense. Their only positive contribution to my freedom will be if I can dominate or exploit them, so that they serve my interests. But again my freedom is then secured at the expense of theirs.

The matter appears quite different when we understand freedom as given and exercised within relationships. Other people do not restrict but enable my freedom when I receive my freedom from them and exercise my freedom as freedom for them. In this way of thinking, freedom is inseparable from love. Then we can think also quite differently about transcending limits. I encounter other people as limits to my own being. But when I go out of myself in love for others, I both accept those limits and transcend them. Indeed, it is by accepting those limits in love, affirming other people, and finding myself in loving relationships with them, that I transcend limits. Instead of the freedom to abolish all limits, I discover the freedom that is enabled by the acceptance and transcendence of limits in love.

---

[12]Cf. J. S. Begbie, *Theology, Music, and Time* (Cambridge: Cambridge University Press, 2000), 186: "constraints are not intrinsically inimical to our freedom but are required for its actualisation." He explicates this claim by using musical improvization as a model (chapters 7–8). It is a claim that could be developed in relation to constraints other than those I discuss here (human relationships, nature, and God), for example, those given to us in each person's physical form and capacities.

Jürgen Moltmann makes the same point:

> In a community of mutual respect, of liking, friendship and love, the other person is no longer a restriction of my personal freedom. That person is the social complement of my own limited freedom. The result is reciprocal participation in the life of other people. People become free beyond the frontiers of their own life, and the outcome of this mutual participation is shared life, "the good life."[13]

We can apply the same concept to our relationship with the natural world. The modern attempt to abolish all limits saw our dependence on nature as limiting our freedom and sought to free us from nature by subjecting it to our interests. But nature, like human society, can also be a sphere in which we can rediscover the freedom of belonging. In acknowledging again our place as finite creatures among others and in lovingly letting other creatures be, we can experience them as limits to our humanness that we transcend as we accept them in love.

Finally, we consider the question of relationship to God, the most difficult relationship for modern thinking about freedom and also the most fundamental, because the modern aspiration to godlike freedom from all limits was possible precisely through the rejection of God as a limit on human transcendence. It is in the recognition of God's infinity that human beings have usually been able to recognize and accept their own finitude. Only forgetfulness of God makes possible the dream of infinite freedom for humanity. But this dream is an alienating illusion. In liberating us from it, relationship with God does not restrict our freedom but enables our truly human freedom.

The crux is the question of obedience to God's will. Is this a kind of heteronomy (subjection to another) that contradicts human autonomy (self-determination)? Many modern people think so. But, properly understood, obedience to God transcends this contradiction. When I love God and freely make God's will my own, I am not forfeiting my freedom but fulfilling it. God's will is not the will of another in any ordinary sense. It is the moral truth of all reality. To conform ourselves freely to that truth is also to conform to the inner law of our own created being. To learn obedience to God involves, of course, a long and painful struggle, as it did for Jesus (Heb. 5:8), who exercised his freedom as Son never more fully than in his acceptance of his Father's will in Gethsemane (Mark 14:36). But it is a journey into the fullest freedom: the goal of our salvation in which theonomy (obedience to God's will) and autonomy

---

[13]J. Moltmann, *God for a Secular Society*, trans. M. Kohl (London: SCM Press, 1999), 158; cf. also J. Moltmann, *The Trinity and the Kingdom of God*, trans. M. Kohl (London: SCM Press, 1981), 216.

will fully coincide. This is why the Anglican collect for peace says that "to serve you is perfect freedom."

Once again the key is love. The limit constituted by God's will is not a restriction on our freedom when we accept it by loving God, by freely embracing God's will, by making God's will our own. We transcend the limit by accepting it. In this way we fulfill through love of God the freedom we receive from God through God's love for us.

Freedom to choose and freedom to choose well

Freedom to choose is essential to authentic humanity. But its value does not consist merely in itself. No doubt there is some value in being able to make some choices between equally good alternatives; for example, to choose strawberry or pistachio ice cream, not because I consistently prefer one to the other flavor, but just because I fancy one or the other today. Such trivial choices add interest to the surface of life. The problem is not that we have more of them than any human society has had before—though some observers detect a degree of "selection fatigue" setting in, as people tire of the constant demands and the time and energy needed for decision making in every aspect of life.

The really serious danger is of reducing all choice to this level. We are forgetting that, at a much more serious and important level, the point is not simply to have choice but to make good rather than bad choices. If we reduce the value of choice simply to that of having a choice, then choice becomes arbitrary and empty. Choosing how to spend one's time, choosing a friend or marriage partner, choosing the values, the philosophy, or the religion one lives by—all become matters of trivial whim, like choosing among fifteen flavors of ice cream. Freedom is supposed to be increased by increasing the number of flavors available and secured by retaining the freedom to choose a different flavor whenever one wishes. We live our lives like a teenager with the television remote, idling switching from channel to channel, attending to nothing and settling for nothing, merely indulging the itch for empty choice.

Freedom of choice is valuable not merely in itself but because it is freedom to make the right choice. The freedom to marry whom one chooses—an important freedom for most people in Western cultures, though not one for which most other cultures have felt the need—would not really be extended by the opportunity to choose between thousands upon thousands of potential spouses. What most people value is the freedom to marry the right person when they do meet that person. It is the freedom of making the right choice—which of course incurs the risk of making the wrong choice—that matters.

At the deepest level, it is the freedom to choose good and thereby to become good that matters. No one can be good without freedom of choice.

This is the significance of the Genesis story of paradise, in which Adam and Eve were free to eat of the tree of the knowledge of good and evil but were commanded not to do so (Gen. 2:17). Without that freedom they could have been innocent. But only by freely choosing to obey God could they become good. This is ultimately why serious freedom of choice must at all costs be protected and valued. Human goodness cannot come about through coercion or magic but only as the result of the continual free choice of good.

However, it is for the sake of this choosing of good that freedom of choice is important. Real freedom is enhanced not so much by the extension of choice as by the making of right choices. In fact, there is a sense in which, as real freedom increases, fewer choices need be made. As Grace Jantzen explains:

> A person who has developed sensitivity and kindness, for instance, does not have to make a choice about whether to help a wailing child in a department store, or whether instead to box its ears when nobody is looking. Kindness is (or has become) natural; there is no decision, no weighing up of pros and cons. But if there is no decision, is kindness to the child not free? On the contrary, it is the self-expression of an autonomous person.[14]

This, rather than in the aspiration to abolish all limits, is the way in which human beings may appropriately approach participation in the freedom of God. For God's freedom is not to choose good or evil. It is the freedom to express the perfect goodness of God's own being. Our freedom is perfected when, through the choice of good rather than evil, we finally attain the freedom simply to be good.

Kierkegaard puts it with characteristic paradox:

> Christianity teaches that you should choose the one thing needful, but in such a way that there must be no question of any choice. That is, if you fool around a long time, then you are not really choosing the one thing needful. Consequently, the very fact that there is no choice expresses the tremendous passion or intensity with which one chooses. Can there be a more accurate expression for the fact that freedom of choice is only a formal condition of freedom and that emphasizing freedom of choice as such means the sure loss of freedom? The very truth of freedom of choice is that there must be no choice, even though there is a choice.[15]

---

[14]Jantzen, "Human Autonomy," 189.
[15]C. E. Moore ed., *Provocations: Spiritual Writings of Kierkegaard* (Farmington, Pa.: Plough Publishing House, 1999), 289.

Conclusion

To sum up:

Freedom from is important: freedom from oppression and domination, freedom from poverty and disease, even relative independence of other people. But liberation from others is true freedom only if it is also liberation for others.

Freedom of is important: freedom of choice, freedom of speech, freedom of worship. But these are no more than the necessary condition for becoming fully free by freely choosing good.

True freedom is freedom in relationships or *freedom with belonging:*
Freedom given by God, other people, and nature;
Freedom with God, other people, and nature;
Freedom for God, other people, and nature.

3

Authority and Scripture

The discussion of authority has a long history in the Christian tradition, and disagreements about authority of course account for some of the denominational divisions in Christianity. But before the modern period the range of discussion was relatively narrow. Taken for granted and undisputed were the authority of God, the authority of truth revealed by God, the authority of God's commandments, including moral principles, to require our obedience. Debates were about the locus of authority in Scripture, tradition, and ecclesiastical institutions. Ecumenical discussions still tend to locate the subject wholly within ecclesiastical boundaries.[1] But if we are to face the real issues of authority for Christian faith and within Christian faith today, we have to take a much wider view. We must come to terms with what has happened to authority in the secular cultural context in which the churches find themselves in Western societies today. Don Cupitt, post-Christian postmodernist, declares, "The age of Authority, of grand institutions, of legitimating myths, and capital T-Truth, is over."[2] That is an aspect of postmodernity, and it makes Christianity not believable. Richard Holloway, former bishop of Edinburgh, arguing that morality must be radically separated from religion because the collapse of authority in our time has enlightened us as to the oppressive nature of the command moralities of religion, asserts, "[W]e now understand that

---

[1]E.g., most recently, the Anglican-Roman Catholic International Commission (ARCIC), *The Gift of Authority: Authority in the Church III* (London: Catholic Truth Society/Toronto: Anglican Book Centre/New York: Church Publishing Incorporated, 1999).
[2]In P. Heelas, ed., *Religion, Modernity, and Postmodernity* (Oxford: Blackwell, 1998), 218.

most moral systems reflected and gave support to external structures of authority, because until very recent times most human systems were systems of command: domination systems, based on an ethic of obedience to authority. Obeying is what people did."[3] He means to imply that this is no longer what people do, and rightly so. By contrast, a great Scottish Christian writer, George Macdonald, writing more than a century earlier, could declare, "Obedience is the one key of life."[4] Just how culturally accessible such a statement was in late nineteenth-century Britain may be debatable, but few statements could be less culturally accessible in the late modern and postmodern climate we now inhabit. For our culture, freedom, not obedience, is the one key of life, and freedom is understood as entirely incompatible with obedience. Some would agree with W. K. Clifford: "There is one thing in the world more wicked than the desire to command and that is the will to obey."[5] The age of authority is over. What then of authority in Christian faith, and—first and foremost for all Christian traditions—what of the authority of Scripture?

Scripture, tradition, and reason: a threefold cord unravelling

A convenient starting point, which need not limit the relevance of the discussion to Anglicans, is a traditional Anglican one: the well-worn claim within the Anglican tradition that the authorities for Anglican doctrine and practice are the so-called threefold cord of Scripture, tradition, and reason. (We can leave aside for the purposes of our present discussion the question of institutional authority in the church, because even for Roman Catholics this is secondary to the more fundamental authority of Scripture and tradition.) It is important to recognize that in the pre-Enlightenment period, when the quintessentially Anglican theologian Richard Hooker bequeathed this threefold notion of authority to the Church of England and thence to other Anglican churches, the three authorities were conceived as harmonious. Those who were not convinced by this view of the matter—Puritans and later Nonconformists—were not convinced because they perceived serious conflict between Scripture and tradition. Within the concept of the threefold cord, reason was not deployed as a critical principle, only as an expository one. Reason helped the church to understand Scripture and tradition, not to challenge their authority by means of a rival authority, that of a form of reason quite independent of them. The

---

[3] R. Holloway, *Godless Morality: Keeping Religion out of Ethics* (Edinburgh: Canongate, 1999), 152.
[4] G. Macdonald, *Unspoken Sermons: Series I, II, III* (Whitethorn, Calif.: Johannesen, 1997) 226.
[5] Quoted in Y. R. Simon, *A General Theory of Authority* (Notre Dame/London: University of Notre Dame Press, 1962), 148.

assumption of an easy harmony between revelation and reason continued in the Roman Catholic tradition right down to Vatican II. In that context reason meant mainly Aristotelianism, already thoroughly tamed by Christian philosophers so as to serve rather than critique the faith.

With the advent of Enlightenment rationality in the eighteenth century, the nature of the threefold cord changed, because reason now came to mean thinking in the Enlightenment mode. People who appeal to this Anglican principle, especially those who are in any particular instance pressing the claims of reason to a part in the trialogue, rarely notice that the meaning of reason in the threefold formula is not constant. It changes historically. Reason does not exist for humans in a purely abstract universal form; it is always embodied in particular traditions of thought, which are different ways of formulating and deploying reasoning. Enlightenment rationality is one, very successful form of reason, but not the only form. However, Enlightenment rationality characteristically understood itself as reason per se. Critical of the claims of all other authorities and traditions, Enlightenment rationality claimed to be universal rationality, propounding truths that would be accessible to any rational person. This is why those influenced by the Enlightenment who claim to be pressing the claims of reason within the Anglican trialogue of Scripture, tradition, and reason rarely recognize that reason is a variable category: Enlightenment reason sees itself as universal—or at least as universalizable—reason.

The advent of Enlightenment reason produced the three ways of deploying the threefold cord that are characteristic of modern Anglicanism. (This term does not here refer to contemporary Anglicanism, but to the Anglicanism of yesterday, still highly influential but also subject now to quite radical change.) (1) The Catholic tradition, deeply rooted in tradition, assumed the harmony of Scripture and tradition and, still to a large extent, reason, defending itself, we might think in retrospect, against Enlightenment rationalism's corrosive effect by shoring up the defenses of tradition. (2) The Evangelical tradition, sitting relatively loose to tradition and therefore able actually to ally itself, though not very consciously, with the Enlightenment prejudice against all traditions, stood firm on the unquestionable authority of Scripture and increasingly adopted the methods that were applied by Enlightenment reason to critique Scripture in order to use the same methods to defend Scripture. (3) The Liberal tradition, very conscious of the clash of Enlightenment rationality with Christian tradition, was generous in the weight it allowed to the former and was ready to dispense with inessential elements of Scripture and tradition as unbelievable in the modern age, while trying to define the essence of Christianity in a way not vulnerable to rational criticism.

These three options are probably how most of the older generation of presently living Anglicans see the matter. But the discussion is dated, because it reflects a period when Christianity was still much more dominant in Western societies than it is in most today and when those societies were still weakly christianized, even in their overtly secular areas. We need to observe the effect of greater and greater secularization, which means, initially, the increasing triumph of Enlightenment rationalism and, later, the partial transition from modernity to postmodern pluralism that is happening at present. (Relevant aspects of postmodernity will be explained later in this chapter.)

It may well be that the continuing advance of Enlightenment rationalism's prejudice against tradition is partly what accounts for the remarkable decline of the Catholic tradition in Anglicanism in the period since the Second World War. With advancing secularization, the old intra-Christian issue of Scripture and tradition has paled in significance beside the more prominent issue of belief and unbelief. Christian belief can hardly get by with the authority only of reason, and it may be that, in the context of belief confronted with secularization, Scripture has come to seem the more secure authority (by comparison with tradition), accounting in part for the growth of Evangelicalism in recent decades.

Christianity and culture: where are we now?

While these remarks have been Anglican in form, somewhat similar points could probably be made about other Christian traditions. Where are we now? Although the degree and nature of secularization varies in various parts of the Western world, it is generally true that secular culture has distanced itself from its Christian past to an extent that many Christians of the older generation do not sufficiently recognize, obvious though it is to younger people. Increasingly we find ourselves in a context, not only of widespread cultural ignorance of Christianity, but also of real cultural hostility to Christianity. In the still weakly Christianized Britain of my early youth, the old-style Christian liberal could feel relatively at home, since his or her social ideals were widely shared by nonchurchgoers. This is no longer true. Undoubtedly there are many significant issues on which Christians can make common cause with others, but the dominant cultural trends have left large swaths of Western culture entirely post-Christian. This is why we are now in a situation in which it will not do to discuss authority in a purely intraecclesiastical way. Authority is a very dubious notion in much of contemporary culture, both modern and postmodern, but especially postmodern, and, since Christianity is no longer culturally dominant, it is the secular culture's problem with authority that influences many people in the churches today.

Among Christians who are thoughtful about their faith, two recognizable categories are particularly significant for understanding an issue of this kind.

One group is of people who, having grown up within a strongly Christian culture and taken it largely for granted, then discover the power and plausibility of various secular views of major issues. They welcome approaches, like Richard Holloway's, which seem to take the secular world seriously, to face up to what's going on in society entirely independently of the church, and to offer some kind of accommodation of secular values or insights with Christian faith. This is the classic Christian liberal response, but in a new kind of situation, one in which it is more difficult than it used to be to straddle the divide between Christian and secular thinking. Often such people are unduly impressed by the anti-Christian propaganda abroad in contemporary Western societies, especially that which blames Christianity for all the evils and failings of Western culture. Motivated by an admirable humility and openness, but therefore influenced by an exaggerated sense of the disastrous effects of Christianity in the past and present, such Christians are strongly inclined to adopt a secular view of any matter on which secular and traditional Christian values conflict.

The other category is of people, often converts, who seek in Christianity primarily an alternative to the secular world they know. For these people the authority of Scripture is often especially important, because it provides their basis for ways of thinking about and living life that are quite different from those of secular culture. These are primarily people who have crossed the cultural divide, not people who want to straddle it.

Both dynamics are at work in contemporary Western Christianity. Both have their characteristic dangers. The first runs the risk of dissipating Christianity into something indistinguishable from other options in Western culture. Richard Holloway is a good example, because he does what few liberal Christians before him would have done: he claims that to base morality on religion is actually very bad for morality. In the sphere of morality he explicitly opts out of being a Christian, because this is the only way he thinks he can do justice to what he has learned from secular culture and its critique of Christian morality as oppressive. Here is no old-fashioned liberal at home in the secular world because its moral values largely coincide with those of the Christian tradition. Here is a man of liberal temperament in a situation of much greater cultural pluralism and of much stronger antagonism to key aspects of Christianity. The point is relevant because the issue of authority is very much in play in Holloway's thesis about religion and morality. It is the allegedly authoritarian nature of the Christian moral tradition that is the problem for its postmodern critics with whom Holloway agrees. We shall return to that.

The second dynamic runs its own risk of fundamentalism. I hesitate to use the word, because it is so readily used by people at any point on the Christian spectrum to deplore all opinions more conservative than their own. But there is a significant issue about fundamentalism, authority, and the postmodern world. The sociologist Zigmunt Bauman argues that the growth of fundamentalism (meaning not only Christian fundamentalism, but equivalent tendencies in other religions, especially Islam) is not an anomalous feature of the contemporary, postmodern world, "not an outburst," as he puts it, "of premodern irrationality," but an "alternative rationality" produced by the postmodern cultural situation.[6] It is the route taken by those who find postmodern individualist freedom threatening and intolerable: "the misery of life composed of risky choices, which always means taking some chances while forfeiting others, or incurable uncertainty built into every choice, of the unbearable, because unshared, responsibility for the unknown consequences of every choice, of the constant fear of foreclosing the future and yet unforeseen possibilities."[7] The "fundamentalist rationality puts security and certainty first and condemns everything that undermines that certainty—the vagaries of individual freedom first and foremost."[8] In this analysis we should notice especially the polarity of freedom, which belongs to the postmodern, free-market type of rationality, as Bauman puts it, and authority, which is the fundamentalist's alternative to freedom. We shall have to consider later that contemporary opposition between freedom and authority.

If Bauman's account corresponds to anything in reality, one danger of the fundamentalist reaction to postmodernity is evidently a mere repudiation of secular culture, with no possibility of constructive dialogue. We should not be too ready to blame those who take that route. In a period of increasing cultural hostility to Christianity, it may be that constructive dialogue will become a luxury, so much more difficult will it become simply to maintain the faith.

However, the kind of position I described as valuing Christianity as an alternative to secular culture does not need to be fundamentalist. I would prefer to call it confident orthodoxy. It has what the liberal response in a critic such as Holloway lacks: a secure position from which to critique and to engage in dialogue with secular culture, with the various other options available in our pluralist culture. Such a secure position (which does not mean a rigidly unchangeable one) makes it possible to learn from others without losing Christian identity, as well as to critique others in ways that cannot be done from within the cultural paradigm that needs critique. It is what is needed if Christians in contemporary Western culture are not simply to be blown by every cultural wind that blows and not to succumb to a typically postmodern instability and fragmentariness that makes it impossible to take a stand on

---

[6]Z. Bauman, *Postmodernity and Its Discontents* (Cambridge: Polity Press, 1997), 185.
[7]Bauman, *Postmodernity*, 183.
[8]Bauman, *Postmodernity*, 185.

anything. The Christian church's calling in contemporary Western culture must be to be in many respects a countercultural movement. But what is also needed, if confident orthodoxy is to be confident without lapsing into authoritarianism, is an adequate understanding of authority, one that takes account of the way our contemporary culture has radically problematized the notion of authority.

Before looking more closely at the modern and postmodern attitudes to authority, it will be useful first to analyze two types of authority that are constantly encountered in ordinary life.

Authority—extrinsic and intrinsic

There is a well-established and very useful distinction between extrinsic and intrinsic authority. If one accepts a statement as true, not because the statement in itself can convince one of its truth, but because the person making the statement is qualified to make it, has the authority to say what is true in this case, then the statement depends on authority external to it—extrinsic authority. If one obeys a command, not because one can see the point or purpose of what one is being required to do, but because the person making the command has the authority to command one, then the command relies on extrinsic authority. Someone who is sick and goes to a medical doctor, who diagnoses his condition, tells him what is wrong, and prescribes medicine for him, may well be quite unable to judge for himself whether the doctor's diagnosis is correct or whether her prescription is likely to work, but because she has medical qualifications and is regarded as reliable by the community, he trusts her diagnosis and obeys her orders. This is extrinsic authority. If, on the other hand, someone observed that my poor state of health could well be due to the overwork and stress I have been suffering recently and that I really ought to take a holiday, I might find this a convincing diagnosis and be able to see that the advice is sensible. In this case it would not matter who made the observation; they need no particular expertise or authority to back up their statements. The statement itself convinces me, so that I accept it as true and do what it requires of me. The statement has intrinsic authority.

It is also worth noticing that in many everyday situations extrinsic and intrinsic authority are both operative in varying degrees. Imagine yourself the pupil of an expert teacher, whose authority to speak about his subject is not merely textbook knowledge but is also based on half a lifetime's experience of the subject. He will give you factual knowledge, which you can in fact check for yourself from the books if you feel the need. But you will also benefit from his powers of judgment, his accumulated knowledge of what works in the subject. This you have to trust, though gradually, as you become expert yourself, you will be able to verify such things from your own experience. But finally there may also be personal knowledge that you cannot check or verify for yourself. A teacher of modern art who had known Picasso personally might tell you anecdotes about the artist or report what Picasso had told him about his work. Here you or anyone else could only take his word for it. This does not at all mean that you have to be credulous or uncritical. You may have grounds for trusting your teacher's accounts, because you have been impressed by him as a reliable person. What he tells you may cohere with whatever else you know of Picasso and so be plausible. It may, as it were, ring true. But in the end you take what the teacher says on trust. In this example there is, in some areas of the knowledge you gain, a shift from more reliance on extrinsic to more reliance on intrinsic authority, as you yourself come to understand the subject more profoundly, but there are also areas in which extrinsic authority is irreplaceable. In a mature understanding of the subject, as much of what you have been taught you come to find convincing in itself, so also your grounds for trusting what you cannot in principle verify become more substantial.

If we apply this kind of analysis of authority to the Bible, it seems to me that for most believers the Bible's authority is a combination of extrinsic and intrinsic elements, and that this is also how the contents of the Bible represent themselves. Surprisingly rarely do the biblical writers demand obedience or belief by sheer appeal to the authority of God. They appeal in all kinds of ways to reason, imagination, and experience. They persuade and convince in all the ways in which literature can persuade and convince. Certainly there is a major dimension that can only be taken on trust, but it is constantly admixed with the intrinsic authoritativeness of what is said. Moreover, much of what Christians, like the pupils of the expert teacher, must begin by taking simply on trust gains a degree of intrinsic authority for them as they grow more deeply into and practice the faith. (Moreover, we should think of the community of faith as much as of the individual. The community's experience of the intrinsic authoritativeness of Scripture far surpasses the individual's.) The Bible claims an irreplaceable and important element of extrinsic authority, but it does not rely on this alone.

In summary, then, the Bible combines internal convincingness and the requirement on us to trust the truth of its message. This combination is a complex and intimate one. All too easily people make a simple distinction between extrinsic authority as oppressive and intrinsic authority as consistent with human autonomy. As we have seen, it is not as simple as that. Both in everyday life and in Christian experience of the Bible, the two go together in various different combinations.

This seems to me broadly consistent with traditional doctrines of Scripture. Perhaps these have emphasized the extrinsic authority of Scripture too one-sidedly: Scripture has the authority of God's Word, and what it says should be believed because God has the authority to say it. But traditionally the inspiration of Scripture had as its corollary the inspiration of the reader of Scripture or the reading community. The Spirit who inspired the Scripture also inspires its believing readers to accept it as God's message and to understand it. This should not be understood as a kind of magic that makes credible to us what would otherwise have no credibility. It can be understood to mean that as the Spirit inspires our Christian living and thinking, leading us further into the experience of what the Bible teaches, so we find the Bible making more sense to us—existentially, intellectually, imaginatively. As the Spirit actualizes the Word of God in our lives, so the Word of God authenticates itself to us. There is a kind of hermeneutical circle of authority and experience.

I suppose that, for people growing up in a Christian context, it has often been the case that they start by regarding the Bible as an extrinsic authority, because everyone they learn from does. Then there comes a point when it begins to penetrate their experience—some might call this their conversion—and the Bible, they might say, comes alive for them, speaks to them; they feel for the first time that they know what it is really about. That is recognition of intrinsic authority or convincingness. Maybe now for many people things happen the other way around. In a secular culture they are not inclined to treat the Bible as authoritative at all, and it is only when its message in some form (not of course necessarily as the text of the Bible itself) strikes home for them that it first gains any authority for them at all. They start with the existential convincingness of the gospel message, but they also then need to acquire a trust in the word of this God they have begun to know. There has to come for all of us a taking, on authority, of what we cannot exhaustively verify. For the new convert an important dimension of that is becoming part of the Christian community for whom as a whole the Bible has authority.

The modernist rejection of authority

As we have already noted, authority is not a concept that has fared well in the modern period. To speak, as Richard Holloway does, of a crisis of authority in society[9] has become virtually platitudinous. Indeed, we seem to have reached a stage in Western cultural history at which for many people authority is indistinguishable from authoritarianism. Authority, which was once a good word, has acquired largely negative connotations. So, if we are to understand the dynamics of people's problems with authority and defenses of authority within the churches, we need to understand this broader cultural context from which such problems stem. In particular, it is essential to distinguish what I shall call

---

[9]Holloway, *Godless Morality*, 30.

modernist forms of rejection of authority from postmodernist ones. These are significantly different.

I use the term *modernist* to refer to the characteristic worldview that stems from the European Enlightenment and has spread from Europe to much of the world in some degree. I shall use the term *postmodernist* to refer to the intellectual and cultural outlook that has recently been superseding modernism. I stress at the outset that the two outlooks overlap. Western societies are in a period of cultural transition in which modernist attitudes are still influentially present alongside the postmodernist ones. It is probably not yet clear whether postmodernism will become the enduring successor to modernist culture, but it is certainly at present a strong contender.

According to Immanuel Kant, the motto of the Enlightenment is: "Have the courage to use your own intelligence!" The Enlightenment rejected traditional authorities, both institutional and intellectual, in the name of autonomous reason. What is worthy of belief is what can in principle be established by rational argument by any intelligent person. What is worthy of moral obedience is what can be discerned as the moral imperative by any rational person. Submission to extrinsic authority—believing or acting merely on someone else's say-so—is incompatible with the autonomy of the individual rational person.

It may look as though modernism, therefore, rejects extrinsic authority and affirms intrinsic authority, but it is not quite so simple. With regard to extrinsic authority, in practice the modern world is heavily dependent on the authority of the expert, especially the scientist. The modern project of extending rational control over human life and the rest of the world requires the accumulation of knowledge—indeed, the formation of traditions of knowledge and practice—that it is impossible for individuals to verify for themselves. Not only the laypeople but even scientists rely on the work of their predecessors and could not practicably verify all of their conclusions for themselves. However, they could *in principle* be verified. What modernism rejects is authority that cannot be checked, tested, and criticized.

But it is important also to notice that for modernism what counts as the criterion for intrinsic authority is a particular and rather narrow concept of reason. One should be convinced only of what can be demonstrated empirically or from first principles in a way that is universally accessible. Hence, in part, the enormous prestige of natural science as the model of true knowledge in modernism. Hence also the attempt to establish moral values as universally recognizable independently of particular cultural and religious traditions. Enlightenment rationality aims to replace all particular traditions of thought and practice, whose inherited wisdom and insights seem to it to have no rational foundation. Such traditions' complex combinations of extrinsic authority and intrinsic authoritativeness are missed and dismissed, since they do not allow the abstract universal verification that modernism demands.

So, having specified in what the modernist rejection of authority consists, we may ask how the authority of the Bible fares in encounter with it. The Bible clearly represents a particular tradition of faith, rooted in a particular history and its interpretation. Its truth claims do not seem open to universal verification in accordance with modernist requirements. However, the Bible was too central to European culture to be dismissed as easily as European cultural imperialists dismissed the traditions of their subject peoples. So, about the Bible's encounter with modernist canons of rational belief, I will make three points:

(1) Much effort in nineteenth-century biblical studies and theology was devoted to the attempt to reconstruct the Bible's value for Christian faith in a way that escapes the modern rejection of authority. There are two main aspects to this. One is historical criticism in its typical nineteenth- and early twentieth-century form (also still with us, of course), that is, the attempt to get behind the way the Bible interprets the story it tells to "what really happened"—a purely objective account of the historical facts from which rational modern people may draw their own conclusions. The historical Jesus—reconstructed by critical historical method—replaces the biblical Christ as the basis of Christian faith. Secondly, there is the attempt to understand the message of the Bible as the proclamation of moral values that are universally accessible to reason but of which the biblical history is a useful instantiation.

Modernism dies hard, and so these issues are still with us. Witness the continuing popularity of pseudoscholarly books that purport to uncover the real and sensational historical facts behind the biblical story or, more respectably, the current flourishing of historical Jesus research especially in America. But there is an intriguing point about the latter. While rooted in modernism (with its naively objectivist view of history), it could be seen as hovering on the brink of postmodernism (with just the opposite view of history). The old criticism of the quest of the historical Jesus, that its practitioners merely find the kind of Jesus they are looking for, could actually recommend the quest in postmodernist eyes. We may see the quest explicitly reformulating itself as the unfettered construction of the variety of Jesus figures a pluralist Christian culture needs.[10] The future for unscholarly, frankly loony books about Jesus ought to be even brighter in the postmodern era.

---

[10]L. T. Johnson, *The Real Jesus* (San Francisco: HarperSanFrancisco, 1997), 8, points out that, despite the historical objectivism of its methodology as generally publicized, the Jesus Seminar's founder Robert Funk is also explicit in viewing its work in thoroughly postmodern constructivist terms: "We need a fiction [i.e., a fictional Jesus] that we recognize to be fictive."

(2) My second and third points concern the way in which discussion of the authority of the Bible ought to respond to the modernist critique of authority. In the first place, within the Enlightenment's rejection of authority, there was a necessary critique of authoritarianism, the coercive imposition of authority. The problem is that the way modernism formulated the opposition between freedom (autonomy) and authority made all forms of extrinsic authority seem to contradict freedom. All extrinsic authority seems authoritarian. If we are to distinguish the Bible's authority from authoritarianism, we need to think about authority and freedom differently from modernism.

(3) The crux of the problem of biblical authority in the context of modernism is the modernist prejudice against the particular and in favor of universal reason. But here postmodernism's critique of modernism turns the whole issue on its head, as we shall now see.

The postmodernist rejection of authority

In a sense, postmodernism takes modernism's rejection of authority for the sake of autonomy to an extreme that subverts modernism. For postmodernists the modern project is itself authoritarian. Behind the Enlightenment's rhetoric of autonomy lies a project of domination.

What postmodernists contend is that the tradition of Enlightenment thought is precisely a *particular tradition* of thought, like any other. Its claim to universality is the attempt to impose some people's particular perspective on others. It is part and parcel of the West's attempt to dominate the world, in which Western science, technology, and education are seen as equally applicable to any society, overriding and replacing indigenous cultural traditions. The purported universality of Enlightenment reason has been hand in glove with colonialism of all kinds, down to the economic and consumerist imperialism ("McWorld" as it has appropriately been called) that is dominant today. The story of the modern project is at least as much a story of domination as it is of enlightenment. The alleged progress of Enlightenment rationality has been an exercise of power.

Thus, in our terms, postmodernism extends the Enlightenment's rejection of authority not only to all extrinsic authority but also to the intrinsic authoritativeness of science and other forms of modern knowledge. The elitism that the modern exaltation of experts entails is the means by which some gain power over others. In other words, all pretensions to truth which others should accept, even when autonomous reason is supposed to be the criterion, are unmasked as means of domination. Hence, in postmodernism, freedom or autonomy comes to be opposed to every kind of authority, even the purported authority of truth. All truth is *somebody's* truth. I must be free to believe my own truth. The Enlightenment principle that there is no authority outside oneself is taken to its fullest possible extreme.

Famously, postmodern literary criticism (initially in the person of Roland Barthes) proclaimed the death of the author. It is no accident, certainly, that the word *author* is related to *authority*. The death of the author means that texts are not communications of meaning intended by an author for readers. Texts freed from authors are for readers to make what they wish of. To the death of the author, a characterization of postmodernism by Judith Squires adds the death of Man, the death of history, and the death of metaphysics:

> This involves the rejection of all essentialist and transcendental conceptions of human nature; the rejection of unity, homogeneity, totality, closure and identity; the rejection of the pursuit of the real and the true. In place of these illusory ideals we find the assertion that man [sic] is a social, historical or linguistic artifact; the celebration of fragmentation, particularity and difference; the acceptance of the contingent and apparent.[11]

Thus, against Enlightenment universality, postmodernism celebrates particularity and diversity. The empowering of individuals and minority groups entails their epistemological autonomy over against the authoritarian claims of Enlightenment rationality. Groups and their traditions that have been marginalized and suppressed by the modern tradition receive affirmative action to reinstate them.

In principle, postmodernism gives all groups and individuals the freedom and space to believe their own truths. But it does so by unmasking all beliefs as instruments in the struggle of diverse interest groups for power. In the pluralism of postmodern society there is no basis on which to argue or persuade. Stripping away the illusory pretensions of the Enlightenment to universal reason has left us with nothing but naked group self-interest and power politics. The roots of this shift may derive from a radical Marxist view of society, but postmodernism ends up with an intellectual world suspiciously like the unbridled capitalist free market with whose triumph it has coincided. Postmodernism, it seems, offers no realistic alternative to McWorld.

Because some people still think postmodernism is a rarefied intellectual game irrelevant to understanding our societies, let me illustrate its general cultural effects, which now seem to me blatantly clear. Modernists happily accepted their medical doctors' diagnoses and followed doctors' orders. Medicine was a major feature of the progress of Enlightenment reason. But the authority of modernist medicine and its experts has suffered remarkably in the last decade or so. More and more people are shopping around in a free market of alternative medicines. What modernist medicine pushed to the margins

---

[11]Quoted in Heelas, ed., *Religion*, 8.

is increasingly coming in from the margins, and the choice between alternative forms of diagnosis and treatment is not made in the way modern rationality would require. It is just as much a judgment of preference as of reason. Alternative medicines profit from an image of the institutional structures of modernist medicine as structures of power that preserve the privileges of those who belong to them and exclude alternatives.

One could think more generally also about the declining reputation of science, but let me bring us closer to home with a comment on postmodernist religion. In the modern period all religious authorities suffered a rationalist critique. Their claims could not pass the test of Enlightenment reason. At the popular level in this century the prestige of science was standardly pitted against religion, and in some respects this approach is still with us, as in the popular works of Richard Dawkins. But scientism is waning. Postmodern people believe all kinds of (by Enlightenment standards) irrational things: astrology, UFOs, crystals, and reincarnation. But they reject any kind of authority beyond their free preference, which is often exercised in a pick-and-mix choice of seemingly (by modernist standards) incompatible elements. Certainly in hitherto secular northern Europe religious beliefs are resurgent (though "religious" is a potentially misleading term here), but in a context in which talk of the authority of the Bible or of anything else is quite alien.

So in postmodern religion truth does not depend on any authoritative embodiment. Truth is highly individualistic, pragmatic, relative, and freely chosen. Truth is seen in terms of "what works for me." It is relative to what satisfies my particular requirements, which may be quite different from another person's. Spiritual experience is valued but need not carry any particular religious beliefs with it. Paul Heelas comments:

> [In a postmodern context] Religion can only too readily be swallowed up by individual desire. . . . The more people come to treat religion as a consumer item, the less likely they are to be attracted to the "real" thing. It might well be claimed that the omens for [real] *religion*—as something requiring discipline, obedience and the exercise of the supra-individual, authorial—are not too good.[12]

I said at the conclusion of the last section that the problem of biblical authority in the context of modernism is the modernist prejudice against the particular and in favor of universal reason. Postmodernism represents a radical reaction against universal reason in favor of the particular. In that sense, it may look more friendly to the biblical tradition. But postmodern relativism

---

[12]In Heelas, ed., *Religion*, 16.

favors the particular only by reducing all truth claims to preference. To the authority of the Bible's claim to truth that is valid for all people, post-modernism is probably even less hospitable than modernism.

Finally, it is worth noting that postmodern autonomy is very far from what it's cracked up to be. Most postmodern people are in fact strongly constrained by cultural trends, the media, the commercial interests that promote advertising and fashion, and peer expectations. Moreover, while choice is constantly multiplied, the real choices involved are often in fact rather trivial ones. People becoming Christians can sometimes find Christian faith an enormous liberation from all that: to put oneself under the authority of God is a way of breaking with the cultural pressure, the demands of other people's opinions and expectations, the interiorized demands of the advertisers, the need to get on and get ahead. It is a way of making for once a thoroughly nontrivial choice about the whole way one sees and lives life.

The authority of the biblical story

Too often we think of authority either in relation to commands or laws which we must obey or in relation to doctrines we must believe. To some extent that is a legacy of the Enlightenment. But the Bible is not primarily a book of timeless doctrines or a book of moral laws. It is primarily a story. The one comprehensive category within which we can locate all the biblical materials is that of story, meaning the total biblical story of the world and God's purposes for it, stretching from creation to new creation. A key place within this overarching story is occupied by the Gospel story of Jesus, but the Gospel story is incomplete and lacks its fully biblical meaning apart from the more comprehensive story in which the Bible places it. The category of story includes not only biblical narratives—the many smaller narratives, many of them relatively self-contained but canonically placed within the Bible's total story—but also prophecy and apostolic teaching insofar as these illuminate the meaning of the story and point its direction towards its still future completion. This total biblical story is also the context within which other biblical genres—law, wisdom, psalms, ethical instruction, parables, and so on—are canonically placed. Story is the overarching category in which others are contextualized.

If we are to think of the Bible as authoritative, we must think primarily of the authority of this story. What does it mean to call this story authoritative? Postmodernism gives us a useful term here: metanarrative. (We shall come back to postmodernism's use of the term. For the moment we merely borrow the category.) The Bible's total story is a metanarrative. That is, it sketches in narrative form the meaning of all reality. To accept the authority of this story is to enter it and to inhabit it. It is to live in the world as the world is portrayed in this story. It is to let this story define our identity and our relationship to God and to others. It is to read the narratives of our own lives and of the societies in which we live as narratives that take their meaning from this metanarrative that overarches them all. To accept this metanarrative as the one within which we live is to see the world differently and to live within it differently from the way we would if we inhabited another metanarrative or framework of universal meaning.

The Bible's narrative does not simply require assent. Like all stories, it draws us into its world, engages us imaginatively, allows us at our own pace to grow accustomed to it. But to accept it as authoritative metanarrative means more than to indwell it, as we might a novel, imaginatively for the duration of our reading. Such an experience of a story may well affect our understanding and experience of the world. But to accept the Bible's metanarrative as authoritative is to privilege it above all other stories. It is to find our own identity as characters in that story, characters whose lives are an as yet untold part of the story. For the metanarrative is, of course, no more than a sketch. The Bible tells that part of the plot that makes the general meaning of the whole clear and points us ahead to the way the plot must be finally resolved. But it leaves the story open to the inclusion of all other stories, including those we play some part in writing.

This biblical metanarrative is the biblical way of combining particularity and universality. The metanarrative hinges on highly particular events—the history of Israel, the Gospel story of Jesus—but reads these events as decisive for the meaning of the whole of reality. It links an imaginative sketch of the story of the whole world—from creation to the kingdom of God—with a highly particular story that is constitutive for the salvation of the world. The particularity is alien to modernism, the universality to postmodernism.

In a famous sentence the French philosopher Jean-François Lyotard defined the postmodern as "incredulity towards metanarratives."[13] At first sight it might seem that modernism was also incredulous of metanarratives. It rejected all religious myths that told a story of the meaning of the world. But in fact modernism created its own metanarrative: the idea of historical progress. Confidence in Enlightenment rationality was inseparable from the myth of enlightenment itself, the march of reason towards an ever more rational and better future. In the wake of the failure of this story, in both its progressivist and its Marxist revolutionary forms, in the twentieth century, postmodernism not only pronounces it incredible but unmasks it as a myth legitimating domination. The onward march of progress was the legitimation for suppressing difference and dissent. Generalizing from this exposure of the Enlightenment myth, postmodernism considers all metanarratives oppressive, since their claim to

---

[13]J.-F. Lyotard, *The Postmodern Condition*, trans. G. Bennington and B. Massumi (Minneapolis: University of Minnesota Press, 1984), xxiv.

universal truth must be in reality the imposition of somebody's truth on others. As Steven Connor puts it, postmodernism marks "a shift from the muffled majesty of grand narratives to the splintering autonomy of micronarratives."[14]

Whether postmodernists themselves can or do live without any kind of metanarrative may be questioned. It is instructive to find that Friedrich Nietzsche, pioneer of postmodernism before its time, frequently embodies his sense of what it means to live after the death of God and after the death of the Enlightenment myth of progress in imaginative narratives. For example, he tells the parable of the three metamorphoses of the human spirit: the camel, the lion, and the child.[15] The camel is the weight-laden spirit, kneeling down to assume its burden and carrying its weight, the heavier the better, into the desert. The camel represents moral humanity, willingly taking on itself the burden of moral duty, to the point of asceticism. The lion, however, the next metamorphosis of the spirit, "wants to capture freedom and to be lord." It struggles for victory over the great dragon it no longer wishes to call "lord" and God, the dragon that says, "Thou shalt." The great dragon is called, "Thou shalt," but the lion says, "I will." The victory of the lion means no more "Thou shalt," only "I will." The lion is needed to create freedom for the human spirit, freedom from given values, freedom to create its own values. But the actual creation of new values lies not with the lion, but with the child, who is the third and last metamorphosis. The child is a new beginning, humanity as truly self-created. "The spirit now wills *its own* will. The spirit sundered from the world now wins *its own* world." The child is the superman, whose will is absolute, who creates his own values, his own world. The parable is a metanarrative that presumably escapes the charge of totalizing oppression by leading not to predetermined closure but to the absolute freedom from constraint, the freedom to make one's own world, that the postmodern spirit craves. If such a metanarrative escapes the postmodern incredulity toward all grand stories, it is worth asking whether a Christian alternative, just as alive to the issues of authority, obedience, and freedom but construing their nature and relationships differently, may likewise, in its own terms, escape the charge of totalizing oppression. In the next section we shall suggest the way in which this could be done.

The case for the Christian metanarrative is not helped by the way it became entwined with the modern myth of progress in the nineteenth century. But the abject failure of that alliance with modernism should warn us against too easy an alliance with postmodernism, reducing the biblical narrative to no more than the story we Christians choose to tell about ourselves, a modest micro-

---

[14]Quoted in Heelas, ed., *Religion*, 7.
[15]F. Nietzsche, *Thus Spoke Zarathustra*, trans. R. J. Hollingdale (London: Penguin, 1969), 54–56.

narrative, an unpretentious local fiction without truth claims. The challenge of postmodernism is to show how the biblical metanarrative liberates rather than oppresses. Is it a story that must suppress all others or a story that in some sense holds open space for all others?

The modernist metanarrative of progress was a narrative of mastery. Enlightenment reason was always essentially aimed at mastering the world through knowledge in order to master it by technology. Autonomous reason in thought aimed at implementing and securing human freedom in the world, that is, the freedom of the master who subjects the slave to his will. The project was to subject the world to human will in order to remake it according to human desires. Increasingly the future would be subjected to human control. It is not surprising that this myth of progress through human domination of the rest of creation entailed also progress through the domination of some humans over others.

The myth lives on in such increasingly dangerous forms as biotechnology. It is noteworthy, once again, that postmodernism, while it unmasks the myth of the Enlightenment, offers no real resistance to its effects. The reason is that postmodernism itself represents a further step along the line of thinking in which freedom or autonomy entails mastery. The modernist mastered the world through science and technology; the postmodernist constructs it textually. Retreating into a purely linguistic world of arbitrary signs, the postmodernist gains freedom from all authority, but leaves the modernist free to continue subjecting the extralinguistic world to abuse.

The problem caused by the Enlightenment's concept of autonomy as freedom from all extrinsic authority is not solved by pushing further in the same direction, as postmodernism does. In this light we can see that the biblical metanarrative offers not another legitimation of domination but a genuine alternative. This metanarrative, by placing the future in God's hands, liberates us from the need for mastery or control, restoring to us a properly human way of living in relationship with the rest of reality, neither subjecting it to our will nor constructing it at will. This depends on recognizing the kind of authority the metanarrative attributes to God as the authority of grace.

The authority of grace

This category is a key element in biblical authority. It is how the Bible transcends the contemporary dilemma of a total incompatibility of freedom and authority, conceived as total autonomy versus oppressive authoritarianism.

The authority that inheres in the biblical story is the authority of *grace*.[16]

---

[16]The phrase is also used by E. D. Reed, *The Genesis of Ethics: On the Authority of God as the Origin of Christian Ethics* (London: Darton, Longman & Todd, 2000), 87. It was

In other words, the biblical metanarrative is a story not of the assertion of autonomy in domination, but of grace and free response. In this story all is given by God, including freedom. The world, our being in it, our redemption from the evil we make of it—all are God's gift, which always precedes God's requirements of us. This is part of the significance of the fact that law and commands in the Bible are contextualized within its narrative. Authority belongs in the first place to the story of God's gracious self-giving to us. In that context the authority of God's will for us expressed in commands is the authority of God's grace. As Walter Brueggemann states, it is "not coercive but generative, not repressive but emancipatory."[17]

Our response to grace is not the coerced submission of the slave, but the free obedience of love.[18] Its paradigm is: "I delight to do your will, O my God; your law is within my heart" (Ps. 40:8). This is neither the autonomy that is contradicted by any authority nor the heteronomy that experiences authority as alien subjection to the will of another. It is the obedience to God of those who already glimpse the eschatological identity of their best desires with God's, who recognize God's will as the desire of their own hearts, whose experience of God's love makes love the freely chosen goal of their lives. Freedom is here not the rejection of all limits, but the free acceptance of those limits that enable loving relationships. Obedience is demanding, but it is no more heteronomous than the athlete's acceptance of the demanding regime that she knows to be the way to the goals she has set herself. (The postmodernist critique at this point consists in the appeal to diversity: there is an indefinite variety of life-goals one may choose, and to pronounce one better than others is to impose one's own choice on others. But this is, as so often turns out to be the case with postmodernism, the philosophy of consumerism,[19] which exalts choice as the supreme value in itself, irrespective of the content of choice.)

Because obedience to God, whose will is the true law of my own being, is

---

also the title of a collection of essays by W. A. Whitehouse, ed. A. Loades: *The Authority of Grace: Essays in Response to Karl Barth* (Edinburgh: T. & T. Clark, 1981), in which P. T. Forsyth is quoted: "The last authority of the soul for ever is the grace of a holy God, the holiness of his gracious love in Jesus Christ" (242).

[17]W. Brueggemann, *Theology of the Old Testament* (Minneapolis: Fortress Press, 1997), 200. The whole section, 198–201, is worth reading on this issue; and cf. Reed, *The Genesis*, 47.

[18]Cf. what Paul Ricoeur calls "the only acceptable sense of the notion of theonomy": that "love obliges" and "that to which it obliges is a loving obedience" (P. Ricoeur, "Theonomy and/or Autonomy," in M. Volf, C. Krieg, and T. Kucharz, eds., *The Future of Theology*, FS J. Moltmann [Grand Rapids: Eerdmans, 1996], 296).

[19]Cf. A. Storkey, "Post-Modernism Is Consumption," in C. Bartholomew and T. Moritz, eds., *Christ and Consumerism: A Critical Analysis of the Spirit of the Age* (Carlisle: Paternoster, 2000), 100–117.

different in kind from obedience to human authorities, the biblical writers struggle with analogies for it. The analogy of servants' or slaves' obedience to their master or subjects' obedience to their king is frequent but also transmuted by paradox: "As servants of God, live as free people" (1 Pet. 2:16); "the perfect law, the law of liberty" (Jas. 1:25). In John 15:14–15 Jesus says, "You are my friends if you do what I command you. I do not call you servants any longer, because the servant does not know what the master is doing; but I have called you friends, because I have made known to you everything that I have heard from my Father." What Jesus here drops from the image of the servant is not the language of command and obedience but the requirement of *blind* obedience that is made of the mere slave. Like Jesus himself in obedience to his Father, his friends know the aim his commandments have in view, and they accept that aim.

But within the relationship of grace, which enables this kind of enlightened obedience to God's will, there remain, while we still live by faith, occasions for obedience in sheer faith without understanding. Jesus, who obeyed his Father's will in perfect understanding of it (so that the paradigm of Ps. 40:8 applies preeminently to him), is the limit-case on the one side. Abraham, the friend of God (Isa. 41:8) to whom God made known his purposes (Gen. 18:17–19), but who had to obey the command to sacrifice Isaac in completely uncomprehending trust (Gen. 22:1–14), is the limit-case on the other side. But, despite the offense the command to sacrifice Isaac unavoidably causes to modernist and postmodernist outlooks alike, even it is not the subjection to heteronomy it would be if it stood alone, outside the context of the wider story of Abraham and the wider story of the Bible. In context it is obedience to the God who, the story of his grace shows, can be trusted in spite of appearances. Abraham's obedience is the measure of the extent to which he has made this gracious God's will the desire of his own heart. While we rightly experience, in reading the story, the conflict of autonomy and heteronomy that we all know, in its wider context the story points us beyond this conflict. Both it and its polar opposite, the obedience of Jesus as the alternative limit-case, point to the eschatological goal beyond autonomy and heteronomy, the final identity of our freedom with God's authority.

In summary of this section, the authority of the Bible is the authority of God's grace to which we respond in the free obedience of love. This authority is not so much about subjection as about gift. Its effect is therefore not repressive but liberating.

Story, commands, and doctrines

The Bible's authority belongs, I have argued, primarily in the metanarrative that is the most inclusive way of characterizing the Bible's content. We acknowledge this authority as we inhabit the narrative and relate to God and the world as we find them portrayed in this narrative. What then of the authority of commands and doctrines, with which we more commonly associate the term *authority*?

I have already shown to some degree the importance of the location of biblical laws and commands within the narrative of God's grace. It is from this narrative that we "know what God is doing," such that our obedience, in Johannine terms, transcends the blind obedience of the servant and resembles the understanding obedience of the son, the daughter, or the friend. That biblical commands are not arbitrary decrees but correspond to the way the world is and will be is fully appreciable only as we inhabit the Bible's narrative and appropriate its perspective on how the world is and will be. The point is important because it will by no means necessarily be evident within the worldviews of our society that biblical commands correspond to the way the world is. Theories of natural law that attempt to demonstrate this independently of the biblical narrative have a certain value, but they are never completely successful, and in a postmodern society are unlikely to carry much conviction at all. Recognizing the importance of the biblical metanarrative enables us to see that inhabiting it is learning to see the world significantly differently (though not of course in every respect differently) from the way the cultural traditions of our context see it. Biblical laws that "make no sense" in relation to the world as those traditions portray it may do so in relation to the world as the biblical story portrays it.

However, there is another important point to make about biblical commands. An obvious problem about the authority of biblical commands is that there is a very large number of such commands that Christians recognize no obligation to obey. The following are some examples selected to illustrate the diversity of such commands. (I include more New Testament than Old Testament examples in order to forestall an obvious but unsatisfactory response to the problem.)

> You shall not eat flesh with its life, that is, its blood (Gen. 9:4).
>
> Do not be too righteous, and do not act too wise (Eccl. 7:16).
>
> You shall not sow your field with two kinds of seed; nor shall you put on a garment made of two different materials (Lev. 19:19).
>
> Greet all the brothers and sisters with a holy kiss (1 Thess. 5:26).
>
> Do not adorn yourselves outwardly by braiding your hair (1 Pet. 3:3, addressed to women).
>
> Let a widow be put on the list if she is not less than sixty years old and has been married only once (1 Tim. 5:9).
>
> Anyone unwilling to work should not eat (2 Thess. 3:10).

> Slaves, obey your earthly masters with fear and trembling (Eph. 6:5).
>
> If anyone will not welcome you or listen to your words, shake off the dust from your feet as you leave that house or town (Matt. 10:14)
>
> Give to everyone who begs from you (Luke 6:30).

Christians of all kinds turn out to be very selective about which biblical commands they consider themselves obliged to obey—or at least to obey literally. Are they therefore recognizing no authority in these commands? The problem with an approach to biblical authority that emphasizes authoritative commands apart from the biblical story is that it must simply ignore these many commands that do not seem to oblige us to obey them. If, however, they are read within their context in the biblical story, then the story defines their authority contextually. This approach enables us to learn from commands that we do not think require our literal obedience. Their place in the story may delimit or relativize their authority as commands. They may not be instructions addressed to us, but they can still be instructive for us.

A different, though not unrelated, problem frequently encountered in respect to biblical commands is that, on many aspects of life where we would expect an authoritative scripture to guide our decision making and practice, the Bible simply does not—however hard the interpreters try to make it—speak with a single, clear voice. On war and peace, on the relationships of men and women, on slavery, on the ethics of material possessions, and a host of other issues of great importance for living in obedience to God, the Bible contains a disturbing diversity of statements and approaches, including various commands and instructions as well as narrative examples and wisdom reflections. Unless we are to pick and choose arbitrarily among these relevant biblical materials, we need a perspective in which the diversity acquires an intelligible shape, in which, one might say, a *direction* of biblical teaching becomes apparent and the texts can be read dynamically, as pointing us in that direction, even though some go less far in that direction than others.[20] Such an approach makes sense in the context of our recognition that it is as a meta-narrative that the Bible is authoritative, not exclusively but primarily. A biblical approach to an issue may then be expected to emerge in the course of the story, taking shape as we observe different aspects of such an approach appearing in different contexts, and even as we take account of a variety of approaches that, on an obvious reading, might seem contradictory. What may seem, when one text is read alone, to be that text's straightforward answer to a question we are asking may have to be relativized by other perspectives on the matter given

---

[20]For the hermeneutical principle of discerning the *direction* of biblical thought, see chapter 1 above, and for a worked example, see chapter 6 below.

us by other texts. All this may seem a frustratingly oblique way of providing us with the teaching we seek to live by, but we can come to appreciate its advantages when we read the Bible in such a way as to let it involve us in its story and in the dynamism of the way God's will for his people and for the world comes to be known. In discerning the direction in the diversity we come to a richer understanding of an issue and its outworking in the diversity of historical human life than a single straightforward pronouncement could afford us.

If the problem of looking in the Bible for authoritative *commands* is that there appear to be far too many of them, then the problem of looking in the Bible for authoritative *doctrines* is that there appear to be far too few of them. But this is because, once again, the story is primary, such that the Bible's theological teaching about who God is and who we are in relation to God and the world is inseparable from the story of God and the world that it tells. This is why, for example, the Bible both does and does not teach the doctrine of the Trinity. Even though I myself think the New Testament more explicitly Trinitarian than most New Testament scholars do, still the New Testament does not provide explicit confessions of the Trinitarian being of God in God's self. But the story of God's acting and suffering in the world in the Gospel story of Jesus is Trinitarian in form. That God is Trinitarian emerges, as it were, from the story. A doctrine of the Trinity represents what we need to say about God in God's self for the biblical story about God to be a true story. It is authorized by the story in that it follows from taking the story seriously as authoritative metanarrative.

Finally, it is important to note that neither what the Bible obliges us to believe nor what the Bible obliges us to do can be known from isolated texts, but requires their total context in the biblical metanarrative.

Other modes of authority

Once we begin to explore the great variety of kinds of literature that the Bible contains, we must come to realize that the sense in which we can attribute authority to Scripture must vary considerably according to the kind of content we find in the various biblical books and passages. It is not only narrative that escapes our habitual thinking about authority in terms of commands and doctrines.

In the Wisdom literature, for example, it will not do to treat the aphorisms in Proverbs as divine commands to be obeyed or the wise reflection on experience of life in Ecclesiastes as doctrine to be believed. It might be more appropriate to formulate the authority attaching to such inspired thoughtfulness as the authority to recommend, "Think about this!" While commandments are formed to be obeyed, aphorisms are formed to be savored and pondered.

In the case of the Psalms, again, neither commandment nor doctrine is an appropriate model. As Israel's temple hymnbook, the authoritative recommendation with which they come is, most generally, "This is how you should pray; make use of these vehicles of prayer for every occasion." But in some cases, it might be better understood as, "You can even say that to God!" The imprecatory or other difficult psalms, so problematic if we attribute an inappropriate mode of authority to them, come into their own as soon as we see that their authority is such as to give us permission to be honest with God, to bring all our concerns to God, and to let God deal with them. For some psalms, the authoritative recommendation must surely be, "Join in this so that you may learn experientially to appreciate and to praise God!" Theirs is an authority such as to enable worship and to empower us to join creation's praise.

Fictional stories, such as Jesus' parables or (as I take it to be) the book of Jonah, do not have the authority of historical reports, but that of appeal to the imagination such as to change our perspective on things. The way such stories creep up on us and make their point by taking us unawares and the way they use humor to startle us out of familiar ways of thinking do not fit any conventional notion of authority at all. They ask only to be heard by those willing to open the ears of their imagination.

While we often think of authority as obliging us, it is also possible to think of authority as *authorizing* us. There are many ways in which we can apply such a notion within the varieties of biblical literature. Gospel stories of people like ourselves coming to Jesus with their needs or their questions *authorize* us to do the same. A command such as the Great Commission at the end of Matthew's Gospel *authorizes* us to act with the delegated authority of the Lord Jesus in making disciples of all nations for the kingdom of God. Much that we often think of as obedience can also be construed as being authorized, a construal that may restore to our thinking the sense of privilege and responsibility that often attaches in biblical thought to the vocabulary of obedience. More generally, the way the Bible speaks of God—which, since God is the transcendent and incomprehensible One, beyond all our language and categories of thought, should never be taken for granted but received as a constant source of amazement and gratitude—*authorizes* us to do what we should never otherwise think ourselves able to do: to speak of God. There is much more that would bear exploration along these lines.

Authority and freedom in biblical interpretation

It is potentially disastrous to speak of the authority of the Bible without also raising hermeneutical questions. It has been a not uncommon phenomenon in the history of interpretation for biblical authority to be used to authorize whatever views the interpreters have wanted the Bible to express. At worst, the Bible has in this way been abused as an ideological tool of self-interest and domination. Yet a certain degree of freedom in interpretation is inescapable. We need to see how this can serve rather than subvert the authority of the Bible.

Insofar as biblical scholarship until recently was concerned with the meaning of the text, rather than with historical reconstruction behind the text, its efforts were directed to establishing the "original" meaning, which is often defined as the meaning intended by the original author, though it might be better defined as the meaning that the first readers could be expected to find in the text (since authors can fail to express what they really mean and can entertain private meanings inaccessible to any reader). The historical scholarship deployed in this task is a form of Enlightenment rationality. This is not a reason to denigrate it; its achievement has been massive, and no responsible hermeneutic can leave it aside. It had, however, limitations typical of Enlightenment thinking. It ignored the perspective of the interpreter, giving the illusion of complete objectivity. It therefore pursued the expectation that disinterested scholarship could achieve agreement on the one and only original meaning of the text. The aim was to specify the historical meaning of the text as precisely as possible, thereby identifying "an immovable textual basis for Christian existence."[21] This attempt to pin down, as it were, once and for all the meaning of the text looks suspiciously like an attempt to master and to control the text.

Despite its enormous achievements, in its ultimate aim this pursuit of the original meaning (now continued also with new methods, such as social scientific methods) has failed. Rather than achieving a consensus, the nature of this scholarly enterprise seems perpetually to incite new interpretations and unending interpretative debates. There is real progress, but not as much as many practitioners like to think. Moreover, the aim of establishing a secure meaning to which the Bible's authority for faith and practice can be attached is frustrated, not only by the plurality of original meanings propounded, but also by the fact that, very often, the more precisely the meaning of the text for its original readers in their precise historical context is specified, the less relevance the text appears to have for any other readers.

Postmodern reading is altogether different. From the naive historical objectivism of modernist reading postmodernist readers are freed to create meaning for themselves. The text is explicitly subjected to the reader's authority.

Thus in modernist reading the attempt to tie the text's meaning down to the one original reading determined by the interpreter effectively controls the

---

[21]T. A. Hart, *Faith Thinking: The Dynamics of Christian Theology* (London: SPCK, 1995/Downers Grove, Ill.: InterVarsity Press, 1996), 119.

text by disallowing any fresh meaning it may acquire in other contexts. An historical reconstruction of the original meaning replaces the text. In postmodernist reading the text's meaning is not tied down but opened up to as many interpretations as there are readers. Here it is readers' creation of meaning that replaces the text. In neither case can the text itself speak with authority to a contemporary context.

For this to be seen as possible, we must recognize that meaning does not simply reside in the text (as it does for modernist reading) nor is it simply created by readers (as it is in postmodernist reading). It happens in interaction between the text itself and its readers. Readers encounter the text as genuinely other than themselves. Historical exegesis helps them to perceive this other, but its otherness is not limited to its historical meaning. Reading the text not only with disciplined historical imagination but also with the prejudices and the concerns of their own contexts, readers experience it as speaking to those contexts. In a sense, this gives space for the freedom of readers in interpretation. They are free to bring their own perspectives to the text. But the same space that allows such freedom to readers also allows the text the freedom to transcend its original historical context and to mean what it can mean to other contexts. Indeed, in such fresh occurrence of meaning, God himself is free to speak God's word with authority.

In summary, this is a hermeneutic that requires the interpreter seriously to listen to the text and to do so as someone who listens, not in abstraction from their own context, but in deliberate awareness of their own context. The listening allows the text to speak with authority, and the context allows the text to speak with relevance.

Of course, in the church individuals do not come to the text in isolation from the community, nor do they read the text as though it had never been interpreted before. Interpretation should normally be the activity of the community, in which individuals play various specific parts, and it should normally be in recognizable continuity with the tradition. These dimensions help interpretation to avoid the idiosyncrasy to which the hermeneutic we have described could be subject were it practiced by individuals apart from the tradition and the life of the church. But there is an important qualification. Scripture may speak freshly to a lone individual or a marginal group in a way that challenges tradition and community and in a way that the church is initially unwilling to hear. We must allow for the Jeremiahs and the Luthers.

Recognizing the Bible's authority entails, in the first place, listening. Although the Bible insists that hearing without doing is worthless (Matt. 7:24–27; Jas. 1:22–25; Rev. 1:3), it also insists that the hearing that leads to practice must be attentive listening: "Let anyone with ears to hear listen!" (Mark 4:9 and elsewhere); "Let anyone who has an ear listen to what the Spirit is saying to the churches" (Rev. 2:7 and elsewhere). Fundamental to the Bible's authority is this claim to be heard as a matter both of urgency and of continuing attention. It is attentive and extended listening to the text that both the modern and the postmodern approaches to interpretation tend to impede, but which the practices of reading of Scripture in the context of the life of the church have usually endeavored to promote. While postmodern reading hastens to make meaning of its own out of the text and cannot wait for the text itself to yield meaning, modern reading sees the task of interpretation as done once it has pinned down the original meaning once and for all—or at least until the next historical critic proposes a rival meaning. Attentive listening, on the other hand, remains open to the unlimited possibilities of meaning which can occur. "We must return to the text again and again and submit our interpretations to it, never resting content that we have the meaning pinned down for good. If we fall into the latter trap we cease to be faithful in our submission to the authority of scripture as such, and exalt our best readings of it instead."[22] Practices of attentive listening have also helped the church to avoid the kind of entrenched traditionalism that merely repeats in the present what was said in the past in the way that it was said in the past. For the attentive listener, the Bible's authoritative voice does not come only from the past, but is a living voice in the present, calling us into the future.

Serious listening entails dialogue, in which the listener interrogates the text and the text interrogates the listener. Such a process brings all kinds of aspects of the attentive listener's context into relationship to the text in order to discover how to live within the biblical metanarrative at precisely its present juncture. Here it is perhaps important to use the image of inhabiting the world of the biblical story with some care. It does not mean living in a purely textual world unrelated to the contemporary world in which others live. Rather, by living within the biblical story we can construe our contemporary world in the unique configuration it has when viewed as the world that must become what it will in the final purpose of God.

The *unfinished* nature of the biblical story—or, more positively, the eschatological hope as the ultimate future God will give to his world—is what creates the space for finding ourselves and our contemporary world in the biblical story. It is what enables and requires the hermeneutic of listening in context that we have briefly suggested. It is what resists the premature closure that would stifle the freedom of obedient Christian living in the contemporary world. It is what both keeps the story open to the inclusion of all other stories and invites all other stories to find the ending that will give them meaning in

---

[22]Hart, *Faith Thinking*, 142.

the coming kingdom of God. Properly to grasp the way the authority of the biblical text and the freedom of ecclesial interpreters relate without contradiction, we must appeal not just to general hermeneutical principles, but to the nature of the metanarrative in which the Bible's authority primarily inheres.[23]

---

[23]The works to which I am most conscious of being indebted in this chapter are:

W. Brueggemann, "The Commandments and Liberated, Liberating Bonding," in *Interpretation and Obedience* (Minneapolis: Fortress, 1991), 145–58.

J. Goldingay, *Models for Scripture* (Grand Rapids: Eerdmans/Carlisle: Paternoster, 1994).

C. Gunton, *Enlightenment and Alienation* (Basingstoke: Marshall Morgan & Scott, 1985).

T. A. Hart, *Faith Thinking: The Dynamics of Christian Theology* (London: SPCK, 1995/Downers Grove: InterVarsity Press, 1996).

T. A. Hart, "(Probably) the Greatest Story Ever Told?: Reflections on Brueggemann's *The Bible and Postmodern Imagination*," in A. N. S. Lane, ed., *Interpreting the Bible: Historical and Theological Studies in Honour of David F. Wright* (Leicester: Apollos, 1997), 181–204.

N. Lash, *Voices of Authority* (London: Sheed & Ward, 1976).

J. R. Middleton and B. J. Walsh, *Truth Is Stranger Than It Used to Be: Biblical Faith in a Postmodern Age* (Downers Grove: InterVarsity Press, 1995).

A. C. Thiselton, "Authority and Hermeneutics: Some Proposals for a More Creative Agenda," in P. E. Satterthwaite and D. F. Wright, eds., *A Pathway into the Holy Scripture* (Grand Rapids: Eerdmans, 1994) 107–41.

4

Authority and Morality

In 1999, Richard Holloway, then bishop of Edinburgh and Primus of the Scottish Episcopal Church, published a book called *Godless Morality: Keeping Religion out of Ethics.*[1] Its central argument—that God should be kept out of morality—is worth discussing in the context of the present book, because it responds to the moral confusion that Holloway discerns in contemporary British society as a result of the discrediting of traditional authorities and that he also describes as a crisis of authority in contemporary society. The book well illustrates the gross misunderstandings and misrepresentations of the Christian tradition of spirituality and morality that are abroad in Western society—all the more strikingly in that it is a bishop who here adopts, endorses, and expresses them with all the rhetoric of enthusiastic conviction and polemical intent. Holloway is not only entirely uncritical of the contemporary misrepresentation of religious ethics as authoritarian and heteronomous; the most remarkable aspect of the book is his open contempt for the tradition with which he has lived his life. His familiarity with the tradition suggests that he can surely not be innocently ignorant of its values and its true character for those who love and obey God. It suggests that he must be wilfully ignorant, intent on blackening the reputation of the entire approach to life that he now disdains. At least he admits the volte-face he has performed: "It is one of the deepest ironies of my life that I have

---

[1]Edinburgh: Canongate, 1999. For a collection of essays responding in a variety of ways to this book, see the *Scottish Episcopal Church Review* 8, 2 (2001). Those by Trevor Hart and Michael Northcott cohere very closely with my argument in the present chapter.

ended up, in my 60s, as the kind of bishop that I despised when I was a priest in my 30s."[2]

Keeping God out of morality

In this chapter we shall be concerned not with the specific moral issues Holloway addresses in his book, but with his fundamental approach to the nature of ethics and the making of ethical judgments. His thesis is that God not only can but should and must be left out of all consideration of morality. The point is not that unbelievers can think and act morally, which is not, of course, to be doubted. Nor is the point that religious believers can usefully engage in moral discussion with unbelievers on common premises without referring to God. The point is that morality cannot and should not be related to God, by believers or unbelievers.

It is important, before entering any critique, to set out as accurately as possible the reasons he adduces for this radical claim (not, as we shall see, a courtesy he accords those with whom he disagrees in the book). The following are the main reasons he gives for the need to keep God out of morality:

(1) Many people no longer connect morality with religion (see 3–4, 19–20). This is a result of the erosion of belief in the great traditions of religion and morality, a "process of disintegration" that "has now reached a critical stage" (153, cf. 30). Consequently the only prospect of a new moral consensus lies with a morality not based on religious belief.

(2) One problem with the religious traditions, which in part accounts for their declining credibility, is that they have not recognized the historically relative character of morality. Moral traditions are in fact "human creations . . . in response to particular circumstances and their challenges" (31), but by appealing to divine authority as the basis for morality, they absolutize their moral principles so that change in response to changing circumstances becomes difficult or impossible (see 4, 69–73). For the same reason they cannot allow validity to moral views other than their own: "they associate God exclusively with their opinions" (72). In short, God-based morality is inflexible. That this inflexibility is unacceptable is shown by the fact that "many claims made on behalf of God have been subsequently rejected for moral reasons" (9). Holloway's parade example is the subordination of women in the Christian tradition (e.g., 4). By contrast with the absolutism of traditional moral systems, morality, in Holloway's view, needs "versatility" and "ability to improvise" (16, 87).

(3) Along with "the erosion of tradition," the most relevant aspect of the

---

[2]Quoted in *Church Times*, Nov. 3, 2000.

contemporary cultural situation is "the crisis of authority" (30, cf. 154). Traditional moralities were "command moralities" (33) requiring obedience to
authority, divine and human, ecclesiastical and secular. Such command moralities have often in fact been oppressive systems of domination, subjecting the
many to the will of the few, who use them to bolster their own power and privileges (cf. 9, 152). The discrediting of authority in this sense of external
authority (distinguished from the intrinsic authoritativeness of arguments and
insights that convince us) means that a new morality must be one of consent
rather than command and obedience. In place of "unthinking" obedience to
divine commands (7), "our own moral and rational assent" is required (8).

(4) Another way of characterizing "command moralities" is that they are
based on fear: "By claiming divine authority for their commandments and pro-
hibitions, with eternal punishment for those who disobey them, religious
moral systems operate on the basis of fear" (17). But divine sanctions of this
kind are no longer credible.

(5) Moral principles or claims are moral only if they can be justified in ways
that anyone can accept: "Saying that an act is wrong, because it is forbidden
by God, is not sufficient unless we can also justify it on moral grounds" (15).
To claim that demands particular to a religious tradition require observance
beyond that tradition is to confuse sin with morality, Holloway explains (5–6,
12–14). In this way he actually *defines* morality as "godless." How then can
moral claims be justified in a way that anyone in our society can find valid?
"The challenge . . . is to separate the basic principles that might help guide us
through what has been called the moral maze from" the absolute systems of
traditional morality (16). He can say that it "is not yet obvious to anyone today
what the basis for a new moral understanding might be" (31), but in some tension with this he also confidently treats "the idea of harm as our moral criterion" (15, cf. 159) and seems to treat it as a quite sufficient criterion to guide
him and any reasonable reader through the moral debates he enters in the
book. On several occasions he spells out what it means: "A wrong act is one
that manifestly harms others or their interests, or violates their rights or causes
injustice" (14, cf. 57, 71). Nowhere in the book does he refer to any other
moral principle he considers valid.

(6) Modern historical study of scriptural texts, such as the Bible, have made
it impossible any longer to see them as "the permanent expression of the mind
of God" (27). Like all traditions, they reflect particular social and historical
contexts.

The contemporary moral task

Presupposed in all these arguments is a particular view of the task of moral
thinking in the contemporary context. Our society is in a state of serious moral

confusion: "it would be difficult to exaggerate the moral confusions of our day" (151). Holloway seems to have two different accounts of why this is so. One attributes it to the erosion of tradition and the crisis of authority (see points 1 and 3 above), such that what is required is a morality not based on tradition or extrinsic authority. The other account speaks of the unprecedented moral pluralism in our society, in which no one traditional moral system is any longer dominant, so that moral systems compete and conflict. It is not clear how these two accounts cohere, since the second seems to suggest that many people still accept the authority of the traditions in which they stand. But Holloway appears to think that the authority of all traditions is fatally undermined in a pluralist society in which they may be chosen but no longer appear self-evident. In any case, the situation is one in which God no longer provides the moral cohesion society requires. What is urgently needed is to discover an "agreed basis" for a common morality (151). Holloway's aim is "to unite those who believe with those who do not in the discovery of a workable ethic for our time" (5).

This aim requires some reflection. A tempting interpretation of the book is that Holloway is simply addressing the task of identifying some common moral values in a democratic and pluralistic society, the degree of moral consensus required for legislation and other public matters, while leaving untouched the much fuller and richer moral traditions that believers find in religious faiths. Jonathan Sacks, the British chief rabbi, has argued eloquently and persuasively for the importance of particular moral communities and moral traditions as the contexts in which people are nurtured in moral understanding and behavior, while also urging that even in our secular and pluralistic society there remains sufficient consensus on key moral values for the degree of moral cohesion any society requires.[3]

But careful attention to Holloway's argument shows that this is clearly not his view. For the various reasons listed above, the religious moral systems are discredited and cannot command the assent even of religious believers other than by habit or because of the psychological frailty that craves the absolute certainties of the resurgent fundamentalisms. The salient fact about our society is not so much the coexistence of several moral traditions, but that it is "post-traditional" (88). It is not just that religious believers should not appeal to God when discussing moral issues with nonbelievers, but also that religious believers cannot plausibly regard God as the source of or the authority for their own moral convictions and principles. Holloway, as we have seen, defines morality as what can be justified for any member of our

---

[3]J. Sacks, *The Politics of Hope* (London: Jonathan Cape, 1977).

society without appeal to any beliefs not held by all. In other words, the pluralistic moral debate is the defining context for morality as such. As far as morality goes, we must all leave God out, we must all be secular, we must all find our moral community in secular society as such, and we must all search for "a new, lightweight moral tradition," "less solid," "more makeshift and provisional" than traditional moralities, based on the principle of consent rather than obedience to authority (156). In this scenario, there can by definition be no such thing as Christian morality or Islamic morality or even humanist morality, insofar as this last is a particular moral tradition. In effect, secular, posttraditional people—"those of us who are unimpressed by the truth claims of traditionalist systems" (11)—dictate the rules of the game for all of us.

Seeking the moral consensus

Despite his quite frequent references to moral pluralism, it is clear that Holloway has no genuine place for a real pluralism of moral traditions. It may seem a surprising observation, but Holloway's arguments all fall into place once one recognizes that his model for the relationship of morality and society is a Christendom model. In the long period when Western societies defined themselves as Christian societies, there was an agreed basis for a common morality. With the excetion of dissident minorities, such as the Jews, who were therefore not properly members of the society, there were moral principles and moral rules which could be justified to anyone on common premises. But the modern collapse of Christendom means that these premises are no longer common. Since most people no longer accept the authority of the Christian revelation, it is no longer a viable basis for morality. So a new basis must be found for a secular morality—a morality of consent rather than authority—that will function for us just as Christian morality once did for Christendom. (The argument does not have to be made with reference to Christianity in particular. Holloway's general arguments always in fact scrupulously refer to "religion" rather than to a particular religion, though examples are usually drawn from Christianity. But a parallel argument could be presented with reference to, for example, Islamic societies. Since he is thinking primarily of European and American society, Holloway's argument is in fact mainly about the transition from Christendom to pluralistic or secular society.)

Another way of putting the point is to say that Holloway's position is the "traditional" (!) Enlightenment one, undaunted and unaffected by any postmodern qualifications. (His occasional references to Nietzsche show no awareness of Nietzsche's radically anti-Enlightenment aims.) Enlightenment thinkers were convinced that traditional moralities could and would be super-

seded by a genuinely universal morality as self-evident to all rational people as
Christian morality had seemed in Christendom when its revelatory authority
was unquestioned. It is odd to find Holloway essentially positioning himself at
the point in history at which the task of discovering this new, posttraditional
morality has allegedly become urgent, without reference to the fact that it has
been high on the agenda of the Western Enlightenment for two centuries.

The only respect in which Holloway's position approaches a more postmodern position is his insistence that morality necessarily changes with historical circumstances. But in his optimistic pursuit of a reasoned consensus
beyond mere relativism and mere pluralism, he is a largely unreconstructed
Enlightenment moralist who makes little attempt to take seriously the postmodern critique of the Enlightenment or to reckon with the ideologically
based moral cynicism abroad in postmodern culture. Despite his perception
of serious moral confusion in society, he has a typically Enlightenment optimism as to the achievement of moral consensus, provided the religious traditions withdraw from the field and leave rational people free to agree on the
basic principle of not harming others.

In this scenario Holloway clearly has no place at all for the church as a distinctive moral community committed to the distinctive ethical way taught by
Jesus and the apostles. He does concede that people "have the right to opt for
what is called an intact moral community," that is, a group that "chooses to
maintain an existing tradition in its entirety, in spite of the critical erosions of
time and change upon it," but this is merely a "way of avoiding the pain and
expenditure of time that moral dilemmas place us in" (74). We come back once
again to the clear message Holloway has for his Christian—as well as all
other—readers: unless we wish to incur the charge of intellectual cowardice
and avoidance of responsibility, we may not base our moral convictions and
principles on any premises other than those shared by all people in our society. Society as a whole is the only legitimate moral community, and morality
can emerge only from the kind of rational debate that is possible in this now
highly secular world.

Despite his perception of serious moral confusion in our society, the out-
come of Holloway's approach is largely to affirm the prevailing moral climate
in our society. It is hard to see how it could really have been otherwise. Holloway has no place to stand from which to critique this moral climate. The criterion of not harming others, the sole basis offered for the new consensus he
seeks, would indeed probably be very widely accepted. But its effect is merely
to put a fence around the highly individualistic pursuit of a chosen form of self-
fulfillment that is the currently accepted goal of life. I can live solely for my
own self-gratification in whatever way I choose, just so long as I do not
infringe anyone else's rights. My responsibility for others is purely negative.

The moral consensus of a modern society is unlikely, in fact, to offer an adequate ethic for all people to live by, but we might at least have expected of Holloway something like the civic morality of positive duties and responsibilities in the public sphere that once characterized modern society. Even the kind of situationist ethics popular in radical Christian circles of the '60s maintained the positive principle of love as the only moral criterion. That was an ethic in tune with the idealism of the '60s. By comparison it is all too obvious that Holloway's ethic is tailored to the acquisitive and hedonistic individualism of the me generation. He is deeply embroiled in the contemporary moral dilemma that arises from exalting freedom of choice as the highest good while attempting to restrain its antisocial consequences by setting harm to others as a limit on freedom. Perhaps it is not too surprising to find Holloway, the quondam socialist, applauding global capitalism for the free-market morality it is promoting worldwide (88–89).

Moral systems are relative to particular perspectives on the meaning and purpose of human life. This is why they have usually been aspects of a religious tradition, but with the decline of religion they have not become self-sufficient and, as it were, neutral with respect to the rest of a worldview or life orientation. Marxist ethics, if the term is appropriate at all, cohere with Marxist ideology in general and humanist ethics with the humanist view of human nature that has suffered so heavily from the postmodern attack pioneered by Nietzsche. Nietzschean—and quite a lot of postmodern—ethics are based on the Nietzschean idea of the will to power as the overriding human good. The new moral consensus Holloway seeks is inconceivable apart from some shared way of thinking about the nature and purpose of human life. By detaching morality from God without attaching it to some secular alternative to religion, Holloway inevitably leaves it at the mercy of the consumerist individualism that is the dominant form of life orientation in our culture and that his moral proposals do nothing to challenge.

This is not to deny that it is important for a democratic and pluralist society to achieve some degree of moral consensus. But the consensus must be one that emerges from the ways in which the various moral traditions in a pluralist society actually converge in significant ways. It will not result from denying the various moral traditions their own integrity and bases. It cannot be a substitute for them because it cannot provide the grounding of ethics in a worldview. It will be a modest consensus identified for the purpose of regulating public life. It cannot offer what the riches and the wisdom of particular moral traditions can; it cannot provide a moral vision for individuals and groups to live by. For that, there must always be moral communities (even if some of them are now virtual) in which people learn, not just the rules, but to be moral people.

A caricature of Christian morality

Holloway's argument (see especially points 3 and 4 above) depends crucially on serious misrepresentation of the traditional Christian understanding of morality. (He himself is happy to write disparagingly of all religious moralities in general; I shall respond only from the Christian perspective.) Take, to begin with, his characterization of Christian morality as a "command morality" based on external authority and on fear and requiring unthinking obedience to divine commands. This representation of religious (he applies it generally) morality is crucial to the first stage of his argument for not basing morality on religion. He takes it for granted (3, cf. 17) that the only difference belief in God could make to morality would be to deter people, through fear, from committing acts they believe God will punish. The technique of caricaturing religious morality is essential to the argument that nonreligious morality, the only morality now worthy of the name, is a morality of rational consent rather than of fearful and unreasoning obedience.

The false polarities Holloway sets up have much to do with his typically contemporary equation of authority with authoritarianism and of obedience with coercion, such that authority is inimical to freedom and obedience to rational consent.[4] In reality, it is coercion, not obedience, that is the opposite of consent. The idea that any requirement of obedience to an external norm is an authoritarian imposition inimical to my freedom is an aspect of the postmodern sense of autonomy for which the only authentic values are those I individually create for myself. If moral values are nothing but freely created ideals that we fashion, change, and exchange at will or whim, then of course they do not oblige us. The sense of moral obligation, intrinsic to all but this extreme relativist and constructivist view of morality, is then abolished. But if there are in any sense objective moral goods that oblige us to strive for them, then the language of obedience is entirely appropriate and has been used by many moralists who do not think of the commands of a personal God but merely of objective moral values that require our assent and obedience. Obedience is the language of moral obligation, not of coercion or fear, though

---

[4]E. D. Reed, *The Genesis of Ethics: On the Authority of God as the Origin of Christian Ethics* (London: Darton, Longman & Todd, 2000), provides an excellent account of divine authority in ethics as noncoercive and nonauthoritarian: God's "authority is not of a controlling or hegemonic kind but of the dialogic, answerable kind which draws persons into relationship" (xxiv); it "does not destroy personal, moral freedom but enables and fulfils it" (xxv); "a clear conceptual distinction is needed between the freedom of individuals who seek autonomy and self-gratification, and the freedom of persons who seek fulfilment of their God-given potential in Christ in communion with God and others" (xxv–xxvi); "divine authority and a relationship of delight between creator and created imply each other" (40).

naturally authoritarian regimes can misuse it in the latter sense. For Christian believers, objective moral goods are formulated as divine commands, but this does not make obedience to them slavish. God is the source and embodiment of all moral good. To obey God is to consent with all one's heart and mind to the good that is the moral truth of reality and the moral truth of our own human being.

Good citizens obey laws because they think they are a good idea and want to be good citizens, not merely because they fear punishment. Moreover, not even good citizens could be good citizens without laws. As an analogy for obedience to divine laws, this analogy is of limited use, but it does show that the notion of obeying laws need have nothing to do with the blind and fearful obedience of the slave. Three further points can be made specifically about obedience to God in biblical and Christian morality. Firstly, the greatest and comprehensive commandment, including all others, is to love God with one's whole being. Part of this love of God is the love of moral good for its own sake. Whether the good is good because it is what God wants, or God wants it because it is good, is a conundrum that rarely occurs to believers in practice. In either case, to love God and thereby to want what God wants is to desire the moral good to which the world has been created to conform, to align oneself with the moral truth of God's self and of our own being.

Secondly, true obedience to God is always response to God's grace: "We love because he first loved us" (1 John 4:19). The free and glad response to God's overwhelming generosity calls forth our gratitude and trust as well as obedience. Ideas of coercion and fear have no place here: "There is no room for fear in love, but perfect love casts out fear" (1 John 4:18). A paradigm biblical expression of the nature of true obedience to God (which Hebrews 10:5–7 applies to Jesus) is Psalm 40:8: "I delight to do your will, O my God; your law is within my heart." The goal of Christian life in the Spirit is to become attuned to God's will, at the same time finding it to be the law of our own being, such that we come to know for ourselves that the paradox is true: "your service is perfect freedom."

What Holloway entirely ignores, yet is absolutely central to the Christian moral tradition, is what Paul Ricoeur calls "the only acceptable sense of the notion of theonomy," which is that "love obliges," and "that to which it obliges is a loving obedience."[5] (As evidence from the tradition, it is worth noting also that the Rule of St. Benedict, the main source of the emphasis on obedience

---

[5]P. Ricoeur, "Theonomy and/or Autonomy," in M. Volf, C. Krieg, and T. Kucharz, eds., *The Future of Theology*, FS J. Moltmann (Grand Rapids: Eerdmans, 1996), 296. Ricoeur argues that theonomy is not a form of heteronomy and is not opposed to autonomy, provided the notion of self-sufficiency is excluded from the latter.

in the Western tradition of monastic spirituality, stresses that Christian and monastic obedience is the obedience of love. According to the Prologue, with spiritual progress "our hearts shall be enlarged, and we shall run with unspeakable sweetness of love in the way of God's commandments."[6])

Thirdly, divine commandments provide a framework for Christian moral judgments and practice, but Christian morality has never been what Holloway calls it: "simply a matter of offering obedience to a series of divine commandments that were laid down to govern every human eventuality" (23). Divine commandments do not exclude the necessity for exercising moral judgment and wisdom in particular contexts and circumstances. They do not provide ready-made answers even to some very old moral dilemmas, such as the morality of war, which has been debated throughout Christian history between pacifists and defenders of the notion of a just war. Even less do the divine commandments in Scripture provide ready-made answers to new dilemmas such as those raised by some aspects of modern medicine. In Scripture and tradition divine commands have always been complemented (without contradiction or tension) in moral discourse and practice by moral wisdom, the rich tradition of reflection and experience in both the Bible and tradition, and by the formation of moral character—in all of which the Holy Spirit is believed to be at work in the hearts and minds of believers, both corporately and individually. To say that, in a "command morality," "our role is one of simple surrender and obedience" (27) is a travesty designed to establish the false polarity between "simply" obeying divine commandments and all other ways of exercising moral discernment.

Scripture and tradition

There is space here for only brief remarks on the way Holloway brings Scripture and tradition into his argument (see points 6 and 2 above). His rather naive appeal to biblical scholarship seems to be supposing that, just because the contents of Scripture were written in various times and places and so in specific contexts (which no one has ever denied), they cannot include permanent moral principles. For all his emphasis on ethical improvization, Holloway does seem to believe in some permanent moral principles, at least that it is wrong to harm others and their interests. If this principle does not transcend particular contexts in which it is enunciated, how could one, for example, criticize the abuse of human rights in China, a very different culture from our own? If Holloway can formulate a moral principle he considers applicable across major cultural differences, why should the biblical teachers not have

---

[6]Translation by J. McCann, *The Rule of St. Benedict* (London: Sheed & Ward, 1976), 4.

been able to do so, and have been inspired by God to do so? Traditional Christian theology and ethics have always recognized that the Bible does contain some rules appropriate only to the first readers' particular context. But, conversely, only an extreme form of postmodern relativism could deny that commandments such as "You shall not steal" or "You shall not bear false witness" or "Love your enemies" could be permanent moral principles.

The Christian tradition is a very large and complex historical phenomenon, and it would be foolish to suppose one could or should defend it against every moral criticism. But for the most part it manifests both a considerable consistency in its moral teaching over time and a willingness to take changing circumstances into account. (On sexuality, for example, there have been changes but only within the scope of the—at least until very recently—unchanging conviction that sexual acts are appropriate only within monogamous, heterosexual, and intentionally permanent union.) It also contains self-critical principles, such as the primacy of scriptural authority. These self-critical principles are essential to understanding, for example, the issue of the role of women in the church, to which Holloway more than once draws attention. The case for the ordination of women appealed to the fundamental principles of the equality of women and men both in creation (Gen. 1:27) and in redemption (Gal. 3:28), as well as to examples of women's leadership in both Scripture and tradition, and based on these intra-Christian criteria its critique of the practice of most of the church in most of its history. This was not arbitrary adaptation to change, but a reform inspired by authentically Christian concerns central to Scripture and tradition. Undoubtedly, people outside the church were important for this process, alerting those within to evils to which the church itself had grown far too accustomed. Openness to learning from others is a significant part of the church's openness to God, but such openness is only part of a constructively Christian discernment when it is at the same time a rediscovery of the direction in which the scriptural word of God points God's people.

Rediscovering the church as a distinctive moral community

Important as the task of nurturing a moral consensus in our pluralistic society is, it cannot be the Christian church's first priority, and the Christian church's particular contribution to it actually cannot be made unless the church puts first things first. First and foremost, the church's vocation is to live faithfully to the gospel of God's love and salvation in Jesus Christ. As far as morality goes, this means living according to the distinctive ethic taught by Jesus and his apostles (and not without reference to the law and the prophets, which their teaching presupposed). In responses to preliminary versions of this essay, some readers have been puzzled as to what I mean by this distinctive Christian ethic. The best answer I can give is to point to some classic New Testament expressions of it, such as Matthew 5, Romans 12:9–21, and 1 Corinthians 13:4–7. The ethic of Christian discipleship given in such passages is distinctive, for one thing, in its radically demanding character, which goes much further than the ethical standards by which most secular people strive to live and certainly much further than the minimal ethical principles Holloway proposes. But this Christian ethic is also distinctive in its content, such as love of enemies, sexual chastity, thoroughgoing truthfulness, nonretaliation, unlimited forgiveness, peaceableness, humility, readiness to renounce rights, concern for the most marginal and the most wretched in society. Of course, such qualities overlap with other moral traditions, but the Christian configuration of these and other principles and qualities is distinctive. Many Christians who practice such ethics may not think of them as distinctive, but this is because in the centuries of Christianization they became to some extent the common property of Western culture. But this is less and less the case. More and more, the distinctiveness of the Christian ethical way emerges in a post-Christian culture, as it did in the late Roman Empire and in many other cultural contexts in which Christians have been a distinctive minority.

This Christian ethic is much more than a set of rules; it is a way of life lived in the devotion of one's whole life to God. (It is preposterous to suggest that someone seeking in that sense to live Christianly could possibly leave God out of it.) It involves the radical realignment of the will and the formation of Christlike character, both possible only through the Spirit of Christ. It entails also a fundamental communal aspect. The church is the community committed to living its distinctive ethic both together in the community's own life and in relation to the world that both individuals and the community inhabit.

This does not mean that the Christian ethic is sectarian in the sense of not being applicable beyond the Christian community itself. Nor does it mean that Christians do not need to learn from the wisdom and experience of others.[7] But the Christian ethic is the ethic that is coherent with the Christian understanding of God, humanity, and the world. Therefore the most important way in which the church can recommend its moral tradition to others is to recommend the gospel itself, without which some of the demands of Christian morality may well make no sense or seem oppressive. It is the Christian way as free and glad response to the overwhelming generosity of God in the

---

[7]For a moderate defense of the distinctiveness of the Christian ethic and the importance of the church as a moral community, which also acknowledges that the church can and should find some common ground with secular liberalism, see D. Fergusson, *Community, Liberalism, and Christian Ethics* (Cambridge: Cambridge University Press, 1998).

gospel that is the church's authentically Christian moral recommendation. Otherwise put, the church's primary vocation in a secular and pluralist society is missionary.

Of course, there is an important need in our society for informed moral debate among people of all persuasions, especially on new questions such as those raised by biotechnology. But such debates are not the substance of the moral life and do not determine the fundamental convictions by which people live. Moral example is probably more important to moral formation and to moral persuasion, and in a culture inclined to treat all truth as relative, it seems plausible to think that the church may recommend the Christian ethic to others less by moral debate than by living out a compelling alternative to the moral confusions and moral cynicism of our culture. By banishing God from morality, Holloway's approach deprives the church of its basis for living this alternative and subverts the church's vocation to live for God in a society sorely in need both of God and of moral inspiration.

5

Authority and Tradition

For as long as some people have claimed the support of the so-called threefold cord of Scripture, tradition, and reason,[1] others have been busy unraveling it. In the history of the by no means always harmonious relationships between these three "authorities," it is tradition which has most often suffered discredit, at any rate since the Reformation. One could represent the history of the modern West, not entirely accurately but not without insight nonetheless, as a progressive liberation from the power of tradition: the Reformation liberated Scripture from tradition, the Enlightenment liberated reason from tradition, while postmodernism proposes that we see even Enlightenment rationality as itself a tradition from which we need liberation. This history, which has surrounded the notion of tradition with intimations of the reactionary and the oppressive, has problematized the role of Christian tradition in the church and especially its relationship to its alleged partners in the threefold cord. Any attempt to define and to defend tradition's authority for the church today must examine rather carefully its relationship to Scripture and to reason.

---

[1] I do not know any attempt to discover the first use of the formula "Scripture, tradition, and reason." The passage usually quoted from Richard Hooker (*Laws of Ecclesiastical Polity* 5.8.2) scarcely qualifies. Hooker undoubtedly worked with the concept of the three authorities (though he was also preoccupied [as in *Laws* 5.8.2] with ecclesiastical authority over *adiaphora*), and he may plausibly be thought partly responsible for the prevalence of the concept in later Anglican thought (so J. E. Booty, "Hooker and Anglicanism," in W. Speed Hill, ed., *Studies in Richard Hooker* [Cleveland/London: Press of Case Western Reserve University, 1972], 207–39). But he never used the term *tradition* in the sense of the formula, preferring *antiquity*: see O. Loyer, *L'Anglicanisme de Richard Hooker* (Lille/Paris: University of Lille, 1979), 129–47.

Tradition in relation to Scripture

The history of views on the relation of Scripture and tradition has been the subject of much research and discussion, usually with its ecumenical implications in view.[2] In a most useful critical synthesis,[3] Tony Lane has classified the views on this subject to be found in Western Christian history[4] until recently as four, which he calls the coincidence view, the supplementary view, the ancillary view, and the unfolding view. He also, correctly, observes that these views of the relation of Scripture and tradition cannot be adequately understood without reference to a third factor, the contemporary teaching of the church. For our purposes it will be sufficient briefly to summarize the four views:

(1) The *coincidence view*,[5] which prevailed from the time of Irenaeus and Tertullian, holds that the content of apostolic tradition coincides with the content of Scripture. This view first emerges clearly in Irenaeus's defense of the Catholic church's teaching against Gnosticism, in which his concern was to show that this teaching, unlike that of the gnostics, preserved the true apostolic message. True apostolic tradition, as distinct from the pretended tradition of the gnostics, could be found both in written form in the apostolic writings (the emerging New Testament canon) and in oral form in the tradition handed down from the apostles to their episcopal successors in the apostolic see. In this argument, the fact that the apostolic writings and the apostolic tradition coincide in their content is important but subsidiary to the main point, that both coincide with the teaching of the bishops, who are the custodians of Scripture and tradition and whose teaching is therefore vindicated as the true apostolic message.

Although in this early period the "rule of faith"—as a summary of the contemporary church's teaching assumed to be identical with tradition from the apostles—can function as a guide to the correct interpretation of Scripture, against the misuse of Scripture by heretics, this does not mean that Scripture

---

[2]Books include E. Flesseman-van Leer, *Tradition and Scripture in the Early Church* (Assen: Van Gorcum, 1955); F. W. Dillistone, ed., *Scripture and Tradition* (London: Lutterworth, 1955); G. H. Tavard, *Holy Writ or Holy Church* (London: Burns & Oates, 1959); R. P. C. Hanson, *Tradition in the Early Church* (London: SCM Press, 1962); Y. M.-J. Congar, *Tradition and Traditions* (London: Burns & Oates, 1966); F. F. Bruce and E. G. Rupp, eds., *Holy Book and Holy Tradition* (Manchester: Manchester University Press, 1968); F. F. Bruce, *Tradition Old and New* (Exeter: Paternoster, 1970). For further literature, see Congar, *Tradition*, 459–60; A. N. S. Lane, "Scripture, Tradition, and Church: An Historical Survey," *Vox Evangelica* 9 (1975): 37–55.

[3]Lane, "Scripture, Tradition."

[4]In the Eastern Orthodox tradition the problems with which Western theology has had to deal have not arisen.

[5]Tavard, *Holy Writ*, refers to the "coinherence" of Scripture and tradition.

was regarded as requiring authoritative interpretation in order to be understood.[6] But this was the form that the coincidence view came to take, as in its classic expression by Vincent of Lérins in the fifth century, who makes it clear that, although Scripture is *materially* sufficient (its content does not need to be supplemented from tradition), it is *formally* insufficient (it needs authoritative interpretation). As numerous heretics demonstrate, Scripture "seems to be capable of as many interpretations as there are interpreters": a point echoed by Roman Catholic theologians from the sixteenth century to the present day. Therefore Scripture must be interpreted according to "the tradition of the Catholic church," which Vincent identifies by means of his famous triple test of universality, antiquity, and consent. Catholic tradition is "what has been believed everywhere, always, by all" (*quod ubique, quod semper, quod ab omnibus creditum est*). Vincent is not entirely unaware of the difficulties of ascertaining a tradition so defined. But whereas they may seem to us to render tradition even more obscure than Scripture, so that, as Newman observed, "the solution [which the Vincentian canon] offers is as difficult as the original problem,"[7] Vincent is not deterred by these difficulties, because his real concern is to vindicate the teaching of the contemporary church. Hence, in his understanding of consensus, not everyone counts equally: priests count more than laypersons, bishops more than priests, synods and councils more than individual bishops. In particular, the decrees of ecumenical councils he considers authoritative expressions of the Christian consensus, so that no one who dissents from these can count against the consensus.[8] The coincidence view as it derives from Vincent already uses the notion of apostolic tradition as a justification for the magisterium's role as the authoritative interpreter of Scripture.

(2) The *supplementary view* is also commonly known as the "two-source theory" of revelation. Though some traces of it can be found in patristic writers, it really gained ground during the Middle Ages, when it coexisted with the "coincidence view," and triumphed in post-Tridentine Roman Catholicism. It holds that Scripture is not only formally, but also materially insufficient. The full content of revelation is to be found not in Scripture alone, but in Scripture and unwritten apostolic traditions. The development of this view is intelligible when we remember that the primary concern, in discussion of tradition, was to vindicate the teaching of the contemporary church as substantially identical with that of the apostles. The presupposition is that the Holy Spirit maintains the church in the truth by guaranteeing the teaching of the magisterium. If the

---

[6]Hanson, *Tradition*, 105–8, 125–26.
[7]J. H. Newman, *As Essay on the Development of Christian Doctrine: The Edition of 1845* (Harmondsworth: Penguin, 1974), 88.
[8]*Commonitorium* 2:4–6; 27:70–29:77.

latter is perceived as no longer coinciding with the content of Scripture, but going beyond it, then unwritten traditions must fill the perceived gap between Scripture and the teaching of the contemporary church.

Such a doctrine was especially appealing in response to the late medieval heretics and the sixteenth-century Reformers, who, in maintaining that the teaching of the contemporary church both contradicted Scripture and went beyond it, appealed to Scripture *against* the authority of the church's contemporary teaching. Although the coincidence view could be and was used to vindicate the latter as the only correct *interpretation* of Scripture, the supplementary view appeared to many a more cogent means of defending the church's teaching, particularly because, in the climate of sixteenth-century humanist exegesis, appealing to an allegorical reading of Scripture as the basis for contested doctrines was not good apologetic. When Protestants, who rejected medieval allegorizing, claimed that Roman Catholic teaching could not be supported from the literal, historical meaning of Scripture, the response was that it did not need to be, because apostolic teaching was to be found not only in the New Testament, but also in unwritten traditions, which could often be supported by patristic evidence but in the last resort were identifiable from the fact that the church teaches them.[9]

The Council of Trent produced a decree whose wording, controversial as its interpretation has become,[10] seems compatible with both the coincidence and the supplementary views, and this has allowed modern Roman Catholic theologians to return to a form of the coincidence view.[11] Nevertheless the fact that the majority of the Council fathers actually held the supplementary view[12] shows that the tide of Roman Catholic theology, reacting against the Reformers, was then moving strongly in its favor.[13] After Trent, its decree was almost universally interpreted by Roman Catholic theologians from the sixteenth to the nineteenth century as teaching the supplementary view.

(3) The *ancillary view* is Lane's term for the sixteenth-century Protestant view, in which tradition functions as an aid, but not a norm, for the interpretation of Scripture. The Reformation principle of *sola scriptura* was not primarily

---

[9]Congar, *Tradition*, 56–61, gives lists of the examples given by sixteenth-century Roman Catholic apologists of the doctrines and practices that they thought defensible only as unwritten tradition.

[10]Cf. Congar, *Tradition*, 164–69; G. Moran, *Scripture and Tradition: A Survey of the Controversy* (New York: Herder & Herder, 1963), 34–38, 48–54, 63–68.

[11]K. Rahner, "Scripture and Tradition," in *Theological Investigations* 6 (New York: Crossroad, 1969), 106–8; Congar, *Tradition*, 410–12.

[12]H. Jedin, *A History of the Council of Trent*, vol. 2 (Edinburgh: Nelson, 1961), 75.

[13]So also G. H. Tavard, "Tradition in Early Post-Tridentine Theology," *Theological Studies* 23 (1962): 377–405.

directed against tradition, but against the teaching of the contemporary church. But it was therefore a rejection of those understandings of the role of tradition that served to justify the teaching of the contemporary church as apostolic and to permit no appeal to Scripture against it. In other words, it was a rejection of *both* the coincidence *and* the supplementary views. In spite of claims to the contrary,[14] the Reformers did not return to the coincidence view and could not do so, because that view depends on the harmony and continuity of the contemporary church's teaching with both Scripture and tradition. Once the contemporary church's teaching is judged to be unscriptural and therefore dependent on *corrupt* tradition, it is no longer possible to identify true tradition in the way that the coincidence view requires, by means of the Vincentian canon. True tradition can now be distinguished from corrupt tradition only by testing all tradition according to the standard of its faithfulness to Scripture. Scripture inevitably becomes the norm for the identification of true tradition, rather than tradition the norm for the interpretation of Scripture. The Reformation posited a degree of discontinuity in church history—the possibility and the fact of serious and long continued doctrinal error by the authorities of the church— that necessarily deprived tradition of the normative status it had in both the coincidence and the supplementary views. If Scripture can be pitted against tradition to reveal its corruption, then Scripture must be not only materially (as in the coincidence view) but also formally sufficient.

The great respect that the Reformers had for the Fathers, and especially for the creeds and the councils of the early church, does not contradict this belief in the formal sufficiency of Scripture. Certainly they could appeal to the true tradition of the early church against the corrupt traditions of the medieval period, but in a way that ultimately presupposes the independent authority of Scripture. Only by judging tradition according to the standard of Scripture could they evaluate the first five or six centuries as relatively pure and the succeeding centuries as progressively corrupt. No other principle (such as the notion of an undivided church) made the tradition of the patristic period especially authoritative, since, as article twenty-one of the Church of England's Thirty-nine Articles states, even general councils "may err, and sometimes have erred."

The notion of the formal sufficiency of Scripture does not, of course, mean that Scripture requires no interpretation at all—a motion which anti-Protestant writers have frequently and easily refuted, thus missing the point— but that it requires no *normative* interpretation. Protestant interpretation of

---

[14]H. A. Oberman, "Quo Vadis? Tradition from Irenaeus to Humani Generis," *Scottish Journal of Theology* 16 (1963): 240–44; Tavard, *Holy Writ*, 210–43 (on the English Reformation).

Scripture employed all the ordinary means of interpreting a text, especially the tools that humanist scholarship had developed for interpreting ancient texts, and respected the views of theologians and exegetes of the past as useful, but not normative, guides to understanding Scripture. The real difference between the classic Protestant and the classic Roman Catholic views lies in the Protestant rejection of the view that tradition, expressed in the teaching of the magisterium, possesses a *binding* authority against which there can be no appeal to Scripture. Behind this difference lie, on the one hand, the Reformation's originating experience of a rediscovery of the gospel in Scripture apart from and in contradiction to the teaching of the contemporary church and, on the other hand, the Roman Catholic trust in God's promise to maintain God's church in the truth. On the one hand, tradition was ruptured by an experience of discontinuity between Scripture and the contemporary church, while, on the other hand, an unbroken tradition remained the vehicle of continuity between the teaching of the apostles and that of the contemporary church.

(4) The *unfolding view*, Lane's term for the modern Roman Catholic understanding, stemming from Newman, of the development of doctrine, involves an important break with the three preceding views and thereby takes us decisively into the modern period. The three preceding views assumed that true tradition is essentially static: it *preserves* the teaching of the apostles unchanged. In both the coincidence and the supplementary views, the continuity of tradition means that what the contemporary church teaches must be what the apostles explicitly taught. Modern historical awareness has made this as implausible to modern Roman Catholics as it was, for different reasons, to sixteenth-century Protestants, while Newman's idea of the development of doctrine came to dominate twentieth-century Roman Catholic theology because it seemed to accommodate the facts of historical change in the church's doctrinal teaching within the classical Catholic conviction of the unbroken faithfulness of the church, in its official teaching, to apostolic tradition. Tradition comes to be understood as the process by which the full meaning of the apostolic message is gradually unfolded.

Two implications of this view need to be noted. First, it tends to place even more weight than its predecessors on the contemporary teaching of the magisterium as the real norm for Christian doctrine, since what is only implicit in Scripture and earlier tradition reaches its fullest development here. Newman himself was quite clear that his understanding of development required an infallible developing authority in the form of the Roman Catholic magisterium.[15] Secondly, the model of development has facilitated the repudiation

---

[15]Newman, *Essay*, 165–78.

by most modern Roman Catholic theologians of the supplementary view in favor of a return to the coincidence view, but in this new form, as modified by the notion of development.[16] But in that case it is even more important than ever to maintain the formal insufficiency of Scripture.[17] The same gap between the explicit content of Scripture and the contemporary teaching of the church, which the supplementary view had filled with unwritten apostolic traditions, has now to be filled by the process of development.

Since Vatican II, many writers have spoken of an ecumenical convergence on the subject of Scripture and tradition.[18] Certainly, on the Roman Catholic side, the general abandonment of the supplementary view and, on the Protestant side, a tendency towards more positive appreciation of tradition as the transmission and actualizing of the biblical message in the life of the church down the centuries[19] have brought Roman Catholics and Protestants closer together. The following words of Max Thurian, as well as correctly bringing the subject into the sphere of pneumatology, state the relation of Scripture and tradition in a way that would command general ecumenical agreement:

> The Holy Spirit, who has given the canon of the New Testament to the Church and by the Church, continues ceaselessly to animate the Word of God contained in the Scriptures, and to make it present and efficacious in the Church and the world. Tradition is this unfailing life of Scripture in the Church under the Spirit's influence. Tradition is the Church's life of listening to the Holy Spirit repeating the word of God ever anew.[20]

Nevertheless, the key difference between Protestants and Roman Catholics still tends to emerge when one asks questions about norms. The Word of God does not come to equally adequate expression in all of the church's thought, worship, life, and practice, nor should its expression in one time and place of the church's existence necessarily be transmitted without change to other

---

[16]Congar, *Tradition*, 413; Moran, *Scripture*, 72–73.

[17]Cf. Rahner, "Scripture," 107–8.

[18]G. H. Tavard, "The Authority of Scripture and Tradition," in J. M. Todd, ed., *Problems of Authority* (Baltimore: Helicon Press/London: Darton, Longman & Todd, 1962), 30; E. Flesseman-van Leer, "Present-Day Frontiers in the Discussion about Tradition," in Bruce and Rupp, eds., *Holy Book*; G. O'Collins, *Fundamental Theology* (London: Darton, Longman & Todd, 1981), 204–7; cf. Anglican-Roman Catholic International Commission, *The Final Report* (London: Catholic Truth Society/SPCK, 1982), 69–71.

[19]E.g., the 1963 Montreal report, *Scripture, Tradition, and Traditions*, of the Fourth World Conference on Faith and Order, discussed in Flesseman-van Leer, "Present-day Frontiers."

[20]Quoted in Congar, *Tradition*, 474.

times and places. How is what is permanently binding to be distinguished from what is in need of revision or reformation, or in Gerald O'Collins's terms, how is "*the* Tradition" (i.e., the Gospel) to be found "within the traditions"?[21] For most Roman Catholics, the norm is still apostolic tradition authoritatively expressed in the teachings of the magisterium, since "the task of authentically interpreting the word of God, whether written or handed on, has been entrusted exclusively to the living teaching office of the Church" (Vatican II, constitution *Dei Verbum* 10).[22] For most Protestants, the norm is still apostolic tradition authoritatively expressed in Scripture alone. But the distinction is no longer as sharp as it was. Many Roman Catholic theologians would give a much more nuanced answer to O'Collins's question, as he himself does,[23] and a good deal of Roman Catholic theology would seem to be moving in the direction of, if not quite reaching, Hans Küng's thoroughly Protestant claim that only Scripture is *norma normans*, while subsequent tradition can be no more than *norma normata*.[24] A few Protestant theologians, on the other hand, seem to be moving in the opposite direction of dissolving any real distinction between Scripture and tradition.[25]

The following critical comments will serve to move the discussion in the direction of the new paradigm to be suggested in section 3:

(1) The Bible is not simply the first part of the tradition. Of course, historically it is the written deposit of a tradition that continued without a break. But it is also true that, even historically, the church's recognition of the canon of Scripture created a real break, which gave the origin of the tradition, in this written form, a uniquely normative status in relation to the rest of the tradition.[26] One cannot take the tradition seriously without taking seriously its basically *interpretative* relation to Scripture, which (with only the partial excep-

---

[21]O'Collins, *Fundamental Theology*, 208–10.

[22]Translation in W. M. Abbott, ed., *The Documents of Vatican II* (London/Dublin: G. Chapman, 1966), 117–18.

[23]O'Collins, *Fundamental Theology*, 210–24.

[24]H. Küng, "Toward a New Consensus in Catholic (and Ecumenical) Theology," in L. Swidler, ed., *Consensus in Theology? A Dialogue with Hans Küng and Edward Schillebeeckx* (Philadelphia: Westminster, 1980), 17.

[25]E.g., D. Ritschl, "A Plea for the Maxim: Scripture and Tradition," *Interpretation* 25 (1971): 113–28; idem, *The Logic of Theology* (London: SCM Press, 1986), 69–71. Ritschl's criticisms of the traditional approach to the normativity of Scripture need to be heeded but in my view do not require surrendering the tradition's own witness to its qualitative distinction from Scripture. Cf. the comments of E. Flesseman-van Leer in M. Hooker and C. Hickling, eds., *What About the New Testament? Essays in Honour of Christopher Evans* (London: SCM Press, 1975), 234–42.

[26]Cf. J. B. Torrance, "Authority, Scripture, and Tradition," *Evangelical Quarterly* 59 (1987): 249–50.

tion of the supplementary view) the tradition itself has fully recognized. This is required by the nature of the Christian revelation: that in the history of Jesus God's revelation of God's self reached a climax that is unsurpassable this side of the parousia.

However, the traditional notion that revelation ceased with the death of the apostles may be a misleading expression of this, which lends itself to the accusation of "a cryptic deism" in "the idea that God has set in motion a dynamic or a mechanism . . . which has already come to a conclusion or a climax and which since then needs only to be unrolled and developed through theological interpretation."[27] It is better to adopt some such distinction as that which O'Collins makes between "foundational revelation" (in the biblical period) and "dependent revelation" (in the history of the church),[28] which gives full recognition to the revelatory activity of the Spirit since the apostles but sees this as a contemporization and contextualization of the foundational revelation. The tradition as in *this* sense interpretative of Scripture is no mere repetition or translation of Scripture, but really creative of the fresh meaning that is generated in the encounter between Scripture and each new context in which its message is heard. God's revelation of God's self in the history of Jesus is never surpassed, nor is its meaning ever exhausted this side of the *parousia*. Yet the process by which it gains ever fresh meaning must remain *subject* to the apostolic account of its fundamental meaning. This is not to restrict the work of the Spirit but to recognize its consistency with the revelation of God in Jesus. It is also a phenomenologically accurate description of the structure of the Christian religion since the second century.

(2) Tradition is now widely and correctly understood as essentially a hermeneutical process, in which the message of Scripture is interpreted and developed. As such it takes place in a tension between the guidance of the Spirit, who preserves the church from irreparable apostasy, and the fallibility of the church as a human society. No one who takes seriously, as many Roman Catholics now do, the experience of the Reformation (to take only the most obvious example), can doubt that the Spirit's guidance occurs not only through the continuity of tradition but also through radical and painful breaks with tradition.

Thus, on the one hand, we can acknowledge the Roman Catholic concern that the Bible be heard and interpreted within the church's tradition of listening to its message under the Spirit's guidance. It does not come to us as a book that has never been interpreted before but as a book whose meaning has

---

[27]Ritschl, *Logic*, 71.
[28]O'Collins, *Fundamental Theology*, 101–2.

been actualized in a rich variety of ways to and by Christians in many different circumstances of the past. But, on the other hand, we must also acknowledge the Protestant concern that the Bible be allowed to challenge tradition. The Reformation was due in large part to reading the Bible in fresh translations that no longer carried the associations medieval theology had built around the text of the Vulgate, so that it could be read *without* the spectacles of tradition and its message heard as though for the first time. Historical-critical study of the Bible in the nineteenth and twentieth centuries has, at its best, had a similarly liberating effect. Liberation theology has again read the Bible in the light of an understanding of its contemporary situation that demands a significant break with the interpretative tradition. Such ruptures with tradition, which of course create their own forms of the tradition, witness to the fact that the Bible is not absorbed by but always transcends its interpretation in the tradition.

(3) The need for such challenges of and ruptures with tradition could be understood in connection with the phenomenon of the "refunctioning" of tradition that David Gross discusses with reference to tradition in general (rather than Christian tradition in particular).[29] He refers to the way in which in the modern period both the political state and the economic market, fundamentally antitraditional agents, have refunctioned traditions and parts of traditions for their own ends. Such refunctioning does not designate the small and gradual processes of change, which all traditions undergo over time, but the deliberate production of extreme changes in the tradition, which subvert the tradition's original ends and appropriate it for political or economic benefit, as perceived from the perspective of the state and the market. That such refunctioning has occurred (and even continues to occur) in the Christian tradition seems likely, in view of the various kinds of deep entanglement with political and economic interests to which the Christian tradition has been subject at many times and places. Movements of renewal and reformation in the Christian tradition can represent instances of the restoration of the original ends of the tradition when it has suffered refunctioning for ends fundamentally alien to it. Given the vulnerability of tradition to refunctioning, it is of the highest importance that the Christian tradition contains, in its recognition of the Bible as uniquely normative, a self-critical element integral and essential to it. The

---

[29]D. Gross, *The Past in Ruins: Tradition and the Critique of Modernity* (Amherst: University of Massachusetts Press, 1992), chap. 7. He is borrowing the German concept of *Umfunkionierung*, used by Bertolt Brecht, Ernst Bloch, and other German Marxists in the 1920s; for them it "referred to a process of refashioning bourgeois values in such a way as to use them against their original intention" (108), a process that they attempted to implement in their own work.

role of the Bible in this respect is not to expunge tradition in some kind of unhistorical attempt to reproduce the biblical past, but to restore to the tradition its authentic and original intentions and ends, releasing their critical power to challenge concrete instances of the appropriation of the tradition by other interests.

(4) In the past, much of the discussion of tradition, shaped as it was by the concern to distinguish Catholic orthodoxy from heresy, was too narrowly focused on the question of universally and permanently normative expressions of tradition. The situation was not much improved by the notion of development of doctrine, which incorporated historical change only in the form of the accumulation of normative tradition, which grows, in Richard Hanson's picture, like a coral reef.[30] Once developed and authoritatively taught by the magisterium, doctrines are of universal and permanent validity.

Thereby most of the real value of tradition was ignored. Tradition is the process by which the gospel takes *particular* form in the various times and places of the church's history. We ought now to be able to see that the evolutionary model of tradition was suspiciously close to European-centered nineteenth-century views of cultural progress. In the churches of the Third World, the imposition of supposedly universal norms, developed in the Western Christian tradition, looks like just another form of Western cultural imperialism, mistaking, according to Western intellectual habit, its own particularity for universality. So not only does the notion of "development by expansion" need supplementing with that of "development by pruning,"[31] but a much more complex process of *contextualization*[32] needs to be envisaged. As Robert Schreiter puts it, the tradition is really "a series of local theologies,

---

[30]R. P. C. Hanson, *The Continuity of Christian Doctrine* (New York: Seabury, 1981), 26.
[31]N. Lash, *Change in Focus* (London: Sheed & Ward, 1973), 145–46.
[32]"Contextualization"—a term that originated in missiological discussion of the relationship of Christianity to non-Western cultural contexts—seems to have acquired different nuances for different people. For example, R. J. Schreiter, *Constructing Local Theologies* (London: SCM Press, 1985), 12–15, considers "Liberation approaches" to be a form of "the contextual model," while T. Witvliet, *The Way of the Black Messiah* (London: SCM Press, 1987), 42–43, sharply distinguishes contextualization from liberation theology. I am certainly not claiming (what Witvliet rejects) that the tradition exists in a noncontextualized form that is then contextualized. I use the term much as in the classic article of Shoki Coe ("Contextualizing Theology," in G. H. Anderson and T. F. Stransky, *Missions Trends No. 3: Third World Theologies* (New York: Paulist/Grand Rapids: Eerdmans, 1976), 19–24, for whom "authentic contextualization must be open constantly to the painful process of decontextualization, for the sake of re-contextualization" (24), and who intends the term as a dynamic, future-orientated concept, implying not adaptation to a static culture, but engagement in a process of change.

closely wedded to and responding to different cultural conditions."[33] This suggests that the *real* continuity of the tradition is maintained as much by change as by permanence.[34]

(5) Allied to the tendency to narrow the concept of tradition to universally valid norms was the rather authoritarian dichotomy between the *Ecclesia docens* and the *Ecclesia discens*, which tended to identify tradition with the teaching of the magisterium, since only there could tradition become effective as a norm.[35]Progressive Roman Catholic theology, by giving greater prominence to such notions as the *sensus fidelium*, the variety of charisms, and the *lex orandi* principle, is rapidly moving away from this perspective.[36] The authority of the magisterium is relativized as it is placed in a broader context.

Tradition, as the transmission and actualization of the gospel in the life of the church, consists not only of creeds, council decrees, and the teaching of bishops, but of liturgy, hymns, popular spirituality, art, poetry, stories, preaching, forms of pastoral and missionary activity, academic and popular theology, charitable and educational institutions, and so on. The subject of tradition is the people, Christian believers in local congregations as they experience Christ and live the gospel, and is therefore the "teaching authorities" only as one charism among others.[37] The authority of tradition is not purely juridical but belongs, for example, to the testimony of the martyrs, the life of Francis of Assisi, or the spirituals of American black slaves—in all of which the gospel is remarkably actualized, at least as much as it belongs to any council of bishops.

---

[33]Schreiter, *Constructing*, 93.

[34]Cf. G. Ebeling: "The same word can be said to another time only by being said differently" (quoted in A. C. Thiselton, *The Two Horizons* [Exeter: Paternoster/Grand Rapids: Eerdmans, 1980], 99); Witvliet, *Way*, 7: "What in one context is liberating theological insight can become the opposite in another."

[35]Congar, *Tradition*, 181.

[36]E.g., L. Sartori, "What is the Criterion for the Sensus Fidelium?"; Y. Congar, "Towards a Catholic Synthesis," both in J. Moltmann and H. Kung, eds., *Who Has the Say in the Church?* (Edinburgh: T. & T. Clark, 1981 = *Concilium* 148 [8/1981]), 56–60, 68–80; L. Boff, *Church: Charism and Power* (London: SCM Press, 1985), chaps. 10–13; P. Suess, "The Creative and Normative Role of Popular Religion in the Church," in N. Greinacher and N. Mette, eds., *Popular Religion* (Edinburgh: T. & T. Clark, 1986 = *Concilium* 186 [4/1986]), 122–31.

[37]The claim that the episcopal office, as such, is the special vehicle of tradition is unhistorical; it ignores the fact that the way bishops actually relate to local congregations has varied widely at different times and places (for a sample, see R. P. C. Hanson, *Christian Priesthood Examined* [Guildford/London: Lutterworth, 1979], chap. 3).

Tradition in relation to reason

We shall not here attempt to trace the history of this subject[38] but will focus on the problem of vindicating tradition in the face of the Enlightenment's prejudice against tradition, which still strongly influences attitudes to tradition in contemporary culture, despite the waning influence of Enlightenment rationality and the strong critiques of it which have emerged from various quarters of contemporary thought. For the most part, postmodernism has not really replaced the Enlightenment's prejudice against tradition with a more positive evaluation, even though, as David Gross points out,

> whereas modernism regarded tradition as a still-powerful force that had to be defeated, this is no longer the case in postmodernism. Tradition is now treated more as a curiosity, as something quaint or interesting. The once-passionate opposition to it has lapsed, because tradition no longer seems to be an obstacle to the emergence of the new. Today the sense is that the battle against tradition is over, that modernism was victorious, that the new not only won out but became institutionalized everywhere. This being so, one is now free to be indifferent toward tradition, to discard it as irrelevant, or, if one wants, to casually borrow bits and pieces from it, though without investing them with any special significance.[39]

Clearly this postmodern trivialization of tradition (to be seen, for example, in the marketing of the past for entertainment) presupposes the modern rejection of the authority of tradition that the Enlightenment pioneered. It is therefore with the latter that we must begin.

(1) The Enlightenment was experienced by its protagonists as a liberation of rational thinking from the shackles of tradition. As Kant put it: "'Have the courage to use your own intelligence'; that is the motto of the enlightenment."[40] Or as Diderot, speaking for the radical philosophes of the French Enlightenment, put it more fully: the ideal philosopher is one who "trampling underfoot prejudice, tradition, venerability, universal assent, authority—in a word, everything that overawes the crowd—dares to think for himself, to ascend to the clearest general principles, to examine them, to discuss them, to admit nothing save on the testimony of his own reason and

---

[38]For which see D. A. Pailin, "Reason in Relation to Scripture and Tradition," in B. Drewery and R. Bauckham, eds., *Scripture, Tradition, and Reason: A Study in the Criteria of Christian Doctrine: Essays in Honour of Richard P.C. Hanson* (Edinburgh: T. & T. Clark, 1988), 207–38.

[39]Gross, *The Past*, 59.

[40]Quoted in C. Gunton, *Enlightenment and Alienation* (Basingstoke: Marshall, Morgan & Scott, 1985), 153.

experience."[41] Autonomous critical rationality, accepting only what cannot be doubted, was set in sharp contrast to mere belief on the authority of tradition. The contrast is still with us and gives the notion of tradition its overtones of restriction and oppression. We still suffer from the Enlightenment's conviction that tradition is by its very nature opposed to freedom, identified with the emancipatory value of autonomous rationality. The roots, though not the modern evaluation, of this contrast between critical rationality and the authority of tradition lie in the Middle Ages, and insofar as the Enlightenment's revolt was against an overly *authoritarian* notion of tradition, it was surely justified and a necessary precondition for the very real achievements of modern thought. Ironically, however, it is arguable that "almost as soon as the autonomous self emerged under modern conditions, it was threatened by the very force that once appeared to be emancipatory—namely, the force of triumphant rationality."[42] Gross here refers to the rationalization of economic and social life, which instrumentalized and bureaucratized so much of human activity that people became, if anything, more shaped by powerful outside forces and conditions than had been the case when life was much more governed by the traditions so opposed by Enlightenment rationality.

However, the point of most importance to us here is an epistemological one. The Enlightenment obscured the extent to which all human knowledge and thought is indebted to tradition. In fact, of course, "the anti-traditional bias of modernity is itself a potent tradition, and one of long standing. It is a way of viewing experience and our reflections upon it that is itself a cultural, historical product."[43] The sociology of knowledge, the philosophical hermeneutics of Gadamer, Michael Polanyi's philosophy of science, Alasdair MacIntyre's tradition-related account of rationality concur in reminding us of the point—so obvious once we have grasped it—that we all, even the most critical and original thinkers, depend on a body of corporate knowledge, much of which has to be taken on trust, and a "fiduciary framework" (Polanyi) of fundamental attitudes that shape the way we test and acquire knowledge. A tradition of corporate belief is not, as such, the antithesis of reason, but its condition.[44] This is still

---

[41]Quoted in C. Taylor, *Sources of the Self: The Making of the Modern Identity* (Cambridge: Cambridge University Press, 1989), 323.

[42]Gross, *The Past*, 49.

[43]L. Gilkey, *Catholicism Confronts Modernity: A Protestant View* (New York: Seabury, 1975), 106.

[44]Cf. A. Thiselton, "Knowledge, Myth, and Corporate Memory," in *Believing in the Church: The Corporate Nature of Faith*, A Report by the Doctrine Commission of the Church of England (London: SPCK, 1981), 45–78; N. Lash, *Voices of Authority* (London: Sheed & Ward, 1978), 69–83; T. A. Hart, *Faith Thinking* (London: SPCK, 1995), chaps. 3 and 8.

insufficiently recognized in those areas of intellectual activity still dominated by modernist presuppositions about rationality, aided and abetted by the general loss of real connection with the past that for a variety of reasons, especially economic, is characteristic of contemporary life.

A significant weakness of the Enlightenment, then, was its failure to recognize the historical particularity of all reason. But recognizing the rootedness of all thinking in a particular cultural tradition need not imply the total relativism that has become fashionable in postmodern reactions against modernity. The most diverse cultural traditions share a common world to which all human reasoning relates, as is evident from our ability to understand, learn from, communicate with, and even convert to traditions of thought quite different from those in which we have first learned to understand the world.[45] But recognizing this rootedness does imply—against Enlightenment pretensions to suprahistorical universality—that universality is mediated through the particularity of cultural traditions and that we can transcend our tradition only in dependence on our rootedness in it. To see the world from a particular standpoint that our tradition has given us is the condition of creaturely knowledge. To trust a tradition for the insight and knowledge it has given us, and to go on to appropriate more of what it has to offer, is not irrational, nor is it necessarily conservative. Even revolutionaries, whatever their destination, can see it only from where they are.

(2) However, this vindication of tradition as such provides no very strong reason to trust the *Christian* tradition, which is not *the* cultural tradition of the modern West or of any other culture in which Christians live today. Modern Western culture is itself more pluralistic than most other cultures have been, but from its standpoint Christianity, in dissenting from the shared assumptions of secularity, appears to be not one of its contemporary variants but an anachronistic survival of pre-Enlightenment tradition. That some of the roots of modern Western culture lie in the Christian tradition does not make the latter any less anachronistic, since post-Enlightenment culture is precisely not concerned with returning to its roots but with moving on from them into a new future. The real problem of the relation between the Christian tradition and secular rationality for the Christian in the modern West is therefore not in the realm of particular criticisms leveled at particular aspects of Christian belief or practice, but the problem of the sense it makes for a participant in modern culture to appropriate a tradition which that culture has deliberately left behind. This problem is the relatively novel one of Christianity in a

---

[45]This seems to me the relevant validity of the criticism of "historicism" by O. O'Donovan, *Resurrection and Moral Order* (Leicester: IVP/Grand Rapids: Eerdmans, 1986), 161–62.

post-Christian culture, as distinct from, say, the problem of Christianity in the pagan Roman Empire. In the latter case, Christianity's problem was that of being a novelty in a culture which revered the past; in our case, Christianity's problem is that it belongs to the past of a culture which believes in progress—or at least, in this remnant of the belief in progress: that religion has been superseded.

In such a context, the place of Christianity is that of "productive non-contemporaneity."[46] By drawing on the resources of a tradition outside the parameters of contemporary thought, it can offer alternatives that are not available from within the historically limited world of the present. It shows up the historicity of modernity. If, as a tradition superseded by modernity, it must allow that modernity has rendered it questionable, no longer to be accepted simply as given, it may also, as a past tradition that can prove itself to be not simply used-up but productive past, render *modernity* questionable, not to be accepted simply as given. It can go beyond pointing out the failures of modernity that are in any case everywhere becoming apparent. The dismissal and suppression of questions of transcendent meaning—by Enlightenment rationality and its postmodern successors alike—can be rendered questionable not simply by listening to a tradition of attempted answers to such questions, but by discovering, first by observation and then by experience, how the appropriation of such a tradition enhances human life and opens up prospects for meaningful living beyond the increasingly closed options of modernity.

Thus Christianity, along with some other religious traditions, has a virtually unique relationship to the culture of modernity and postmodernity. It offers the possibility of a critique of modernity from outside modernity. It meets what David Gross sees as the need for a critique that goes beyond the "immanent critique" offered, for example, by Habermas, in which the most "progressive" elements of modernity are employed to move modernity on. What is needed, according to Gross, is

> a critique of modernity from *outside* modernity. Many of today's most astute social and cultural critics seem unable to provide a perspective from beyond the boundaries of the present. They give us at most a modern critique of modernity. But in refusing to base their critiques

---

[46]J. B. Metz, "Productive Noncontemporaneity," in J. Habermas, ed., *Observations on "The Spiritual Situation of the Age": Contemporary German Perspectives* (Cambridge, Mass./London: MIT Press, 1984), 169–77. For the German origins of the term *noncontemporaneity (Ungleichseitung)*, see Gross, *The Past*, 94–95. He does not refer to Metz, but does trace the term back to the art historian Wilhelm Pinder and its use by Karl Mannheim and Ernst Bloch, who insisted that it could be used progressively, despite the regressive practice by the Nazis.

on anything outside the dynamic of modernity itself, they place in question what is given only from within the confines of the given. Even when the "social pathologies" of modern life are superbly diagnosed or criticized, the hidden assumption is that these pathologies somehow contain their own remedies. The cure for modernity is simply—more modernity.[47]

Christianity, as not only a retrievable but also a living tradition, ought to be truly an "other" to modernity,[48] a tradition in the light of which "the givens of modern culture become problematized."[49]

Christianity also has a remarkable advantage in critical potential vis-à-vis modernity and postmodernity. Late modern and especially postmodern culture has proved extraordinarily eclectic, able to draw into itself all kinds of elements of other cultures, past and present. But this is a kind of inclusive eclecticism that absorbs all such elements into either a (modern) homogeneous whole or a (postmodern) cultural supermarket of consumer choice. In either case, such cultural elements are deprived of their otherness and critical potential. But increasingly Christianity is excluded rather than absorbed. (One is reminded of that university department in which, it is claimed, the Bible can be approached and interpreted from virtually any perspective—feminist, ecological, vegetarian—*except* a Christian theological one.) Christianity significantly resists cultural co-option in contemporary Western society, and it is important, even at the cost of marginalization, that it continues to do so. The view from the margin is sometimes one for which things otherwise difficult to see become insistently clear.

(3) It is important, with Metz, to distinguish "productive non-contemporaneity" from two other ways of dealing with Christianity's experience of noncontemporaneity. There is, on the one hand, "the catch-up mentality in theology," which aims at a "consciousness which is as contemporaneous as possible with bourgeois-liberal society and scientific-technological civilization."[50] This is the characteristic temptation of liberal theology, with its instinct for reducing otherness to sameness. On the other hand, there is mere conservative traditionalism, which is fundamentally an attempt to opt out of history by remaining in the past. Both avoid the creative tension of noncontemporaneity, which draws on the resources of the Christian tradition in order to engage critically with modernity for the sake of change. There have been and perhaps increasingly there will be situations of cultural hostility in which

---

[47]Gross, *The Past*, 87, cf. 89, 134.
[48]Gross, *The Past*, 84.
[49]Gross, *The Past*, 100.
[50]Metz, "Productive Noncontemporaneity," 172.

the tradition can be kept alive only in a ghetto, but still it must be kept alive, not merely for the sake of the past, but with a view to the future.

The point to be maintained is that productive noncontemporaneity is not backward-looking. Its resort to the tradition is not in order to reproduce the past but to find future in the past, the possibilities that have been left behind but can be taken up again in a creative way.[51] Not that the tradition is merely to be plundered for what, judged from the standpoint of modernity, seems useful. It must be listened to attentively in its deepest dissent from modernity, for precisely there may be its relevance. But the result must be contextualization, a productive engagement with the present for the sake of a future that can never be the same as the past, though it can have learned from it.

(4) Given that post-Enlightenment culture is itself a tradition or traditions, it is distinguished from most premodern and non-European traditional cultures in its orientation to change, whereas traditional cultures were orientated to stability. Of course, this is a relative difference. But it explains why premodern cultures attributed authority to the past, while the Enlightenment's repudiation of tradition was a rejection of this authority of the past in favor of an orientation to a new future.[52]

The Christian tradition was rather easily assimilated to the ancients' and the medievals' veneration for the past: it became a repetition of a sacred and authoritative origin. The Vincentian canon, at least as Vincent expounds it, is heavily indebted to this concept.[53] Change, which of course occurred in ever new contextualizations of the gospel, had to be assimilated to the model of reproducing or restoring the past. What made Christianity assimilable to this model was its attribution of unique, normative religious significance to a piece of past history—the history culminating in the history of Jesus. Nevertheless, the assimilation was a misapprehension. In the biblical understanding, the authority of the story of Jesus lay in its promise for the future. Its uniqueness was eschatological. In it was disclosed the possibility of a different future—the kingdom of God. Not that this would be reached by any kind of incremental progress, but in living towards it, its possibilities became provisionally actual. The past was remembered in hope, not as an escape from historicity, but as the inspiration and direction for missionary engagement with the world for the sake of its future.[54]

---

[51]J. Moltmann, *God in Creation* (London: SCM Press, 1985), 131–32.

[52]A useful discussion of the question of the authority of the past is Lash, *Voices*, 55–68, which, however, tends to neglect the question of orientation to the future.

[53]O'Collins, *Fundamental Theology*, 211.

[54]J. Moltmann, *Theology of Hope* (London: SCM Press, 1967), 295–303; idem, *The Church in the Power of the Spirit* (London: SCM Press, 1977), 2–3; idem, *On Human Dignity* (London: SCM Press, 1984), 105–6.

Thus the Christian tradition is by no means inevitably traditionalist. Its eschatological hope and its missionary orientation press it towards constantly changing contextualizations of the gospel, in which the resources of the past are brought into critical relationship with the present context with a view to the future. Even in the centuries of European Christendom, in which the general cultural tradition was only weakly Christianized, the Christian tradition itself frequently reemerged as a critical ferment offering fresh vision.

The modern world's break with tradition and orientation towards change, of course, produces conservative reactions. The disorientating effect of constant change—the sense of homelessness in modern culture—can produce a nostalgia for tradition, and religion precisely as traditionalist becomes attractive to the fugitive from modernity. The conflict between desire for progress toward a better future and disillusioned nostalgia for a good past also invades the churches and is reflected in any number of debates over liturgical language or sociopolitical attitudes. Continuity and change are, in any case, interdependent, not mutually exclusive, but Christianity must do better than achieve some tolerable balance between the two. It must find its continuity in the memory of the story of Jesus and its faithfulness to the direction in which the story points, toward the kingdom of God. "Christianity is more than a tradition; it is a hope."[55]

(5) The value of the Christian tradition as a criticism and an alternative to modernity is not intended to suggest that, in its critical conversation with modernity, it can escape criticism from modernity. But in discussion of issues of purely theoretical credibility, it needs to be recognized that modernity's standpoint is not a privileged one. Probably more important is the application of ideology criticism to the Christian tradition to expose its ideological manipulation by those in power in church or society. Traditional doctrines of the ministry, for example, including its limitation to men, must be subject to the suspicion of being self-justification for those who propounded them.[56] Contemporary ideology criticism here proves an ally of important New Testament concerns.[57] Moreover, full and ashamed recognition of "the Janus face of church history"[58]—its character as curse as well as blessing to humanity, which secular historiography as well as the judgment of Scripture can expose—must prevent productive noncontemporaneity from becoming a new sort of triumphalism.

It may be that ideology criticism can also help to rescue the real authority

---

[55]J. Moltmann, in E. Moltmann-Wendel and J. Moltmann, *Humanity in God* (London: SCM Press, 1984), 118.
[56]Boff, *Church*, 43 and passim.
[57]Cf. A. C. Thiselton, *Interpreting God and the Postmodern Self: On Meaning, Manipulation, and Promise* (Edinburgh: T. & T. Clark, 1995).
[58]Ritschl, *Logic*, 63.

of the tradition from authoritarianism. Other interests, such as social conformity, distorted the tradition into a purely external, coercive authority. Its real authority is that of a noncoercive witness to a divine disclosure of truth, an authority that invites by offering the possibility of redemptive meaning and convinces through experience of its ability to engage redemptively with all contexts. David Tracy's account of the authority of "the classic" provides at least an illuminating model of the Christian tradition's claim to attention. Classics, he says, invite "the risk of interpretation," in which interpreters will themselves be interpreted as they struggle to interpret. The real authority of the classic is acknowledged neither by the person who (applying purely historical and social-scientific methods of interpretation) retains his or her complete autonomy over against it, nor by the person who merely repeats the classic in an authoritarian, "fundamentalist" way, but by the person who enters a genuine conversation with the classic and thereby produces a new interpretation of the classic out of his or her own lived experience of it.[59]

(6) Finally, the usefulness of defining the issue as the relation between tradition and reason may be questioned. In the first place, the tradition, of course, includes reason. It includes the work of some of the greatest minds in history. It includes traditions of reflection, practical wisdom, and intuitive insight, as well as rational argument about the faith. Only the narrow understanding of tradition as normative apostolic tradition identified with revelation produced the simple opposition between tradition and reason.

But, secondly, if it is used to label the tradition's encounter with the activity of reason outside the tradition, the term *reason* is potentially misleading, because it disguises the historicity of reason, whose universal validity is always mediated by the particular standpoints of actual traditions of thought. Reason, for the Christian tradition, has meant everything from Platonism to Vedantic philosophy to the critical theory of the Frankfurt school. Moreover, it disguises in fact that this historicity means a standpoint within a social and cultural context. Such problems will be avoided if we think more broadly of Christianity's relation to its *context*. The model of contextualization will include reason both within the Christian tradition from the past that has to be contemporized and in the new contemporary context in which it must be contextualized.

A new model: Scripture, tradition, and context

In a recent discussion Jürgen Moltmann judiciously asserts both the contextuality and the universality of all Christian theology:

---

[59]D. Tracy, *The Analogical Imagination: Christian Theology and the Culture of Pluralism* (London: SCM Press, 1981), chaps. 3–4.

> The forms of theological thinking, theological language and theolog-
> ical metaphors are contextual, always and everywhere. They are deter-
> mined by their situation and are guided by particular interests. . . . But
> on the other hand, every particular and contextual theology . . . is *theo-
> logy*, talk about the one eternal God of all human beings, all creatures
> and times. . . . Every Christian theology, however conditioned by its
> context, *kairos* and culture, says something about God and is impor-
> tant to all who believe in God. Every Christian theology, however
> conditioned by its context, *kairos* and culture, follows and interprets
> the text of the biblical writings.[60]

The consequence is that the theology of one context is not irrelevant or without interest to the church and its theologians in another context. Theology—
and the same could be said of wider areas of the church's life—is both
context-related and context-transcending. Only because it is the latter can it
relate critically to its context. Scripture, as the textually available source and
guide for Christian faith, is one aspect of the commonality that makes it possible for Christians in all places and times to understand and to learn from each
other. The other key aspect is tradition, which functions hermeneutically to
assist the ongoing relationship the church must sustain between Scripture and
contemporary context.

The diagrams[61] represent (in inevitably simplified form) the way in which
the life and thought of the church in any particular time and place is a mediation of the three factors of Scripture, tradition, and context. (Context is used
here in the broadest sense of every aspect of a society in which the church
exists.) In diagram 1, S represents Scripture, and C1, C2, C3 represent three
successive contexts. The three triangles (T1, T2, T3) stand for the life and
thought of the church in each context, as formed by the contextualization of
the message of Scripture in that context. In other words, they are three successive stages of tradition. The continuity of the tradition across these three
stages is represented in two aspects of the diagram. The shaded areas of overlap between the triangles indicate that various contextualizations of the
Gospel are bound to have major common features. The arrows represent the
fact that each contextualization of Scripture is influenced by previous stages of
the tradition, for example, by inherited creeds, liturgies, or theology.

Diagrams 2 and 3 explain how the shaded areas of overlap in diagram 1
come about. There are two dimensions of this continuity in the tradition. In

---

[60]J. Moltmann, *Experiences in Theology*, trans. M. Kohl (London: SCM Press, 2000),
59–60.
[61]The diagrams were inspired by and attempt to refine the diagram in L. Kretschmar,
The Voice of Black Theology in South Africa (Johannesburg: Ravan Press, 1986), 88.

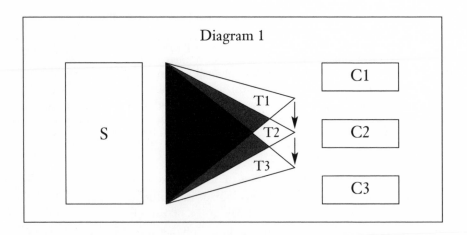

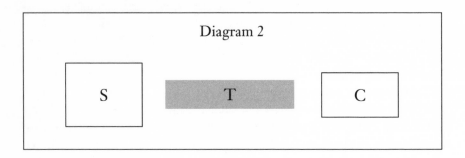

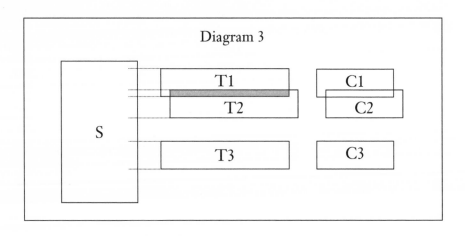

diagram 2, C represents not any particular human society but the common human condition. It represents the extent to which all societies and cultures share a common world, purely by virtue of being human societies on this earth. T therefore represents those insights that the tradition gains through reflection on the relation of Scripture to constant features of the human condition. These are not insights necessarily present in every stage of the tradition, but once gained in one stage of the tradition, they are transferable to others. This is where Newman's theory of the development of doctrine, as an accumulation of "irreformable" dogma, to the extent that it can be allowed any validity, might fit into the diagram.

Diagram 3 illustrates the overlap of contexts, independently of their participation in the common human condition. C1 and C2 might represent, for example, two successive stages of Western European culture, exhibiting both continuity and change, or they could represent contemporary Western culture and a non-Western culture that has been considerably influenced by Western culture. Cultural overlap can also occur coincidentally, in contexts not historically continuous. C3 provides for the possibility of a context not overlapping with others. The shaded area of T1 and T2 represents that dimension of the continuity of the tradition that results from the overlap of contexts. Also represented in the diagram is that fact that different parts or aspects of Scripture become relevant in different contexts. The distinction between the two dimensions of continuity represented in diagrams 2 and 3 is, of course, an abstraction that is by no means always easy to make in actual instances.

Various complexities of the real situation that cannot be represented in the diagrams should be noted: (1) That Scripture itself derives from a tradition with a variety of original contexts is presupposed. (2) Contexts vary not only over time but also across space, and contemporaneous branches of the tradition in different contexts overlap and influence each other. (3) Distinct Christian groups in the same context can evolve relatively different traditions. (4) The diagram does not incorporate Christianity's influence on its context, which can mean, for example, that a particular context may have been partly formed by previous stages of the Christian tradition.

Despite its limitations, the diagrammatic model can be illuminating. For example, it shows the key difference between traditionalism and creative fidelity to the tradition in new contexts. Traditionalism mistakes the unshaded areas of previous stages of the tradition (in diagram 1) for shaded areas, and therefore perpetuates aspects of the tradition that are no longer appropriate. Creative fidelity to the tradition produces an unshaded area whose novelty may offend traditionalists. On the other hand, it has to be recognized that the persistence of features of the tradition that originated to meet the needs of superseded contexts can sometimes prove unexpectedly useful in new contexts. For example, monasticism—whether or not it also fulfills a purpose valid in any context—has performed a remarkable variety of context-related roles.

The dimension represented by diagram 2 is frequently underestimated in modern discussion, but is extremely important.[62] It explains why we can find the most culturally remote parts of the tradition illuminating. The very difference in cultural contexts may help to highlight aspects of life that our own context neglects but that need reemphasis. The interrelation between the common human condition and the particularities of actual human societies makes the cultural variety of the tradition in various times and places, not so much a divisive factor that impedes communication, as a means of enriching adventures; material can be retrieved from all parts of the tradition in the past, and experiences of Christians in quite different contemporary cultures can speak to our own. A familiar example of the former is almost any hymnbook: hymns that certainly could not be written today enrich contemporary worship for precisely that reason. Moreover, the underlying continuity of the human condition can mean that even novel features of a new context, while in some sense requiring novel responses, can also draw out unexpected resources in the tradition. For example, the ecological crisis, caused by attitudes of exploitative domination toward nature that recent Christian tradition has tended to nurture, gives Francis of Assisi's attitude to nature no longer a merely sentimental attraction but the value of contributing to a new form of Christian respect for nature.[63] The adequacy of the tradition is constantly proved in its unexpected resources for interpreting the novel features of new situations—not in such a way as to deny the novelty, but by producing an interpretation of the novelty coherent with the tradition.

The fact that we cannot always easily, and usually do not, distinguish the dimensions represented by diagrams 2 and 3 does not normally matter much. But sometimes problems arise. The sheer length and continuity of the Western Christian tradition—which actually results from contextualization in a long series of more or less overlapping contexts—can create the illusion that long-standing features of it are constant because they are appropriate to the human condition as such and so can be transferred to any context. Of course, the arrogance of European cultural imperialism since the nineteenth century has aided and abetted this, and the discovery of the relativity of the Western Christian tradition has been somewhat painfully combined with the need to repent of the colonial mentality.

---

[62]Cf. R. P. C. Hanson's argument against D. Nineham in "Are We Cut Off from the Past?" chap. 1 of *Continuity*.
[63]See chapter 7 below.

The diagram does not explain *how* Scripture is contextualized, that is, how Scripture and context are mediated, with the aid of previous tradition, to create a new stage of the tradition. In that sense, it is far from prescribing a theological method, just as the old trio of Scripture, tradition, and reason was.[64] A descriptive account of how contextualization has actually happened would uncover a wide variety of forms, which would need critical appraisal in a prescriptive account of contextualization.[65] The latter would have to insist on the critical element in the relationship to context, distinguishing critical assimilation from syncretism and critical engagement from uncritical adaptation. It would need to show how the phenomena that have been described as the *sensus plenior* of Scripture[66] and the development of doctrine can be more adequately understood as the generation of fresh meaning in the encounter between Scripture and new contexts. It would also have to show how contextualization requires a dialectic of movement from the concerns of Scripture and tradition to the context and from the concerns and questions arising from the context to Scripture and tradition.[67] It would have to restore the relevance of aspects of the tradition that theology tends to neglect (such as spirituality, the history of biblical interpretation, or the lives of the saints), as well as explaining the status of relatively universal validity (and therefore *normae normatae*) that some monuments of the tradition, such as the creeds, have acquired. But there are limits to the usefulness of prescribing method. Contextualization is not an exact science, but the difficult art—in which theology may participate—of the church's whole life of faithfulness to the gospel in authentic response to the challenges of a particular situation.[68]

---

[64]Against the claim that this formula constitutes an Anglican theological *method*, see S. W. Sykes, *The Integrity of Anglicanism* (London/Oxford: Mowbray, 1978), 63–75.

[65]For an attempt at a prescriptive account, see Schreiter, *Constructing*.

[66]Cf. O'Collins, *Fundamental Theology*, 256, for this understanding of the *sensus plenior*.

[67]Thus taking account of, but transcending, what Ritschl, *Logic*, 102, calls "the reversal of the question of the relevance of the Gospel."

[68]J. S. Begbie, *Theology, Music, and Time* (Cambridge: Cambridge University Press, 2000), 216–21, offers an illuminating use of musical improvization, with its productive interplay of freedom and constraints, as a model for tradition, incorporating many of the aspects of tradition that have been presented in this chapter.

6

Egalitarianism and
Hierarchy in the Bible

Egalitarianism and hierarchy are two opposed forms of thinking about the structures of human society and the ordering of human relationships. For hierarchical thought, human beings are fundamentally unequal, such that some are entitled to power and privilege over others. The rule of superiors over inferiors is justified either by nature or by divine decree or both. Some humans may be considered to be by nature inherently superior to others and thus designed by nature to rule their inferiors. This is how, for example, Aristotle justified slavery, and how many nineteenth-century Europeans justified their empires. Alternatively or additionally, hierarchical structures of domination and subordination may be justified by divine ordination. Thus, in much medieval thinking about both ecclesiastical and secular political and social hierarchy, the model was of a hierarchy in which God, as the ultimate source of all power, devolved power downwards, in the first place to the pope and/or the emperor, and subsequently through lower levels of God-given authority.

By contrast, for egalitarian thought, human beings are fundamentally equal, such that none is entitled to status and privilege above others. Insofar as the exercise of power and authority by some is necessary, it is justifiable only as a responsibility to be exercised on behalf of all and in the interests of all. Egalitarian thought has inspired the modern search for democratic structures that can place power ultimately in the hands of all people equally and can ensure that rule is exercised with responsibility to and for all.

The most powerful critique of hierarchy is currently the feminist one.[1] Since

---

[1]The kind of feminist critique of hierarchy that is briefly outlined here is common to most feminist thought: for very different examples see R. R. Ruether, *Gaia and God: An*

this critique in many cases extends to the role of the Bible as promoting and sanctioning hierarchy, it is an appropriate point of entry to a consideration of this issue as a biblical hermeneutical issue. The feminist critique, of course, focuses on patriarchy, the hierarchical ideology that in Western Christian societies has sanctioned not only the domination of some men over others but also the domination of men in general over women in general. The feminist critique further recognizes that, in traditional Western Christian thought, these structures of domination in human society belong to a broader hierarchical ideology, which envisages all of reality in a hierarchical structure. The overall hierarchical structure is God–man–woman–nature. In this structure the man-woman hierarchy is legitimized and strengthened by its place in a wider cosmic hierarchy. Male rule over women is justified by seeing men as closer to God and more rational, while women are closer to nature and more physical. The man-woman hierarchy coheres in this way with the hierarchies of human rule over the rest of creation and of the superiority of reason to body, both of which have played key roles, along with patriarchy, in the Western tradition.

It is evident that traditional ideas of God are implicated in this overall hierarchical scheme of thought about cosmic reality and the structures of human society. In the feminist critique, traditional Christian ideas of God belong to the patriarchal system and provide ideological support for it. The image of God as male reflects and reinforces the rule of man over woman. When God is imaged as King or Father, images of male rule are projected onto the deity. ("Father" is as much an image of male domination as "King" is. The father rules his family, and ancient kings often called themselves the fathers of their nations.) The feminist critique of masculine language and imagery for God is badly misunderstood if it is taken to involve only the issue of gender. The critique combines the issues of gender and hierarchical domination, which, according to feminists, have been inseparable in the Western Christian tradition. Male images of God portray not merely a divine male but a divine patriarch, who rules at the summit and source of the whole structure of patriarchal hierarchy. Hence, much feminist theology rejects traditional ideas of divine transcendence, which seem to set God above us and so sanction a generally hierarchical way of thinking.

There can be little doubt that much of the Western Christian tradition is vulnerable to this feminist critique of hierarchy, though it is arguable that there have also been significant egalitarian trends in the tradition. The aim of the present chapter is not to discuss the tradition, but rather to argue that the

---

Ecofeminist Theology of Earth Healing (London: SCM Press, 1993); D. Hampson, *After Christianity* (London: SCM Press, 1996).

Bible itself should not be regarded as the source and guarantor of Western hierarchical ideology. It is a mistake to read the Bible through the lens of hierarchical thinking, as much of the Western Christian tradition in the past has read it and as much feminist theological criticism today reads it. The overall direction of biblical thought, it will be argued, is egalitarian. Its tendency is not in support of but away from hierarchical structures in human society, and biblical images of God's rule function not to legitimate human hierarchy, but to relativize or to delegitimize it.

Two biblical strategies

It is certainly not the case that advocacy of egalitarian social structures is everywhere apparent in the Bible. What can, however, be argued is that running through the biblical traditions is a strongly egalitarian *direction* of thought,[2] operating especially to critique relationships of privilege, which give to one person or class privileges or rights at the expense of others who lack them. This egalitarianism takes, in both testaments, two different forms. One form is radical opposition to hierarchical relationships and structures. It delegitimizes such structures altogether and requires egalitarian relationships and structures instead. The other, less radical form accepts hierarchical structures while trying to ensure that they operate for the good of all, rather than for the particular benefit of the privileged. Instead of radical opposition to hierarchy, this second form of egalitarianism is a strategy of relativizing and transforming hierarchy. Since it involves a pragmatic acceptance of hierarchical structures as a starting point, its egalitarian *direction* can be missed by a static reading of the texts that fails to observe the dynamic of biblical thought. But when this second attitude to hierarchy is recognized as tending in an egalitarian direction, then the two forms of egalitarianism can be seen to be alternative strategies aiming in the same direction. The strategy of radical opposition to hierarchy and the strategy of relativization and transformation of hierarchy are alternative routes towards the same goal.

Both strategies can be observed in both testaments. The difference between the testaments lies in the main focus of the issue of egalitarianism in each case. In the Old Testament, egalitarianism is expressed primarily in the form of the economic equality of family households, while the form of hierarchy that has to be addressed is the political hierarchy constituted by the monarchy. In the New Testament, egalitarianism is expressed primarily in the form of the equal-

---

[2]For the hermeneutical principle of discerning the *direction* of biblical thought, see also chapter 1 above.

ity of individuals in the family of faith, while the form of hierarchy that has to be addressed is that of the household. This is not to say that equality of individuals is in no way a concern in the Old Testament, or that political hierarchy is never addressed in the New Testament. But as a relative difference of focus the contrast just stated is valid and will enable us to observe how the two biblical strategies in relation to equality and hierarchy are both operative in both testaments, though taking different forms because of the different foci of the issue in the two testaments.

Old Testament

In the Old Testament, the *source* of the egalitarian direction lies in the event that made Israel YHWH's people, the exodus.[3] The powerful memory of the exodus, which reverberates through Israel's traditions of faith, was a memory of liberation from slavery. As slaves in Egypt, the Israelites had been at the bottom of a strongly hierarchical social structure, which stretched from the divine Pharaoh, who exercised absolute sovereignty by virtue of his relation to the gods, down to foreign slaves like the Israelites. The value of persons decreased as one moved down the scale. At the exodus, YHWH took the side of the slaves against the divine Pharaoh, overturned the hierarchy, and by emancipating the slaves set his face against oppressive structures based on privilege. The God of the exodus was clearly not the kind of god who devolved power and privilege downward from a divine king. The God of the exodus was the God of freed slaves, and therefore the ideal of society which arose from the exodus was that of a people always mindful of the fact that they had been slaves (e.g., Exod. 23:9; Lev. 19:33–34; 25:42; Deut. 24:18). Such a people should not set up the kinds of structures of privilege and exploitation from which they themselves had suffered. They should form a community free of oppressive structures, and with provisions to protect any who might be vulnerable to exploitation. In this way the exodus was the source of a radically egalitarian ideal, frequently forgotten, but always there to be recovered and applied in criticism of hierarchy and privilege.

In premonarchical Israel the egalitarian ideal seems to have achieved a reasonable—in its historical context, remarkable—degree of practical realization. The *form* that egalitarianism took was the basic economic equality of family households. In this structure the individual featured primarily as a member of a household: the three-generational family unit, of varying size. While this is alien to a modern egalitarian perspective, the Israelite perspective focuses on

---

[3]See, e.g., P. D. Hanson, *The People Called: The Growth of Community in the Bible* (San Francisco: Harper & Row, 1987), 20–24.

the household because this was the economic unit. It is, above all, an economically realistic form of egalitarianism, recognizing that, since power and privilege come from the accumulation of wealth, real equality must have an economic base. The prevalent modern notion that equality in democratic rights can coexist with large-scale economic inequality would have made no sense to anyone in ancient societies, which fully recognized that wealth is what gives some people status and power over others.

In the agrarian society of early Israel, the individual could not normally be economically self-sufficient. The economic unit was the family group, working together, in often harsh conditions, to make a living from its plot of land. The essential need was that each family should have its own portion of land, sufficient for subsistence and inalienable. Israelite land law was designed to ensure that land could not pass permanently out of the kinship group in which it passed down by inheritance.[4] If people were obliged, through debt, to sell land, there were provisions for the redemption of land by relatives, while in the jubilee year all land should revert to its original family. Of course, there could be no mathematical equality of economic resources. But accumulation of land—by which some families grow wealthier and others lose their livelihood—should not, according to the law, happen. When it did happen, in disregard of the law, the prophets denounced it (e.g., Isa. 5:8; Mic. 2:1–2).

Even in this system of inalienable family land ownership, some people would be unable to support themselves. The three groups repeatedly mentioned in the laws and the prophets as paradigmatic are widows, orphans (i.e., categories of people who, if they owned land, could not work it themselves), and resident aliens (i.e., foreign workers who did not own land). Israelite laws in a variety of ways made provision for the support of these people who fell outside the household economic structure. The focus on the household was not therefore to the exclusion of individuals. Most individuals were considered as integral to family units with collective economic resources, but the whole society had to take responsibility for those who were not in this position.

This land-based form of egalitarianism had an important theological basis in the idea that the land was the land YHWH had given to his people, who held it in trust from him. He had apportioned it fairly to provide for the support of all of his people. To deprive Israelites of their family inheritance of land was, in effect, to challenge God's rule over his people. God's rule over Israel was intimately related to God's gift of the land to Israel, since in the ancient world kings were commonly considered to own the whole land they ruled. This was the basis on which they could demand taxes from the land their sub-

---

[4]See, e.g., Hanson, *The People Called*, 63–65.

jects held by their permission, or even reappropriate the land for their own use.[5] In Israel's case, since God was the king who owned the land, there seemed to be no place for a human king. With the absence of a human king went the absence of the other social strata of wealth and privilege that monarchy entailed in ancient practice. God's sole kingship over his people was the foundation for an egalitarian, nonhierarchical structure opposed to human monarchy and the structures of inequality associated with it.

Of course, early Israel had leaders, especially for military purposes, but the so-called judges had no court and founded no dynasty; the opportunities for power and privilege to become entrenched were avoided. The theocratic principle was expressed by Gideon when the people invited him to rule as king: "I will not rule over you, and my son will not rule over you; the LORD will rule over you" (Judg. 8:23). Even more revealing of the antimonarchical principle of Israel's egalitarian tradition is the account of the origins of the monarchy in 1 Samuel 8. Israel wished to abandon her distinctive nonmonarchical egalitarianism and have a king "like other nations" (8:5), thereby rejecting YHWH's rule over them. In a remarkable warning Samuel spelled out what human kingship means: subjection to absolute monarchy, and the growth of a military and bureaucratic elite made rich at the expense of the peasantry (8:11–17). In the climactic summary—"you shall be his slaves" (8:17)—Samuel implied that Israel would, in effect, be reversing the exodus, rejecting the liberating kingship of YHWH in favor of the enslaving rule of a human monarch like Pharaoh. Since this time they were choosing oppression with their eyes open, YHWH would not hear their cry for deliverance as he had at the exodus, but leave them to the fate they had chosen (8:18). In this passage we see how clear-sighted the Israelite tradition of radical opposition to monarchy was about the evils of political hierarchy as it actually developed in Israel: the growth of a rich landowning class, the draining of resources from the peasantry to support the elite, the impoverishment of many of the peasantry, the radical inequality of status and wealth. We can also see clearly why monarchy was seen to threaten the Israelite ideal of a free society of equals, subject only to the liberating rule of YHWH.

From a pragmatic point of view, no doubt there was a certain inevitability about the development of monarchy, if Israel was to survive in a world of strong, centralized states. Stable, centralized political structures that were not monarchical and hierarchical had not been invented. It is not surprising that the monarchy is accepted in much of the Old Testament. But it is accepted

---

[5]This is what Ahab does in 1 Kgs. 21, bringing him into direct conflict with YHWH's own rule over his people.

with major qualifications. In other words, the second strategy of ancient Israelite egalitarianism comes into play. While the first strategy opposes human monarchy as incompatible with YHWH's sole rule, the second attempts to co-opt the monarchy to the service of YHWH's rule over his people. This involves relativizing monarchy's pretensions to absolute power: in Israel, YHWH's people, the king is *not* to rule like the kings of other nations. It also involves insisting that the king's function is to serve his people (cf. 1 Kgs. 12:7). The strategy is to attempt to ensure that, since there is hierarchy, it should be as far as possible benevolent hierarchy, serving not the interests of the privileged but the interests of all, especially the most vulnerable.

Three different examples of this strategy will suffice. First, the only passage about kingship in the Mosaic law (Deut. 17:14–20) envisages a king who is as unlike the kings of the nations and as much like the ideal "judges" of pre-monarchical Israel as possible. The king is not to exalt himself above his fellow Israelites, but to rule *as one of* his people. The king's power and privileges are relativized to the extent of requiring, if it were conceivable, an egalitarian form of monarchy. Here the second strategy is so radically applied as to be virtually the first strategy in disguise.

Secondly, Psalm 72, a coronation psalm, provides, as one might expect, an idealized version of the monarchy. However, this is not an idealization that cloaks oppression, but an idealization that demands justice. The two interwoven themes of the psalm are the prayer that the king should execute God's righteousness for his people and the prayer for the prosperity of the king's reign. It is clear that the prosperity is conditional on the justice, which, since it is God's justice, is justice for the poor and the needy, deliverance for the oppressed, support for the weak and vulnerable (Ps. 72:2, 4, 12–14). The king is not to be the summit of a hierarchy of oppression, in which the poor and the vulnerable are at the bottom. On the contrary, the king's prime duty is to protect and to support the poor and the vulnerable. This is an entirely practicable ideal, since, as the highest judicial authority, the king had the unique power to intervene on behalf of those denied their rights in local courts, where the powerful could all too easily bend justice to their interests. If the king's highest authority were aligned with God's concern for the disadvantaged, then the king could be the hope of justice for the poor. Of course, there is no earthly sanction to ensure that the king fulfills this ideal, but should he do so, monarchy, by adopting the concerns of God's rule, justifies itself as the servant of God's rule. It is no accident that this monarchical ideal became the messianic hope for a king who would execute justice for the poor (Isa. 11:4).

Thirdly, the ideal, such as we see in Psalm 72, of a king who implements God's righteousness, especially in protecting the needy and the vulnerable, is the criterion by which the prophets assessed the actual kings of Judah and

Israel, found many of them severely wanting, and pronounced God's judgment on them.[6] For example, Jeremiah praises Josiah for judging the cause of the poor and needy, but condemns his son Jehoiakim for thinking that being a king consists in building palaces at the expense of his people (Jer. 22:13–17). The prophets never fully accepted the entrenched privilege of a royal dynasty, because for them YHWH remained the true king of his people who intervenes in judgment to remove kings and royal houses who fail to rule as his anointed. Again we see the relativization of royal power and pretensions by means of belief in divine sovereignty.

New Testament

In the New Testament the *source* of the egalitarian direction lies initially in Jesus' understanding of God's fatherly concern for each individual person and subsequently also in the Christian conviction that this love of God was enacted in Jesus' death for each individual person, such that one's brother or sister must be valued as one for whom Christ died.

Jesus appropriated the radical egalitarian tradition of Israel,[7] but instead of focusing on the image of God as king (making Israelites all equally his subjects), he preferred to think of God's rule in terms of the image of God as Father, making all Israelites equally his children, brothers and sisters to each other. (The use of *brother* for fellow Israelite is already an Old Testament usage, but one that comes into its own in the New Testament through the unprecedented extent to which Jesus privileged the image of God as Father.) The family image becomes primary. Instead of the egalitarianism of family units in early Israel, Jesus was concerned with the equality of family members in the renewed community of Israel, envisioned as a family of faith.

It is very striking that, in this context, Jesus disallows human fathers. Just as in the radical form of Old Testament egalitarianism, the equality of all Israelites under the sole rule of YHWH meant there could not be a human king in Israel, so in Jesus' teaching, representing the radical form of New Testament egalitarianism, the equality of all means there cannot be human fathers. Among the new relationships Jesus establishes in the community of his disciples, the renewed Israel, fatherhood is pointedly excluded (Matt. 23:9; Mark 3:35; 10:29–30). It is excluded because it represents hierarchical authority in the family. (The mother's authority over small children did not significantly survive their coming of age, whereas the father held authority over all family members.) Jesus abolishes patriarchal authority in the renewed Israel

---

[6]See, e.g., P. D. Miller, "The Prophetic Critique of Kings," *Ex Auditu* 2 (1986): 82–95.
[7]On what follows, see, in more detail, R. Bauckham, "Kingdom and Church according to Jesus and Paul," *Horizons in Biblical Theology* 18 (1996): 4–13.

because patriarchal authority belongs exclusively to God. This is the necessary corollary of his transposition of the Israelite egalitarianism of divine kingship into the familial image of God's rule as God's fatherhood.

Also indicative of Jesus' radical vision of a society without status or privilege is the way he makes those who had the lowest status or lacked any status in hierarchical society the paradigms or models of what it means to belong to the kingdom of God. He makes slaves the paradigm for status in the kingdom of God, when he acts as a slave to his disciples by washing their feet, and requires them to do the same for each other (John 13:3–15). He makes the poor—i.e. the destitute, who lack any reliable means of support—the paradigm for status in the kingdom of God, when he pronounces them blessed, as those to whom the kingdom belongs (Matt. 5:3; Luke 6:20). And since children had no social status at all, he makes them the model for the lack of status which all must accept on entering the kingdom of God (Matt. 18:1–4; Mark 10:13–16). If the kingdom of God belongs to slaves, the destitute, and the children, then others can enter the kingdom only by accepting the same lack of status. The kingdom of God makes all equal by requiring all to come down to the level of the lowest. In this way Jesus envisages and implements an egalitarianism in radical opposition to the hierarchical structures of his contemporary society.

In the churches of the Pauline mission, which are the churches about which we know most in this respect, Jesus' radical egalitarianism made a strong impact. Christians were a family of faith, brothers and sisters to each other, relating to each other without the structures of privilege and status that subordinated one to another in society around them. This egalitarianism was one of the most strikingly countercultural features of early Christianity, classically expressed in Galatians 3:28, which declares the typical relationships of inequality and privilege (Jew/Greek; slave/free; male/female) to have no validity in Christ (cf. 1 Cor. 12:13; Col. 3:11).

While in many respects this egalitarianism successfully resisted the highly hierarchical structures of the early churches' social environment,[8] the strategy of radical opposition to such structures was not uniformly applied. As in the Old Testament, another strategy also evolved, in which the hierarchy was not rejected from the outset but relativized and transformed. Whereas in the Old Testament the hierarchy in question is monarchy, with the political and social structures it entails, in the New Testament the focus is especially on the hierarchy of the household. This is natural in view of the nature of the early Chris-

---

[8]For other aspects of it in the Pauline literature, see Bauckham, "Kingdom and Church," 16–20.

tian communities, but it also means that the relationships within the household are especially the focus of the tension between egalitarianism and hierarchy in the New Testament: the egalitarianism of the new household of faith had to be related to the hierarchical structures of the old households to which many of its members still belonged. (A revealing point at which the two languages of household relationships are juxtaposed is when Paul asks Philemon to receive Onesimus "no longer as a slave but more than a slave, a beloved brother" [Phlm. 16].)

The second strategy can be seen most clearly in the household codes of Colossians (3:18–4:1), Ephesians (5:21–6:9), and 1 Peter (2:18–3:7), which address Christians in the roles they played in the three main forms of relationship within the household: husbands and wives, parents and children, masters and slaves. All three relationships were understood in contemporary society in strongly hierarchical terms: the husband, the parent, and the master had authority; the wife, the child, and the slave were subordinate. Hierarchical subordination in the household was normally thought essential to order in society, and Christians must have felt strong pressure not to be seen to be disrupting this order. They were in fact accused of breaking up households, in cases where, for example, a wife became a Christian but her husband did not (cf. 1 Cor. 7:13–14; 1 Pet. 3:1–2). In such cases Christian faith unavoidably entailed an act of insubordination: a wife had to reject her husband's gods in order to follow a faith of which her husband disapproved. It is understandable, therefore, that Christians, who could not avoid public disapproval of such breaches of hierarchical order, might wish to reaffirm as far as possible the general hierarchical structure of household relationships.

In the advice given in New Testament letters to the superior partner in each of the hierarchical relationships of the household, we can observe attempts to relativize and to transform the hierarchy. (1) There are attempts to relativize the hierarchy by reference to God's or Christ's authority. Masters are told not to threaten their slaves, "for you know that both of you have the same Master in heaven" (Eph. 6:9; cf. Col. 4:1). Christ's authority here relativizes the human master's, just as in the Old Testament God's kingship can relativize the power of a human king. (The contrast between the two strategies can be seen by comparing this passage with Matthew 23:10. There, from the fact that the disciples have "one instructor, the Messiah," it follows that there may be no human instructors among them. In Ephesians and Colossians masters are still called masters, but their subordination to Christ, the master of all his Christian slaves, relativizes their authority.)

(2) There are also attempts to ensure that the hierarchical relationships operate benevolently and beneficently, not oppressively or exploitatively. The person in authority is instructed to exercise it for the good of the subordinate,

not in his own interests. Thus, whereas wives are told to be subject to their husbands, husbands are not told to rule their wives but to love them (Col. 3:19; Eph. 5:25; 1 Pet. 3:7), and in one case the nature of the love required is developed by means of an elaborate comparison with Christ's love for the church (Eph. 5:25–33). Just as in the Old Testament human kingship can be accepted on condition that it serves the purposes of God's rule, so here the husband's authority is acceptable only insofar as it follows the pattern of Christ's love for his people.

(3) Most interesting is the attempt to transform relationships of dominance and subordination into relationships of *mutual* subordination. The household code in Ephesians 5:21–6:9 puts all the hierarchical relationships of the household under the introductory rubric: "Be subject to one another out of reverence for Christ" (5:21). The meaning is certainly not that some should be subject to others, but rather that there should be mutual subjection. The principle is not worked through in the case of the first two relationships (wives/husbands; children/fathers) but affects the third in a remarkable way. When slaves have been instructed to "render service with enthusiasm, as to the Lord and not to men and women" (6:7), masters are told to "do the same to them" (6:9). This can only mean: to render service to them, to serve them as slaves, as they do you. This is a radical transformation of hierarchy, which, taken fully seriously, would take the second strategy beyond itself and destroy hierarchy. At this point the egalitarian direction of the second strategy clearly converges with that of the first.

This last example is one of the best illustrations of the difference that discerning the *direction* of thought in a text, as in the biblical texts as a whole, can make to interpretation. On a static interpretation, this text (Eph. 5:21–6:9) is likely to be read as simply endorsing hierarchy, but such a reading cannot do justice either to 5:21 or to 6:9a. A static interpretation cannot acknowledge the real tension in the text between the hierarchical structures that are accepted and the principle of mutual subordination that aims to transform them into nonhierarchical structures. A dynamic reading finds precisely in this tension a direction of thought away from hierarchy towards egalitarian relationships of mutual service. The tension in the text authorizes readers to follow its egalitarian direction further than the text itself does.

Divine rule and human society

It remains to draw conclusions about the Bible's use of God-language in relation to our issue. When the Bible depicts God in images of masculine hierarchical power and authority—King, Lord, Father—how do these images function in relation to the structures of human relationships and society? They certainly do *not* function to legitimate human hierarchies. It is not at all the case that the Bible depicts the divine king or father as the summit of cosmic hierarchy that includes the subordination of women to men, slaves to masters, and subjects to kings. Quite the opposite. These images, though drawn from human hierarchy, come to be used as symbols of what is utterly unique to God: that transcendence of God over all creatures that puts all humans on the same level of equality before God, their Creator and Lord.

Thus, in the radical strategy of opposition to hierarchy, that God is king or father means that no human should claim royal or patriarchal authority. To call God king is to recognize that all humans are equally God's subjects. To call God father is to recognize that all humans are equally God's children. It is to forbid humans to claim any status or privilege above their fellows.

Even in the more compromising strategy, the effect of divine kingship or fatherhood is not in the direction of legitimating or bolstering human hierarchical power but of relativizing it. It is accepted that Israel has a royal dynasty, but the king must remember that he and his subjects are equally subject to God's authority. It is accepted that there are Christian masters and slaves, but masters must remember that they are slaves of Christ no less than their slaves are. The tendency is to the leveling of hierarchy, not the entrenching of it.

7

Human Authority in Creation

Introduction

Other chapters on authority in this book have been concerned with authority over and within human life, but there is another crucial area of current discussion that concerns human authority over the nonhuman creation on this planet, often described as the human dominion over creation, following the usual English translation of Genesis 1:28. In the title of this chapter, I have preferred to speak of human authority *in* creation rather than over creation, because, as the chapter makes clear, it is vital for Christians today to recover a lively sense of human creatureliness. In Genesis 1 itself, it is clear that humans, while given a special status and responsibility for other creatures, are themselves creatures alongside their fellow creatures. Their dominion is within the created order, not, like God's, transcendent above it. Distinguished from their fellow creatures in some respects, they are also like them in many respects. A crucial issue that will be highlighted in our exploration here of the history of interpretation of this Genesis text is the extent to which interpreters have retained a sense of the horizontal relationship of humans with their fellow creatures along with the vertical relationship of dominion that sets them in some sense above other creatures on earth. The loss of the horizontal relationship, in effect treating humans as gods in relation to the world, was, we shall argue, probably the most fateful development in Christian attitudes to the nonhuman creation. Only with this development did interpretation of Genesis 1:28 take its place in the ideology of aggressive domination of nature that has characterized the modern West.

The word *dominion* easily enough suggests the charge of domination, that is, of exploitative power by which humans have treated the rest of nature, animate and inanimate, as no more than a resource for human use and material for humans to fashion into whatever kind of world they might prefer to the existing one. Such an attitude has undoubtedly characterized the modern West and has been essential to the course the modern scientific and technological enterprise has taken, with vast implications in the economic sphere. It could well be seen as the ideological root of the ecological crisis of recent decades, and those who have tried to pin a major share of responsibility for our contemporary ecological problems on the Western Christian tradition (with or without its Israelite and Jewish roots) have often focused especially on the notion of human dominion over nature given in Genesis 1. In this they have followed the lead of the celebrated article "The Historical Roots of Our Ecologic Crisis," by the medieval historian (a specialist in the history of medieval technology) Lynn White Jr. This article, first published in 1967 and reprinted a number of times since then,[1] has been hugely influential[2] and is still so in spite of the many attempts to refute its central thesis.[3] It is a very brief article, bursting with confident and ill-substantiated generalizations that cry out for more detailed historical investigation. Yet the very simplicity of its provocative thesis has earned it a great deal of attention and has proved a useful stimulus to some of the more detailed historical study that needs to be done[4] if the thesis is to be accepted, rejected, or qualified.

---

[1]L. White, "The Historical Roots of our Ecologic Crisis," *Science* 155 (1967): 1203–7; reprinted in I. G. Barbour, ed., *Western Man and Environmental Ethics* (Reading, Mass.: Addison-Wesley, 1973), 18–30; and most recently in R. J. Berry, ed., *The Care of Creation* (Leicester: InterVarsity Press, 2000), 31–42.

[2]Although White has subsequently contributed little more to the debate, he is "the most cited author in the field of the eco-theological discussion," according to H. Baranzke and H. Lamberty-Zielinski, "Lynn White und das dominium terrae (Gen. 1,28b): Ein Beitrag zu einer doppelten Wirkungsgeschichte," *Biblische Notizen* 76 (1995): 56. On the influence of White's article in solidifying the view of many environmentalists that the Judeo-Christian religious tradition is the enemy, see the interesting autobiographical comments by M. Oelschlaeger, *Caring for Creation: An Ecumenical Approach to the Environmental Crisis* (New Haven/London: Yale University Press, 1994), 22–27. For White's own later contributions, see R. F. Nash, *The Rights of Nature: A History of Environmental Ethics* (Madison, Wis.: University of Wisconsin Press, 1989), 95.

[3]E.g., B. McKibben, *The Comforting Whirlwind* (Grand Rapids: Eerdmans, 1994), 34–35. D. Worster, *Nature's Economy: A History of Ecological Ideas*, 2d ed. (Cambridge: Cambridge University Press, 1994), 27–31, still follows White, even though in his *The Wealth of Nature: Environmental History and Ecological Imagination* (New York/Oxford: Oxford University Press, 1993), 207–19, he argued that White's thesis was mistaken in that the real roots of the ecological crisis lie not in the Christian tradition but in modernity.

[4]See especially J. Cohen, *"Be Fertile and Increase, Fill the Earth and Master It": The Ancient and Medieval Career of a Biblical Text* (Ithaca/London: Cornell University Press, 1989); C. Wybrow, *The Bible, Baconianism, and Mastery over Nature: The Old Testament and Its*

White's central claim is that Christianity, as "the most anthropocentric religion the world has seen," set human beings above nature (sharing, "in great measure, God's transcendence of nature"),[5] dedivinized and desacralized nature,[6] and thus made nature into mere raw material for human exploitation ("no item in the physical creation had any purpose save to serve man's purposes"). By contrast with religious attitudes which either reverence nature as divine or place human beings within nature alongside other creatures, the Christian view, according to White, has robbed nature of any value other than its usefulness to humanity. Christianity has understood human beings to have been set over the rest of creation by God and given the right and even the duty to subject the whole of nature to human use. This view—based on and appealing to the key biblical text of Genesis 1:26, 28—was in White's view the ideological basis for the arrogant and aggressive domination of nature that has led to the ecological destruction of modern times.[7] Since the rise of Western science and technology, through which this domination of nature has been attempted, dates from the eleventh century, a period in which the traditional Christian view of the world was largely unchallenged in Western Europe, White can argue that the modern attempt at technological conquest of nature derives directly from this traditional Christian view.

The thesis—which Wybrow calls "the mastery hypothesis"[8]—is not peculiar to White, whose original contribution was probably only his association of it with the late medieval beginnings of modern technological development, his own specialist area; other versions of the thesis tend to see at least the ideological impetus for the modern scientific and technological project developing in the early modern period. Essentially the same thesis as White's had, before White, been argued by Christian theologians and historians[9] who

---

Modern Misreading (New York: Peter Lang, 1991). Also in part responding to White is K. Thomas, *Man and the Natural World: Changing Attitudes in England 1500–1800* (London: Penguin, 2d ed. 1984), 22–25.

[5]White, "The Historical Roots," 25.

[6]The word *nature* is problematic for a number of reasons, not least because, as generally used, it seems to presuppose that humans are not part of nature; see R. Bauckham, "First Steps to a Theology of Nature," *Evangelical Quarterly* 58 (1986): 229–31. But the word is almost impossible to avoid and will be used in this chapter in its usual sense in this context, referring to the nonhuman creation (and often limited to this planet).

[7]See also the even more trenchant statement of this case by A. Toynbee, "The Religious Background of the Present Ecological Crisis," in Barbour, ed., *Western Man*, 137–49; also in D. and E. Spring, eds., *Ecology and Religion in History* (New York: Harper, 1974), 137–49.

[8]Wybrow, *The Bible*, Introduction and passim.

[9]Examples in Wybrow, introduction to *The Bible*, and Baranzke and Lamberty-Zielinski, "Lynn White," 50–52.

wished to claim that modern science and technology, regarded positively as the great achievements of the modern age, were the fruit of the Christian world-view. This apologetic approach was part and parcel of a broad Christian theological strategy of justifying modernity—even its secularity—as the product of Christianity. It is ironic that, with the ever more apparent failures of modernity, the same strategy is now adopted by those who blame all the failures and evils of the modern period on Christianity, ignoring the antitheological trend of modernity at the same time as they are themselves deeply indebted to it.

There have been many responses to White's thesis,[10] and the present chapter is another. Insofar as White made a claim about the meaning of Genesis in its own terms, responses from the perspective of biblical exegesis can fairly be said to have refuted it over and again. But the historical claim about the indebtedness of the modern project of dominating nature to long-standing Christian views of the human relationship to nature is a more complex one and not so easily answered. Our focus in this chapter will be on the history of the various and changing Christian interpretations of the Genesis idea of human dominion over the world, in an effort to specify how and to what extent interpretation of this idea is implicated in the beginnings and development of the modern scientific-technological project of the domination of nature. We shall

---

[10]See, e.g., R. Dubos, "Franciscan Conservation versus Benedictine Stewardship," in Barbour, ed., *Western Man*, 114–36; L. W. Moncrief, "The Cultural Basis of our Environmental Crisis," in Barbour, ed., *Western Man*, 31–42; J. Barr, "Man and Nature: The Ecological Controversy and the Old Testament," *Bulletin of the John Rylands Library* 55 (1972): 9–32 (these three articles can also be found in Spring, ed., *Ecology*, 114–36, 76–90, 48–75); W. Leiss, *The Domination of Nature* (New York: George Braziller, 1972); J. Macquarrie, "Creation and Environment," in Spring, ed., *Ecology*, 32–47; J. Passmore, *Man's Responsibility for Nature: Ecological Problems and Western Traditions* (London: Duckworth, 1974); U. Krolzik, *Umweltkrise—Folge des Christentums?* (Stuttgart/Berlin: Kreuz Verlag, 1979); R. Attfield, "Christian Attitudes to Nature," *Journal of the History of Ideas* 44 (1983): 369–86; R. H. Hiers, "Ecology, Biblical Theology, and Methodology: Biblical Perspectives on the Environment," *Zygon* 19 (1984): 43–59; B. W. Anderson, "Creation and Ecology," in B. W. Anderson, ed., *Creation in the Old Testament* (London: SPCK/Philadelphia: Fortress, 1984), 1–24; J. Cohen, "The Bible, Man, and Nature in the History of Western Thought: A Call for Reassessment," *Journal of Religion* 65 (1985): 155–72; C. Wybrow, "The Old Testament and the Conquest of Nature: A Fresh Examination," *Epworth Review* 17 (1990): 77–88; Wybrow, *The Bible*; Cohen, *"Be Fertile"*; T. Cooper, *Green Christianity* (London: Hodder & Stoughton, 1990), 33–38; R. Attfield, *The Ethics of Environmental Concern*, 2d ed. (Athens, Ga./London: University of Georgia Press, 1991), chaps. 2–3; R. Murray, *The Cosmic Covenant* (London: Sheed & Ward, 1992), 161–66; S. R. L. Clark, *How to Think about the Earth* (London: Mowbray, 1993), 8–19; E. Whitney, "Lynn White, Ecotheology and History," *Environmental Ethics* 15 (1993): 151–69; Baranzke and Lamberty-Zielinski, "Lynn White"; T. Hiebert, *The Yahwist's Landscape: Nature and Religion in Early Israel* (New York/Oxford: Oxford University Press, 1996).

make clear from the start that the history of interpretation of Genesis 1:28 and associated biblical themes has been much influenced by nonbiblical ideas about the human relationship to the rest of nature. Only at the end of the chapter will we offer some biblical interpretation that has learned from the history of interpretation and seeks to avoid its fateful errors.

The history of Christian attitudes to the rest of nature and ideas about the human relationship to the nonhuman creation is a complex subject, on which much detailed research still needs to be done.[11] A focus on the idea of human dominion and interpretation of Genesis 1:28 cannot tell us everything, but the prominence Lynn White and his followers and critics have given to this aspect of the matter is not unjustified. It is, however, important to keep in view other aspects of Christian thought about creation that could be seen to qualify or moderate what is said about the human dominion as such. We shall therefore keep the idea of human dominion at the center of attention but notice also the bearing that other aspects of Christian thought had on it. My argument owes a good deal to previous responses to White and other discussions of the matter but attempts a further clarification of the historical development. Jeremy Cohen's claim that, as a result of his study of Jewish and Christian interpretations of Genesis 1:28 in the patristic and medieval periods, Lynn White's thesis "can now be laid to rest"[12] was a little premature. Not only does much remain to be said about those periods, but also the interpretation of Genesis 1:26, 28 in the early modern period (not reached by Cohen's study)[13] is of crucial importance to the debate.[14] Cameron Wybrow's important book[15] partly supplies this latter gap in the discussion, but is rather narrowly focused on the exegetical validity of the interpretations of Genesis that gained ground in the early modern period, while underestimating the extent to which medieval theology prepared the ground for, without determining, the early modern development.

---

[11]Pioneering surveys are C. J. Glacken, *Traces on the Rhodian Shore: Nature and Culture in Western Thought from Ancient Times to the End of the Eighteenth Century* (Berkeley/Los Angeles: University of California Press, 1967) (an immensely learned and valuable resource); H. P. Santmire, *The Travail of Nature: The Ambiguous Ecological Promise of Christian Theology* (Philadelphia: Fortress Press, 1985) (a study of the mainstream theological tradition, which employs a rather questionable interpretative schema).

[12]Cohen, *"Be Fertile,"* 5. Unfortunately for our purposes, this book, though initially stimulated by White's thesis, gives far more attention to the command in Genesis 1:28 to "be fruitful and multiply" than it does to the idea of human dominion.

[13]He makes brief reference to the Protestant Reformers only: *"Be Fertile,"* 306–9.

[14]This is recognized by G. Liedke, *Im Bauch des Fisches: Ökologische Theologie* (Stuttgart/Berlin: Kreuz Verlag, 1979), 66–68; and (though with less reference to exegesis) Passmore, *Man's Responsibility*, 18–23.

[15]Wybrow, *The Bible*, esp. part 3.

My argument will be that White's historical thesis does contain an important element of truth, but that it fails as a whole because White neglected other elements in the traditional Christian attitude (or attitudes) that significantly balance and qualify the features on which he seized, and because White also neglected the new developments in the understanding of the human relationship to nature that occurred in the early modern period and to which the modern project of aggressive domination of nature can be far more directly linked than it can to the Christian tradition of premodern times.

The question of the origins of the contemporary ecological crisis is, of course, a much larger historical question. Answering that question would involve taking account of the modern ideology of progress (to which the ideas we shall discuss contributed only a small ingredient), modern individualism and materialism, industrialization and consumerization, the money economy and globalization—in short, a whole network of factors that characterize modernity.[16] Most of these factors can be understood only as the supersession of Christian ideals, values, and practice by post-Christian and secular modes of thought, goals, and forms of life. On this broad scale, the search for the origins of the contemporary ecological crisis in Christianity is certainly looking in entirely the wrong direction. But much Christian thought in the modern period went along with major aspects of these developments in modernity and in itself gave them Christian justification. Our story, though only a small part of an account of the origins of modernity from an ecological perspective, will throw some light on what can be seen, in retrospect at least, to have been an ideological co-option of biblical and traditional themes to an alien end.

The dominant theological tradition

According to Genesis 1:28, God commanded humanity to "subdue" the earth and to have "dominion" over other living creatures. The interpretation of this notion of human dominion by Christian theologians and exegetes remained fairly consistent from the time of the Fathers, through the Middle Ages, until the early modern period in the West. It was an interpretation strongly influenced by Greek philosophical (mainly Stoic but also Aristotelian) ideas about human uniqueness and superiority over the rest of nature. Since pagan writers who expounded these ideas spoke explicitly of human dominion over the earth (e.g., Cicero, *De natura deorum* 2.60;

---

[16]The best succinct account of the origins of the ecological crisis is M. S. Northcott, *The Environment and Christian Ethics* (Cambridge: Cambridge University Press, 1996), chap. 2; see also Attfield, *The Ethics*, chap. 1.

Hermetica 3.3b) and exalted the special place of humanity in creation, it must have seemed natural to Christian thinkers with a Hellenistic education to read the Genesis account in such terms, especially as the principal philosophical alternative was argued by the Epicureans, whose general worldview seemed much more alien to the biblical Christian view. Indeed, all the ingredients of the Christian reading of Genesis in Aristotelian and Stoic terms are to be found already in the first-century Jewish philosopher Philo of Alexandria, who did so much to interpret Jewish monotheistic faith in Hellenistic philosophical terms and from whom some of the early Fathers learned how to do the same for their Christian faith. Philo not only propounded a Stoic interpretation of human dominion throughout his works,[17] but also in his *De animalibus* he defended, explicitly and at length, the Stoic position against the Epicurean views of his apostate brother Alexander.[18] Similarly, the great third-century Alexandrian Christian theologian Origen explicitly supported the Stoic view against the Epicurean position maintained by his pagan opponent Celsus (*C. Cels.* 4.74).

In this way a series of ideas about the human relationship to the rest of creation that were not of biblical but of Greek philosophical origin came to be associated with the Genesis text and regarded, for most of Christian history, as the Christian view. In the first place, the rest of creation was held to have been made by God for humanity. This highly anthropocentric view of the world derives not from the biblical tradition but from Aristotle (*Polit.* 1.8)[19] and the Stoics (e.g., Cicero, *De natura deorum* 2).[20] It was taken up enthusiastically by early Christian writers (e.g., Origen, *C. Cels.* 4.74–75; Lactantius, *Div. Inst.* 7.4–6; Nemesius, *De natura hominis* 10) and seems to have been thereafter unquestioned until the sixteenth century.[21] In the early modern period it was still dominant. It was, for example, unequivocally and influentially expressed by John Calvin (*Inst.* 2.6.1; Comm. Gen. 1:26).

---

[17]A. Terian, *Philonis Alexandrini De Animalibus: The Armenian Text with an Introduction, Translation and Commentary* (Chico, Calif.: Scholars Press, 1981), 36–45. But P. Borgen, "Man's Sovereignty over Animals and Nature according to Philo of Alexandria," in T. Fornberg and D. Hellholm, eds., *Texts and Contexts*, FS L. Hartman (Oslo/Copenhagen/Stockholm/Boston: Scandinavian University Press), 369–89, stresses Philo's affinities with Jewish literature.

[18]See the translation and introduction in Terian, *Philonis Alexandrini De Animalibus*.

[19]Cf. Glacken, *Traces*, 47–48.

[20]Terian, *Philonis Alexandrini De Animalibus*, 51; Glacken, *Traces*, 57. See also Xenophon, *Mem.* 4.3.2–14, where this idea is attributed to Socrates; this passage influenced the Stoics. It was also adopted by Jewish writers from the first century onwards: Borgen, "Man's Sovereignty," 379.

[21]One sixteenth-century Christian writer who denied it was the English Protestant martyr John Bradford: Thomas, *Man*, 166.

Secondly, the sense in which the world was made for humanity was understood in strongly utilitarian terms.[22] All creatures exist for the sake of their usefulness to humanity.[23] In the face of the objection that many creatures do not seem at all obviously useful for human life, the Stoics were famous for their ingenious explanations of the usefulness of each of the animals: for example, that fleas are useful for preventing oversleeping and mice for preventing carelessness in leaving cheese about.[24] Similar attempts to explain all features of the natural world as deliberately designed by God to supply specific human needs can be found in many Christian writers, from the Fathers (e.g., Origen, *C. Cels.* 4.78; Lactantius, *Div. Inst.* 7.4) to the eighteenth century.[25] It seems to have been only in the seventeenth century that such explanations began to lose their power to convince.[26]

Thirdly, human dominion over the world was therefore understood as the right to make use of all creatures for human benefit. Compare the following statements, the first by Cicero, writing in the Stoic tradition, and the second by the fourth-century Christian theologian Didymus the Blind, commenting on Genesis 1:28:

> The human race has dominion over all the products of the earth. We enjoy the treasures of plains and mountains; ours are the streams, ours the lakes; we cultivate the fruits and plant trees; we give fertility to the soil by works of irrigation; we restrain, straighten or divert our streams—in short, with our hands we set about the fashioning of another nature, as it were, within the bounds and precincts of the one we have (*De natura deorum* 2.60)

> God has made [the gift of dominion to humanity] in order that land for growing and land for mining, rich in numerous, diverse materials, be under the rule of the human being. Actually, the human being receives bronze, iron, silver, gold, and many other metals from the ground; it is also rendered to him so that he can feed and clothe himself. So great is the dominion the human being has received over the land that he transforms it technologically—when he changes it into glass, pottery, and other similar things. This is in effect what it means for the human being to rule the whole earth.[27]

---

[22]Cf. Glacken's comment on Xenophon: Glacken, *Traces*, 44.

[23]Stoic thinkers could also speak of the creation's aesthetic value for humanity: see Glacken, *Traces*, 52, 57.

[24]Terian, *Philonis Alexandrini De Animalibus*, 51; cf. Glacken, *Traces*, 57, 61.

[25]Thomas, *Man*, 19–20.

[26]Thomas, *Man*, 166; cf. Passmore, *Man's Responsibility*, 20–22.

[27]Quoted in Cohen, *"Be Fertile,"* 227 (and see n. 18 on that page for further patristic references).

Both passages express the normal and natural ancient view that human beings have the right to use their environment to sustain and enhance their life, heightened by the typically Greco-Roman enthusiasm for humanity's ingenuity in making something ordered and useful out of wild nature, by landscaping, farming, taming animals, mining, and the technological arts.

Fourthly, this understanding of human dominion was allied to a strongly hierarchical view of the world. Aristotle (*Polit.* 1.8) held that plants were created for the use of animals, animals for the use of humanity, along with the view, generally repudiated by Stoics and Christians, that some human beings are naturally intended to be subjected to others. The Stoics held that the irrational creation (including animals) exists for the sake of the rational, and human beings for the sake of the gods,[28] a view which the Christian writer Lactantius, for example, merely adapted to his belief in the Christian God: the world was made for living creatures, other living creatures for humanity, humanity (who alone can appreciate God's creation and worship the Creator) for the worship of God (*Div. Inst.* 7.4–6).[29] The hierarchical nature of the medieval Christian worldview, along with the influence of Aristotle, appears in Thomas Aquinas, who regarded it as the natural order of things that the imperfect are for the use of the perfect. Hence plants make use of the earth, animals make use of plants, human beings make use of plants and animals: "Therefore it is in keeping with the order of nature, that man should be master over animals." This natural order corresponds to "the order of Divine Providence which always governs inferior things by superior" (*Summa theologiae* 1.96.1; cf. 2.64.1). In this way, Thomas can link the natural hierarchy to the dominion over other creatures given to humanity by God, taking it for granted that this dominion is the right of the superior to make use of the inferior.

Fifthly, humanity was distinguished from the animals by an absolute difference in kind: only human beings are rational.[30] This was a controversial view in the ancient world,[31] since it is so easily challenged from observation of animal behavior, but it was the Stoic view,[32] taken over by most Christian writ-

---

[28]Terian, *Philonis Alexandrini De Animalibus*, 51.

[29]For similar hierarchical thinking in the Fathers, see D. S. Wallace-Hadrill, *The Greek Patristic View of Nature* (Manchester: Manchester University Press/New York: Barnes & Noble, 1968), 114–15.

[30]This is not the general biblical view. Job 35:11 regards humans as more intelligent than animals and birds, but not as the only rational creatures. However, Jude 10 and 2 Peter 2:12 do allude, for their particular polemical purpose, to the Stoic view that animals are irrational (and in the latter case, also to the Stoic view that the irrational animals have been created for the use of rational beings, i.e., humans).

[31]Cf. Terian, *Philonis Alexandrini De Animalibus*, 49–50.

[32]Passmore, *Man's Responsibility*, 15.

ers and associated by them with the idea of humanity's creation in the image of God (Gen. 1:26–27).[33] Human beings uniquely reflect or participate in the divine rationality, and this is what gives them their superiority to the animals by virtue of which they exercise their God-given dominion over the animals (Gen. 1:26).[34] This view did not, of course, mean that animals lacked any sort of consciousness or feeling. Hardly anyone seems to have thought that until the seventeenth-century philosopher René Descartes reduced animals to the status of mere machines.[35] But, in confining to human beings free will, moral responsibility, and the ability to understand and reason, and therefore also immortality and relationship with God, this view did put human beings on a quite different metaphysical level in the hierarchy of creation. They stand between the animals and the angels (who are purely immaterial intellects). Although theoretically the theological tradition's insistence on the goodness of the body as integral to human nature created by God and on the hope of the resurrection of the body should have ensured humanity's solidarity with the rest of the material creation, the emphasis on humanity's distinctiveness as akin to the angels and to God himself in immaterial rationality elevated humanity above nature. Human beings were encouraged to see themselves as a quite different kind of creature ruling over a creation inferior to them.

Finally, the Stoic view was that because irrational animals and rational human beings were radically unequal, there could be no question of justice or injustice in dealings between them.[36] Thomas Aquinas gave this Christian form in his insistence that we can have no duty to love irrational creatures, as we have to love God and our human neighbors (*Summa theologiae* 2.65.3). This is a consistent consequence of the view that animals exist only for our use, but for Christians it raised the problem of the Old Testament's apparent concern for animals in its laws urging consideration for their needs (e.g., Deut. 25:4) and its commendation of kindness to animals (Prov. 12:10). However, Philo had already provided the answer to this difficulty: the value of kindness to animals is only as a way of learning to be kind to human beings (*Virt.* 81, 116, 125–60).[37] Thomas Aquinas (*Summa contra gentiles* 3.113) and other Christian theologians took the same view.[38] This dogma that animals could have no

---

[33] For Augustine's view, see G. Clark, "The Fathers and the Animals: The Rule of Reason?" in A. Linzey and D. Yamamoto, eds., *Animals on the Agenda* (London: SCM Press, 1998), 67–79.

[34] Cohen, *"Be Fertile,"* 226–59; D. Cairns, *The Image of God in Man* (London: Collins, 2d ed. 1973), 116–19. For the early modern period, see Thomas, *Man*, 30–33.

[35] Descartes's view was anticipated by Gomez Pereira in 1554: Thomas, *Man*, 33.

[36] Terian, *Philonis Alexandrini De Animalibus*, 52.

[37] Terian, *Philonis Alexandrini De Animalibus*, 45.

[38] Thomas, *Man*, 151.

rights could lead good people to take callous views, such as the seventeenth-century Anglican divine Isaac Barrow's description of vivisection as "a most innocent cruelty, and easily excusable ferocity."[39]

Though all derived from Greek philosophical rather than biblical thought, this set of ideas dominated the Christian theological tradition up to the early modern period and is certainly not without its influence today. As we shall see, this interpretation of the human dominion over nature did provide the ground on which the theoretical foundations for the modern technological project of aggressive domination of nature would be erected by others. However, it did not in itself provide the ideological impetus to that project. In order to appreciate this point, we need to notice some important qualifications of the view we have outlined.

In the first place, neither the theological tradition nor the exegetical tradition of commentaries on Genesis 1 was very interested in the human relationship with nature.[40] They were much more interested in interpreting the image of God in humanity in terms of humanity's relationship to God than in terms of humanity's relationship to the rest of creation.[41] Though this in itself is evidence of the theological tendency to detach human beings from the natural world, it hardly provides a theological impetus to the implementation of human dominion by conquest of nature.

Secondly, the human dominion over nature was generally understood as a static fact (at any rate since the fall, which impaired it). The theologians convey no sense of a divine command that human beings are obligated to fulfill by extending their exploitation of nature.[42] They take it for granted that the text refers merely to the usual ways in which people were using nature in their time. Their interpretation of the dominion simply gives a rather conventional blessing to what their contemporaries were doing in their fields and their workshops with no need for special theological motivation. Thus, even though the rhetoric, as in the quotation from Didymus above, might try to match the apparently large scope of the biblical text, the concept of human dominion was in fact severely limited.

Thirdly, the fundamental notion was of a world created ready for and adapted to human use, not of a world open to radical reshaping for human purposes.[43] Cicero's remarkable idea (quoted above) of a human transformation of nature, such as to constitute the creation of a kind of second nature,[44] was to be

---

[39]Quoted in Thomas, *Man*, 21.
[40]Cohen, *"Be Fertile,"* 268.
[41]Cohen, *"Be Fertile,"* 309–10.
[42]Liedke, *Im Bauch*, 65.
[43]Passmore, *Man's Responsibility*, 17.
[44]On the theme, see Glacken, *Traces*, chap. 3.

taken up, as we shall see, in the Renaissance but notably does not find echoes in the Christian tradition up to that time. Certainly human ingenuity and inventiveness, as proof of our superiority over the animals, were a conventional theme inherited from classical sources. Nature provides scope for this inventiveness by not providing us with clothing and shelter directly, thus obliging us to find out how to make our own.[45] But the twelfth-century theologian Hugh of St. Victor shows how this inventiveness was understood (*Didascalion* 1.9).[46] He specifies three kinds of work: the creative work of God, who brings things into being out of nothing; the work of nature, which brings hidden potentialities into actuality; and the work of human artificers, who merely put together things disjoined or disjoin what is put together. They cannot do the work of God or of nature, but can only imitate nature. The person who first invented clothes, for example, observed how nature clothes growing things and followed her example. This is a very long way from the interpretation of the divine image in humanity and the human dominion over the world as a kind of participation in the divine creativity by which human beings can recreate the world. Only the latter would lead to the modern technological project.

Fourthly, it must be remembered that, although this tradition of thought offers a highly anthropocentric interpretation of the world, the anthropocentricity belongs within a broader theocentricity. This allowed the Stoic notion that all other creatures exist only for human benefit to be combined with a rather different theme in Christian tradition: that nature reflects and exists for the glory of God.[47] From this point of view the natural world serves humanity not only in the Stoic, utilitarian sense, but also by revealing its Creator and assisting human contemplation of God. Thus, when Thomas Aquinas spells out the sense in which all corporeal creatures have been created for humanity's sake, he says, "[T]hey serve man in two ways, first as sustenance of his bodily life, secondly, as helping him to know God, inasmuch as man sees the invisible things of God by the things that are made" (*Summa theologiae* 3.91.1). This sense of the contemplative value of nature as revelation of God was to be lost in the transition to the purely utilitarian attitude to nature, as a resource to be exploited, that informed the modern project of dominating nature.

---

[45]Glacken, *Traces*, 54, 108; Lactantius, *Div. Inst.* 7.4.

[46]Liedke, *Im Bauch*, 65–67, following Krolzik, *Umweltkrise*, 77ff. (I have not been able to see this work), sees in Hugh of St. Victor's *Didascalion* a turning point in the history of interpretation of human dominion. For the first time, he claims, Genesis 1:28 is understood as an imperative to restore dominion over the earth by technological innovation. But I can find no evidence for this view in the text of the *Didascalion*.

[47]For this theme in patristic and medieval writers, see Wallace-Hadrill, *The Greek Patristic View*, 120–21, 128–30; Glacken, *Traces*, chap. 5. There are some classical precedents, e.g., Xenophon, *Mem.* 4.3.14.

Fifthly, there is another sense in which the anthropocentricity of the traditional Christian view was qualified. For there were believed to be a vast number of created beings superior to humanity: the angels.[48] Although the rest of the corporeal creation was made for humanity's sake, this did not by any means make humanity the summit of creation as such, for the purely spiritual beings ranked higher than humanity. The pure anthropocentricity that treats humanity as the summit and goal of all things arose not from the traditional Christian worldview, but from the Renaissance exaltation of humanity above the angels and the Enlightenment rejection of both angels and God.

Sixthly, as the previous two points indicate, the anthropocentric view that the world existed for humanity could not obscure the more fundamental doctrine of creation: that angels, humans and other creatures are all creatures of God the Creator. This came to expression perhaps most clearly in the belief that all creation worships God and that human worship is participation in that worship of God by all creation. This theme was more familiar in the medieval period than in the modern partly because of the frequent liturgical use of the Benedicite,[49] the canticle that calls on each and every creature, in a long catalog of invocation, to worship the Creator. The Benedicite is taken from the Greek version of the book of Daniel (3:52–90), which is one of the Greek additions to the Hebrew/Aramaic text of Daniel. It was therefore part of the canon of the Old Testament for the medieval Western (as also the Eastern) church and included in the Vulgate version, whereas it was not part of the canon of the Jewish Scriptures and would therefore be relegated to the Apocrypha by the Protestant Reformers. But Lynn White, who remarks that it "contradicts the historically dominant Judeo-Christian anthropocentrism," is quite wrong in supposing that it shows the influence of hellenism or was ever thought in the least heretical.[50] On the contrary, it merely develops at length the theme of nature's praise of God to be found in the Psalms (especially Psalm 148). Medieval Christians familiar with it in regular worship would have acquired thereby a strong sense of their horizontal relationship to the rest of creation as fellow creatures, all existing for the glory of God.

---

[48]Cf. H. P. Santmire, *The Travail of Nature: The Ambiguous Ecological Promise of Christian Theology* (Philadelphia: Fortress, 1985), 83, 90–91.

[49]For its use in the Irish church, see T. O. Clancy and G. Márkus, *Iona: The Earliest Poetry of a Celtic Monastery* (Edinburgh: Edinburgh University Press, 1995), 89–90; M. Low, *Celtic Christianity and Nature* (Belfast: Blackstaff Press/Edinburgh: Edinburgh University Press, 1996), 173–74. While the use of the Benedicite has not disappeared altogether in modern liturgy, it is often regarded as tediously repetitious and sometimes used in abbreviated form.

[50]L. White, "Continuing the Conversation," in I. G. Barbour, ed., *Western Man and Environmental Ethics* (Reading, Mass.: Addison-Wesley, 1973), 61–62.

Seventhly, awareness that the creatures over whom humanity exercises dominion are God's creatures could balance and modify the trend to understand dominion as a human right to use them in whatever way serves human needs. This is particularly clear in relation to cruelty to animals. The view cited above that human beings have no duty of kindness to animals was far from universal.[51] For example, the early fifteenth-century treatise on the ten commandments, *Dives and Pauper*, though allowing the slaughter of animals for food, clothing, or protection, warns that unnecessary harm or cruelty to animals is a very serious abuse of God's creatures.[52] Similarly Calvin, while taking the view that all creatures were made for the sake of humanity, nevertheless insisted that when God subjected the animals to human rule, he did so on condition that we treat them considerately, avoiding cruelty, because they are God's creatures.[53] Whether this acknowledgment that animals, as God's creatures, have certain rights we must respect is strictly consistent with the view that they exist only for our benefit is doubtful, but it does set some limit to human dominion. The interpretation of dominion as the right to use the rest of creation for human benefit is unchanged, but it is limited by another principle. A more radical step, which no one seems to have taken before the seventeenth century, would be to reinterpret dominion as stewardship over God's creation. On this view human beings have been given by God the responsibility of caring for the creation.[54] But this was a step decisively beyond the view that dominated Christian thought up to the early modern period.

In summary, the dominant theological tradition before the modern period did articulate a strongly anthropocentric view of the human dominion, largely as a result of imposing on the biblical texts understandings of the human relationship to nature that were of Greek, rather than biblical, origin. However, the facts that the dominion was understood as a static fact, not a mandate for extension, and the world was understood as created ready and adapted to human use, not requiring large-scale technological modification, distinguish this view sharply from the interpretation of the dominion that accompanied the rise of the modern project of technological domination of nature. They show that the medieval view was not itself sufficient to authorize that project. Moreover, the anthropocentricity of the dominant tradition was also significantly qualified by other convictions about the relationship between God, humanity, and the rest of creation: that human beings are part of God's creation, which itself is theocentric, existing for the glory of God; that not

---

[51]Thomas, *Man*, 152–55.
[52]Quoted in Thomas, *Man*, 152–53.
[53]*Sermons on Deuteronomy*, quoted in Thomas, *Man*, 154.
[54]Thomas, *Man*, 155; Glacken, *Traces*, 480–82.

humans, but angels, were the summit of creation; and that all creatures worship God and have the value of creatures created by God. Such qualifications meant the vertical relationship in which the dominion over nature placed humanity to the rest of creation was complemented by a real awareness of the horizontal relationship in which humans relate to their fellow creatures as all creatures of the one Creator. As we shall see, all these qualifications fell away in the Renaissance interpretation of the human dominion that paved the way for the modern subjugation of nature. When any sense of the value of creation for God and of a common creatureliness in which humans share was lost, the idea of human dominion would acquire quite new significance.

However, what we have called the dominant view was never completely dominant, and there is one major premodern tradition of Christian attitudes to the nonhuman creation that, while having some affinity with the dominant view, also diverged significantly from it. Though it has been comparatively neglected in studies of the history of Christian attitudes to nature, it deserves to be taken just as seriously as the dominant view that we have so far described.

An alternative tradition: Saints and nature

In addition to the work of the theologians and exegetes, on which our previous section focused, there is another tradition of Christian literature in which Christian attitudes to the natural world are expressed and the idea of human dominion over nature is interpreted. This is the tradition of stories of hermits, holy men and women who went to live (permanently or temporarily) apart from human society in order to devote themselves entirely to God. Because they deliberately sought out places remote from human habitation, they lived amid wild nature, closer than most people to nature unmodified by human use. There are hundreds of stories of the relationships of these saints to the natural environment in which they lived, especially their relations with wild animals.[55] The tradition of these stories runs from the desert fathers of

---

[55]H. Waddell, *Beasts and Saints* (London: Constable, 1934) is a collection of some of the best of the Latin stories in translation, while D. N. Bell, *Wholly Animals: A Book of Beastly Tales,* Cistercian Studies 128 (Kalamazoo, Mich.: Cistercian Publications, 1992) overlaps with Waddell's collection but also includes many stories from other sources. Many of the stories about the desert fathers can be found in translation in N. Russell and B. Ward, *The Lives of the Desert Fathers* (London and Oxford: Mowbray/Kalamazoo, Mich.: Cistercian Publications, 1981). Some of the stories of the Celtic saints are retold in R. Van de Weyer, *Celtic Fire: An Anthology of Celtic Christian Literature* (London: Darton, Longman & Todd, 1990). Studies of the stories include S. P. Bratton, "The Original Desert Solitaire: Early Christian Monasticism and Wilderness," *Environmental Ethics* 10 (1988): 31–53; R. D. Sorrell, *St. Francis of Assisi and Nature* (New

the fourth century to the Franciscan saints of the thirteenth and fourteenth centuries, the same period as that covered by the dominant theological tradition surveyed in our previous section. Moreover, the tradition has not only a wide chronological range, but also a wide geographical range: from Egypt to Belgium, from Georgia[56] to Ireland. Those who know some of these stories, for example in Helen Waddell's collection of some of the most attractive,[57] have perhaps tended to think of them simply as charming stories. But they are much more than that. They express attitudes to the natural world that, through the considerable popularity of these stories, must have been very influential throughout the medieval Christian world, surely at least as influential at the popular level as the views expressed in works of academic theology and technical exegesis. Nor is the importance of these stories much affected by the view we take of the relation between fact and fiction in the tradition. The tradition must certainly be rooted in the real experiences of many Christian hermits.[58] But the themes certainly also became conventional and many of the actual stories are probably legendary to some degree. Modern readers will find some of the stories plausible and others obviously tall, but in many cases will be unable to judge their historicity. But this need not at all affect their value as witness to a view of the human relationship with nature.[59]

The Christian ascetic tradition has often been blamed for fostering negative attitudes to the natural world. It is true that parts of that tradition in the medieval period were heavily influenced by a Greek dualism of spirit and matter, which denigrated the physical and aspired to spiritual detachment from the physical world to which the human body is akin. But the stories of hermits and

---

York and Oxford: Oxford University Press, 1988), 19–27; A. G. Elliott, *Roads to Paradise: Reading the Lives of the Early Saints* (Hanover and London: University Press of New England, 1987), 144–67, 193–204; S. P. Bratton, "Oaks, Wolves and Love: Celtic Monks and Northern Forests," *Journal of Forest History* 33 (1989): 4–20; and especially W. J. Short, *Saints in the World of Nature: The Animal Story as Spiritual Parable in Medieval Hagiography (900–1200)* (Rome: Gregorian University, 1983) (I am grateful to Dr. Short for providing me with a photocopy of this book, which is unobtainable in Britain). Surprisingly, such stories are not discussed in Low, *Celtic Christianity and Nature*, though cf. 111, 136–37. I am also grateful to James Bruce for comment on my treatment of these stories.

[56]See the stories about David of Garesja in D. M. Lang, *Lives and Legends of the Georgian Saints* (London: Allen & Unwin/New York: Macmillan, 1956), chap. 5.

[57]Waddell, *Beasts*.

[58]Cf. Bratton, "The Original Desert Solitaire," 40–41.

[59]No attempt is made here to plot any chronological development in the attitudes to nature expressed by the stories. They are, of course, evidence primarily of such attitudes at the time of composition or recension of the stories, which is often much later than the time of the saints they describe. Where I have indicated the period in which the saint lived, no implication as to the date of the stories about him is intended.

nature reveal a quite different side to the ascetic tradition, largely unaffected by Platonic dualism. In some of the stories there is a different kind of dualism: a strong sense of the world as a scene of conflict between good and evil. The hermits who went out into the wilderness in order to encounter and defeat the forces of evil sometimes understood aspects of the natural world, such as snakes and scorpions, as emblems of the demonic.[60] But more prominent is their positive appreciation of their natural surroundings. In a period when most people's appreciation of nature was largely limited to nature as cultivated, ordered, and otherwise improved by human art, it was the hermits who, from their experience of living alone in the wild, learned to appreciate the beauty of wild nature and to love the natural world for its own sake as God's creation.[61]

Perhaps the most "conservationist" of all the stories of saints and nature is one of the stories about the Irish saint Kevin (Coemgen, d. 618), who more than any other of the early Irish saints was remembered in later traditions for his love of animals. An angel is sent to tell Kevin that he and his monks are to move to a new place, where the monastery he is to found would be home to thousands of monks until the day of judgment. But the place the angel indicates is well-nigh inaccessible. Kevin protests: "It is impossible for monks to live in that valley, hemmed in by mountains, unless God assists them by his power." The angel promises that God will supply all they need and goes on to picture the future glories of the monastery:

> [T]his place shall be holy and revered. The kings and the great ones of Ireland shall make it glorious to the glory of God because of you, in lands, in silver and gold, in precious stones and silk raiment, in treasures from over the seas. . . . A great city shall rise there. And the burial place of your monks shall be most sacred, and none that lie beneath its soil shall know the pains of hell. Indeed, if you should wish that these four mountains that hem the valley in should be levelled into rich and gentle meadow lands, beyond question your God will do that for you.

But Kevin replies:

> I have no wish that the creatures of God should be moved because of me. My God can help that place in some other fashion. And moreover,

---

[60]Cf. L. Leloir, "Anges et démons chez les Pères du Desert," in J. Ries and H. Limet, eds., *Anges et Démons: Actes du Colloque de Liège et de Louvain-La-Neuve 25–26 novembre 1987* (Louvain-La-Neuve: Centre d'Histoire des Religions, 1989), 330–31; Bratton, "The Original Desert Solitaire," 41–42; Sorrell, *St. Francis*, 21; Short, *Saints*, chaps. 6–7.

[61]See Wallace-Hadrill, *The Greek Patristic View*, 87–91 (on Basil of Caesarea); Short, *Saints*, 25–27.

all the wild creatures on these mountains are my house mates, gentle and familiar with me, and what you have said would make them sad.[62]

Implicit in the whole tradition of these stories—and occasionally explicit—is an understanding of the human dominion over nature. Because the hermits are exemplary righteous people, they relate to nature in the way that God originally intended human beings to do so.[63] Submitting themselves wholly to God's will, they recover the human dominion over the rest of creation in its ideal form. In their relationships with wild nature, paradise is regained and the coming restoration of paradise in the kingdom of God is anticipated.[64]

What this means in practice can sometimes remind us of the theological tradition of hierarchical order. The animals acknowledge the saints as those who have the right to rule and command them. Dangerous animals become tame and revere the saint.[65] They obey the saint's orders. Often they willingly serve the saint.[66] Abba Helle, one of the desert fathers, had only to call out to a herd of wild asses, requiring that one carry his burden for him, and one of them willingly trotted up to undertake the task.[67] For the sixth-century Breton saint Leonoris, when he and his monastic brothers were worn out from working the fields without oxen, twelve stags appeared and spontaneously ploughed for thirty-eight days.[68] The Italian saint William of Montevergine (d. 1085) recruited two wolves to protect his garden from a wild boar.[69]

As often, the most attractive stories are of the Celtic saints. Colman's three friends—the cock, the mouse, and the fly—each assisted his devotions: the cock crowed in the middle of the night to wake him for prayer, the mouse woke him in the morning by nibbling his eyes, and the fly would keep his place on the page of the Scriptures as he meditated on the words.[70] After Cuthbert had prayed all night submerged to his neck in the sea, two

---

[62]Waddell, *Beasts*, 134–36 (translation adapted).

[63]It is notable that none seem to have thought this required complete vegetarianism, even though they protected animals from the hunters.

[64]Glacken, *Traces*, 310–11; G. H. Williams, *Wilderness and Paradise in Christian Thought* (New York: Harper, 1962), 42–46; Sorrell, *St. Francis*, 20; Elliott, *Roads*, 167; Short, *Saints*, passim.

[65]E.g., Short, *Saints*, 11, 13, 33, 35, 51.

[66]Short, *Saints*, chap. 2.

[67]Waddell, *Beasts*, 19; Bell, *Wholly*, 73; *Historia Monachorum* 12.5, translated in Russell and Ward, *The Lives*, 90.

[68]Short, *Saints*, 53–54.

[69]Short, *Saints*, 46.

[70]Waddell, *Beasts*, 145–47; cf. Kenneth (Canice) and the stag whose antlers he used as a lectern: Bell, *Wholly*, 37.

otters warmed his feet with their breath and tried to dry him with their fur.[71] Not only the animals, but even the sea served Cuthbert, throwing up on the shore a plank of exactly the length he needed for the shelter he was constructing. His biographer Bede draws out the significance explicitly in this case: "[I]t is hardly strange that the rest of creation should obey the wishes and commands of a man who dedicated himself with complete sincerity to the Lord's service. We, on the other hand, often lose that dominion over creation which is ours by right through neglecting to serve its Creator."[72]

Such stories presuppose a hierarchical order in which those human beings who obey God have a right to be obeyed by the rest of creation. But this is portrayed as a state of harmony in which the animals willingly serve but are certainly not exploited. Moreover, it is not implied that they exist only for the use of humans. As other stories make clear, the hierarchical order is understood as a state of harmony that benefits all God's creatures. The animals are not the saint's slaves, but are frequently portrayed as friends and companions of the saint, and as objects of the saint's care and concern. In these respects the stories step right outside the theological and exegetical tradition.

Although some of the desert fathers can appear rather severe in their treatment of animals,[73] others took pleasure in the friendly companionship of wild creatures.[74] Several stories of the Celtic saints represent the saint as the abbot of a small monastery of wild animals, who keep him company in the wilderness and obey him as their abbot.[75] This picture puts rather well the ideal relationship the stories envisage: the monks must obey the abbot, but they are also, as fellow monks, his brothers and companions in the service of God, and his rule over them is a matter of pastoral care. The care and concern of the saints for wild animals are the theme of many stories. The famous story of Kevin and the blackbird is an extreme example. As Kevin knelt in prayer with his hand outstretched, a blackbird built her nest on his hand and laid her eggs in it.

---

[71]Bede, *De Vita et Miraculis S. Cudberti* 10, translated in J. F. Webb, *Lives of the Saints* (Harmondsworth: Penguin, 1965), 84–85; Waddell, *Beasts*, 59–61; Bell, *Wholly*, 49–51.
[72]Bede, *De Vita et Miraculis S. Cudberti* 21, translated in Webb, *Lives*, 98–99.
[73]E.g., Abba Bes in *Historia Monachorum* 4.3, translated in Russell and Ward, *The Lives*, 66; Abba Helle and the crocodile: *Historia Monachorum* 12.6–9, translated in Russell and Ward, *The Lives*, 90–91; cf. Waddell, *Beasts*, 20–21; Bell, *Wholly*, 74. Harsh treatment of animals can also be found in some stories of the Celtic saints.
[74]E.g., Theon: *Historia Monachorum* 6.4, translated in Russell and Ward, *The Lives*, 68; Bell, *Wholly*, 120; Macarius and the hyena: *Historia Monachorum* 21.15–16, translated in Russell and Ward, *The Lives*, 110; cf. Waddell, *Beasts*, 13–15; Bell, *Wholly*, 93.
[75]For the Cornish saint Piran, see Van de Weyer, *Celtic Fire*, 60–61; for the Irish saint Ciaran of Saighir, see Waddell, *Beasts*, 104–6; Bell, *Wholly*, 40–42.

Kevin kept his hand open until the chicks were hatched.[76] The twelfth-century English hermit Godric of Finchale is another saint remembered, probably with more historical basis, for his habit of caring for animals in need.[77]

Two themes recur frequently as forms of the saints' care for animals. One is their feeding of wild animals. Several of the desert fathers provided food and water for the animals of the Egyptian desert: lions, wolves, antelope, wild asses, gazelles.[78] In the later, European stories, birds are the most common recipients of food.[79] That timid birds feed from the saint's hand is seen as evidence of his gentleness, as in the case of William Firmat (d. 1179) of Mantilly in France, who also sheltered birds from the cold under his clothes and fed bread crumbs to the fish in the local pond.[80] The account is surely in this case an accurate reminiscence of a man who loved God's creatures, but it also portrays the ideal harmonious relationship of humans and animals: the gentleness of the saint is reciprocated by the tameness of the animals. Sometimes a saint shares his own food with birds, recognizing their common creaturely dependence on the Creator's provision.[81]We are reminded of the biblical stress on the Creator's provision of food for birds (Job 38:41; Ps. 147:9; Matt. 6:26; Luke 12:24). The saints both recognize their common creatureliness with the birds and reflect the Creator's own caring provision for God's creatures the birds.

The other recurrent theme is that of the saint's protection of animals from hunters.[82] Wild boars, bears, partridges, stags, rabbits, and foxes are all saved from the hunters pursuing them when they enter the sanctuary of the hermit's dwelling.[83] The hermitage and its environs are understood as a paradise where all creatures are safe and the violence of the hunt may not intrude. Once again, the ideal relationship of humans and animals is envisaged as peaceful harmony, rather than as the human right to make use of animals, with which the dominant theological tradition underpinned the practice of hunting.

---

[76]Waddell, *Beasts*, 137. Another extreme example is the concern of David of Garesja for a monstrous dragon that was attacking the deer he had befriended: Lang, *Lives*, 85–86. Note also the theme of the blessing of animals by saints: Bratton, "The Original Desert Solitaire," 37; Van de Weyer, *Celtic Fire*, 60.

[77]Bell, *Wholly*, 69–70, 156–57. Sadly, this aspect of Godric does not feature in F. Buechner's novel *Godric* (London: Chatto & Windus, 1981).

[78]*Historia Monachorum* 6.4, translated in Russell and Ward, *The Lives*, 68; Bratton, "The Original Desert Solitaire," 36, 38–39.

[79]But for other examples, see Bell, *Wholly*, 94–95, 96, 100.

[80]Short, *Saints*, 16.

[81]E.g., Short, *Saints*, 18–19; cf. Bratton, "The Original Desert Solitaire," 39.

[82]Short, *Saints*, chap. 3.

[83]Short, *Saints*, 79–87, 95–100; Lang, *Lives*, 88–89.

In summary, we may say that the tradition of stories of hermits and animals understands the human dominion over the rest of creation as a hierarchical relationship of mutual service and care: the animals willingly serve those who serve God, but the servants of God care for and protect the animals. Moreover, the sense of hierarchy is strongly qualified by a sense of common creatureliness. The animals are friends and companions. The saints delight in their company. They recognize their common dependence on their common Creator. When a partridge took refuge with the Georgian saint David of Garesja and the bird's hunters asked David who looked after and fed him there in the uninhabited wilderness, David said, "He whom I believe in and worship looks after and feeds all his creatures, to whom he has given birth. By Him are brought up all men and all animals and all plants, the birds of the sky and the fishes of the sea."[84]

Rarely but significantly, this shared creatureliness is perceived as the common worship of God. The Saxon saint Benno of Meissen (d. 1106) was disturbed in his contemplation by the loud croaking of a frog, and so he commanded it to be silent. But he then remembered the words of the Benedicite, which, among its exhortations to all creatures to worship God, includes, "Bless the Lord you whales and all that swim in the waters" (Dan. 3:79). Reflecting that God might prefer the singing of the frogs to his own prayer, he commanded the frogs to continue praising God in their own way.[85]

Francis of Assisi as representative of the alternative tradition

Lynn White proposed Francis of Assisi as a patron saint for ecologists.[86] The proposal is entirely appropriate. No other figure in Christian history so clearly, vividly, and attractively embodies a sense of the world, including humanity, as a community of God's creatures, mutually interdependent, existing for the praise of their Creator, or has so effectively inspired in Christians an attitude of appreciation, gratitude, respect, and love for all God's creatures.[87] However, when White portrays Francis as a completely exceptional figure in Christian history, he both misrepresents Francis's own views and neglects the extent to which they are anticipated in the tradition of stories of

---

[84]Lang, *Lives*, 89.
[85]Waddell, *Beasts*, 71–72; Bell, *Wholly*, 25–26. Note also the quotation from the Benedicite in the *Voyage of St. Brendan*, discussed by Sorrell, *St. Francis*, 24–25.
[86]White, "The Historical Roots," 30.
[87]The definitive study is now Sorrell, *St. Francis*; but see also E. A. Armstrong, *Saint Francis: Nature Mystic* (Berkeley/Los Angeles/London: University of California Press, 1973); E. Leclerc, *Le Chant des Sources* (Paris: Editions Franciscaines, 3d ed., 1975).

saints and nature. On the one hand, it is not true that "Francis tried to depose man from his monarchy over creation and set up a democracy of all God's creatures" or that he "tried to substitute the equality of all creatures, including man, for the idea of man's limitless rule of creation."[88] Francis did not reject the notion of human dominion over the rest of creation but interpreted it in the way that we have seen that the tradition of stories of saints and nature interpreted it. On the other hand, White misrepresents the latter tradition when he says that the legends of the saints (referring especially to the Irish saints) do not provide a precedent for the stories about Francis, because they told of the saints' dealings with animals only in order "to show their human dominance over creatures."[89] White cannot have read many of the legends of the Irish saints if he has not noticed how much more striking are the saints' delight in the companionship of animals and their loving care for animals. This is not to say that there are not relatively new aspects and emphases in Francis's teaching and behavior, but the novelty emerges from his continuity with the tradition in which he stood.[90] Francis is the climax of a tradition reaching back to the desert fathers. He transcends it only through deep dependence on it.

Many of the stories of Francis's relationships with animals and other creatures continue the theme of the restoration of the paradisal relationship of humans to the rest of creation,[91] and they portray this relationship in much the same ways as the tradition of the stories of the saints had done. Francis frequently acts with authority to command the animals,[92] illustrating Bonaventura's conclusion that "Francis had power not only over men, but also over the

---

[88]White, "The Historical Roots," 28, 29. L. Boff, *Saint Francis: A Model for Human Liberation* (London: SCM Press, 1982), 34, who speaks of "the cosmic democracy," comes rather close to this mistake, though his insights into Francis's confraternity with all creatures are very valuable.

[89]White, "The Historical Roots," 29.

[90]Even Sorrell, who carefully establishes Francis's continuity with the tradition before attempting to specify the really novel elements in his life and message (see the summary: *St. Francis*, 138–39), perhaps fails to show sufficiently how the relatively novel elements develop out of the traditional. Bratton, "Oaks," 17–20, helpfully compares and contrasts Francis with the desert fathers and the Celtic saints.

[91]According to Bonaventura, *Legenda Maior* 8.1, Francis returned "to the state of primeval innocence by restoring man's harmony with the whole of creation" (translation in M. A. Habig, *St. Francis of Assisi: Writings and Early Biographies: English Omnibus of the Sources for the Life of St. Francis* [Chicago: Franciscan Herald Press, 1983], 688). Translations from Francis's works and the early biographies are taken from R. J. Armstrong, J. A. W. Hellmann, and W. J. Short, eds., *Francis of Assisi: Early Documents*, vol. 1: *The Saint* (New York: New City Press, 1999), when the texts are included in this volume, in other cases from Habig, *St. Francis*.

[92]Examples listed in Sorrell, *St. Francis*, 43.

fishes of the sea, the birds of the air and the beasts of the field."[93] The fierce wolf that was terrorizing the town of Gubbio was tamed and became friendly under Francis's influence.[94] Animals serve Francis, like the falcon that during his residence in his hermitage at La Verna used to wake him in time for matins but showed such consideration for the saint that when Francis was tired or ill it would delay waking him until dawn.[95] Like many of the stories in the earlier tradition, this one emphasizes the affectionate friendship between the saint and the bird. The creatures respect Francis's authority, but they do so lovingly and willingly, as friends rather than slaves.

Many stories show Francis's care for animals in relatively traditional ways. Like other saints, he fed and protected his fellow creatures. He wanted Christmas Day, a festival of special importance to Francis, to be honored by the provision of abundant food for birds and more than the usual amount of food for domestic animals.[96] He saw to it that bees were provided with honey or wine lest they die of cold in the winter.[97] Though he is not said to have saved animals from hunters, several stories portray him saving animals from danger or harm, freeing animals that had been caught and brought to him, returning fish to the water, even removing worms from the road lest they be trampled.[98] (But Francis was not a vegetarian, and so cannot have thought the catching of fish and trapping of animals was always wrong.) Such stories are both continuous with the tradition and sufficiently distinctive of Francis to convince us that we are not dealing with a literary topos, but with genuine reminiscences of Francis's concern for creatures, which stemmed from his eremitical experience of living close to wild nature, as many hermits had before him. Like some of the stories in the earlier tradition, those about Francis frequently emphasize the reciprocity of his relationships with animals: they are tame and friendly as he is gentle and concerned. The friendly and nonviolent harmony of paradise is restored.

Francis is reported as saying that "every creature says and proclaims: 'God has created me for you, O man!'" Although this reflects the medieval theological commonplace that the rest of the material creation was made for humanity, the context should be noted. Francis is telling the brother gardener not to plant vegetables everywhere, but to reserve part of the garden for plants whose

---

[93]Habig, *St. Francis*, 1880.

[94]*Fioretti* 1.21 (Habig, *St. Francis*, 1348–51).

[95]Celano, *Vita Secunda* 168 (Habig, *St. Francis*, 497–98).

[96]Celano, *Vita Secunda* 200 (Habig, *St. Francis*, 522).

[97]Celano, *Vita Prima* 80 (Habig, *St. Francis*, 296; Armstrong, Hellmann, and Short, *Francis*, 250).

[98]Listed in Sorrell, *St. Francis*, 44.

scent and flowers "might invite all men who looked at them to praise God."[99] Thus Francis refuses to limit the value of the rest of creation for humanity to its practical usefulness but sees it as consisting also in its assisting humanity's praise of God. But Francis's principle (to be expressed most fully and beautifully at the end of his life in the *Canticle of Brother Sun*) was that because the "creatures minister to our needs every day," and "without them we could not live," therefore we should appreciate them and praise God for them.[100] Thus the theme of human dominion is understood theocentrically rather than anthropocentrically. The creatures' service of humanity is properly received only as cause for praise and thankfulness to God. Therefore the human dominion over the creatures becomes for Francis primarily a matter of dependence on the creatures, with whom humanity shares a common dependence on the Creator. The creatures on whose service we depend are not to be exploited but to be treated with brotherly/sisterly respect and consideration.

This means that in Francis the sense in which humanity has been given a superior status in creation is only to be understood in relationship to his overwhelming sense of the common creatureliness that makes all creatures his "sisters" and "brothers."[101] This usage seems to be distinctive of Francis. The Celtic saints had called the animals who befriended them their brothers in the monastic sense. Francis regards all the creatures (not only animals, but also fire and water, sun and moon, and so on) as brothers and sisters, because they are fellow creatures and fellow members of the family of those who serve God. The terms denote affection and especially affinity. Thus, while there is a residual element of hierarchy in the relationship (humans and other creatures are not regarded as equal members of a democracy), this does not negate the common creatureliness of humans and other creatures. One concept that helped Francis, as a man of the thirteenth century, to understand the relationship of humans and other creatures in terms not of domination but of mutuality was the chivalric notion of "courtesy."[102] Courtesy is the magnanimous, deferential, respectful attitude that enables love to be shown up and down the social hierarchy. In the community of creation, brothers and sisters on different levels of the hierarchy can interact with mutual respect and loving deference. With the chivalric notion of courtesy Francis fused the traditional monastic virtues of obedience and humility,[103] so that he can say that obedience "is

---

[99]*Legenda Perugina* 51 (Habig, *St. Francis*, 1029).
[100]*Legenda Perugina* 43 (Habig, *St. Francis*, 1021).
[101]Sorrell, *St. Francis*, 66, 127–28.
[102]See Sorrell, *St. Francis*, 69–75.
[103]On the relationship of humility (and poverty) to Francis's confraternity with creatures, see Boff, *Saint Francis*, 38–40.

subject and submissive to everyone in the world, not only to people but to every beast and wild animal as well[,] that they may do whatever they want with it insofar as it has been given them from above by the Lord."[104] Here the hierarchy is virtually subverted by mutuality: the obedience that the creatures owe to humanity is reciprocated by an obedience of humanity to the creatures. What Francis envisages, in the end, is a kind of mutual and humble deference in the common service of the creatures to their Creator.

Another theme that has roots in the tradition, as we have seen, but that Francis also made very characteristically his own is the duty of all creatures to praise their Creator and the participation of humans in the worship given by all creation to God. The influence of the Psalms and the Benedicite is unmistakable in Francis's own liturgical compositions that call on all creatures to praise God.[105] Francis was original in that he translated this liturgical usage into an actual practice of addressing the creatures themselves. This began with the famous sermon to the birds in 1211,[106] which initiated a regular practice: "From that day on, he carefully exhorted all birds, all animals, all reptiles, and also insensible creatures, to praise and love their Creator, because daily, invoking the name of the Savior, he observed their obedience in his own experience."[107] In this way Francis put into practice a conviction that every creature has its own God-given worth (as he said to the birds, "God made you noble among His creatures"[108]) that should be returned to its source in praise of the Creator. We should also remember Francis's habit of singing along with cicadas and birds in what he understood as their praise of their Creator.[109] In this way he translated the sentiments of the Benedicite into a real human sol-

---

[104]The Praises of the Virtues (Habig, St. Francis, 134; Armstrong, Hellmann, and Short, Francis, 165).

[105]The Exhortation to the Praise of God (translation in Sorrell, St. Francis, 109; Armstrong, Hellmann, and Short, Francis, 138) and The Praises of God before the Office (Habig, St. Francis, 138–39; Armstrong, Hellmann, and Short, Francis, 161–62). These works echo the Psalms, which call on all creatures to praise God, the Benedicite, and Revelation 5:13. The last was to be used by the friars before each hour of the office. The influence of Psalm 148 and the Benedicite can also be seen in The Canticle of Brother Sun: see Sorrell, St. Francis, 99, 102–5.

[106]Celano, Vita Prima 58 (Habig, St. Francis, 277–78; Armstrong, Hellmann, and Short, Francis, 234); Fioretti 1.16 (Habig, St. Francis, 1336–37).

[107]Celano, Vita Prima 58 (Habig, St. Francis, 278; Armstrong, Hellmann, and Short, Francis, 234); cf. 80–81 (Habig, St. Francis, 296–97; Armstrong, Hellmann, and Short, Francis, 250–51).

[108]Celano, Vita Prima 58 (Habig, St. Francis, 278; Armstrong, Hellmann, and Short, Francis, 234).

[109]Celano, Vita Secunda 171 (Habig, St. Francis, 499–500); Bonaventura, Legenda Maior 8.9 (Habig, St. Francis, 695–96); J. R. H. Moorman, A New Fioretti 57 (Habig, St. Francis, 1881–82).

idarity with the rest of creation, understood as a theocentric community existing for the praise and service of God.[110]

In the famous *Canticle of Brother Sun* or *Canticle of the Creatures*, written at
the end of his life, Francis summed up much of his attitude to creation. It is
important to appreciate fully the opening two stanzas that praise God before
reference is made to the creatures:

> Most High, all-powerful, good Lord,
> Yours are the praises, the glory, and the honor, and all blessing,
> To You alone, Most High, do they belong,
> and no human is worthy to mention Your name.[111]

That God surpasses the creatures in such a way as to be the only praiseworthy
one could not be clearer. So, when the next stanza continues

> Praised be You, my Lord, with all Your creatures

the praising of the creatures can only be a way of praising their Creator, from
whom their praiseworthy features derive. This praise of God *with* the creatures
(stanzas 3–4) is a transition from the praise of God *without* the creatures (stanzas 1–2) to the praises of God *for* the creatures, which occupy stanzas 5–13. In
these stanzas the various qualities of the creatures are lovingly detailed, so that
God may be praised for them. Each of these stanzas begins (in Francis's Italian original), "Laudato si, mi Signore, per . . . ," followed by reference to one
or more of the creatures. There has been controversy over whether the meaning is "Be praised, my Lord, by . . . ," "Be praised, my Lord, through . . . ," or
"Be praised, my Lord, for . . . ." Divergent interpretations of the phrase go
back to soon after Francis's death,[112] and any would be consistent with his
thinking about the creation. But the latest detailed study by Sorrell argues very
convincingly for the translation "Be praised, my Lord, for . . . ."[113] In that case
the canticle does not call on Sister Moon, Brother Wind, Sister Water, and the
rest to praise God, even though Francis, as we have seen, could well have done
this. Rather the canticle takes up Francis's conviction, which we have also
noticed, that human beings should praise God for their fellow creatures. The
creatures are appreciated in three ways: for their practical usefulness in making human life possible and good, for their beauty, and for the way their
distinctive qualities reflect the divine being (in particular, "Sir Brother Sun,"
in his beauty and radiance, resembles God). This is an appreciation of the

---

[110]Cf. Boff, *Saint Francis*, 37–38.
[111]Armstrong, Hellmann, and Short, eds., *Francis*, 113.
[112]Sorrell, *St. Francis*, 116–17, 119.
[113]Sorrell, *St. Francis*, 118–22.

God-given value of creation that goes far beyond a purely utilitarian, anthropocentric view. It celebrates the interdependent harmony of creation. The canticle is designed to teach people to think of creation with gratitude, appreciation, and respect.[114]

We have considered various aspects of Francis's attitude to and relationships with the nonhuman creation, but we have still to register the intensity of delight in the creatures that frequently raised Francis to ecstatic rejoicing in their Creator. Some comments from his early biographers will illustrate this:

> He used to extol the artistry of [the bees'] work and their remarkable ingenuity, giving glory to the Lord. With such an outpouring, he often used up an entire day or more in praise of them and other creatures.[115]

> He had so much love and sympathy for [the creatures] that he was disturbed when they were treated without respect. He spoke to them with a great inner and exterior joy, as if they had been endowed by God with feeling, intelligence, and speech. Very often it was for him the occasion to become enraptured in God.[116] (AP 49).

> [H]e caressed and contemplated [the creatures] with delight, so much so that his spirit seemed to live in heaven and not on earth.[117] (AP 51).

This aspect of Francis's relationship to the creatures seems unprecedented in the Christian tradition and warrants speaking of Francis's creation mysticism.

Creating the modern tradition: (1) Italian Renaissance humanists

A major development in the understanding of the human dominion over nature occurred in the Italian humanist writers of the Renaissance. It was a development that could hardly have taken place except on the basis of the dominant theological tradition of the patristic and medieval periods, which we have already outlined, but it was also a major step beyond that tradition, which has been little enough noticed in discussions of our subject.[118] It is this step that can be said to have created the ethos within which the modern project of aggressive domination of nature has taken place.

---

[114]Sorrell, *St. Francis*, 124.

[115]Celano, *Vita Prima* 80 (Habig, *St. Francis*, 296; Armstrong, Hellmann and Short, *Francis*, 250).

[116]*Legenda Perugina* 49 (Habig, *St. Francis*, 1027).

[117]*Legenda Perugina* 51 (Habig, *St. Francis*, 1029).

[118]Wybrow, *The Bible*, 166–71, is one of the few discussions to give it serious attention.

The Renaissance humanists were preoccupied with the theme of the supreme dignity of humanity, which they not infrequently expounded as exegesis of Genesis 1:26.[119] Even where reference to the text is not explicit, it is frequently implicit. Moreover, the traditional understanding of the human dominion, which these writers knew not only from the theological tradition but also from the classical sources that had influenced that tradition, is taken entirely for granted. The rest of creation was made for humanity (it was, says Petrarch, "dedicated to nothing but your uses, and created solely for the service of man"[120]). The unique superiority of human nature over the rest of creation equips human beings to rule the world.[121] But these traditional themes are given unprecedented emphasis and at the same time developed in a novel direction.

A striking feature of the Renaissance humanist idea of humanity is that the vertical relationship of humanity to nature (human beings as rulers over the rest of creation) is emphasized to the virtual exclusion of the horizontal relationship of humanity to nature (human beings as creatures who share with other creatures a common creaturely relationship to the Creator). Humanity's place within creation is abolished in favor of humanity's exaltation above creation. While this takes to an extreme one aspect of the traditional hierarchical thinking, other aspects of the medieval hierarchical view of creation are left aside. Human beings are no longer regarded as occupying a metaphysical status below that of the angels, but are exalted above the angels, if not by virtue of their creation, then at least by virtue of their deification in Christ.[122] With this is connected a rejection of the idea that humanity occupies a given, fixed place within the created order. Human beings are understood as uniquely free to make of themselves what they will and to transcend all limits.[123] In effect, humanity becomes a kind of god in relation to the world. Human creatureliness is forgotten in the intoxication with human godlikeness. The Renaissance humanist vision of humanity is of a creative and sovereign god over the world.

In writers such as Giannozzo Manetti, Marsilio Ficino, and Pico della Mirandola, the image of God in human nature is understood not simply as the rational or moral capacity that distinguishes humans from other creatures—as the dominant theological tradition had understood it—but as likeness to God

---

[119]See especially C. Trinkaus, *In Our Image and Likeness: Humanity and Divinity in Italian Humanist Thought* (London: Constable, 1970).

[120]*De remediis utriusque fortunae* (1357), quoted in Trinkaus, *In Our Image*, 180.

[121]Cf. Trinkaus, *In Our Image*, 192.

[122]Trinkaus, *In Our Image*, 188–92, 212–13, 511–12.

[123]See the passage from Pico della Mirandola quoted and discussed in chapter 2 above.

in the divine activity of creating and mastering the world. The rather traditional theme, inherited from classical antiquity, of stress on humanity's ingenuity and inventiveness is heightened and emphasized in the typical
Renaissance adulation of the artistic and technological achievements of
humanity. As Manetti commented:

> After that first, new and rude creation of the world, everything seems
> to have been discovered, constructed and completed by us out of some
> singular and outstanding acuteness of the human mind. . . . The world
> and all its beauties seems to have been first invented and established
> by Almighty God for the use of man, and afterwards gratefully
> received by man and rendered much more beautiful, much more
> ornate and far more refined.[124]

This is a relatively restrained adumbration of the idea that humanity's likeness
to God consists in a creative ability to reshape the world, fashioning a kind of
second creation out of the raw materials of the first. Here the idea that we
noticed in Cicero finally comes into its own, with its implication that, as
Manetti quotes from Cicero, human beings, in their special capacity for knowing and doing, act in their dominion over the world "as though a certain mor-
tal god."[125]

This new sense of the godlike creativity of humanity should be contrasted
with the traditional concept, which we have seen in the work of Hugh of St.
Victor, according to which human beings can do neither the work of God nor
that of nature, but can only imitate nature. According to Ficino, "Human arts
make by themselves whatever nature itself makes, so that we seem to be not
servants of nature but competitors. . . . Man at last imitates all the works of
divine nature and perfects, corrects and modifies the works of lower
nature."[126] Human sovereignty over the world in knowing and creating is such
that the human soul must be termed divine:

> The mind in comprehending conceives of as many things in itself as
> God in knowing makes in the world. By speaking it expresses as many
> in the air; with a reed it writes as many on paper. By making it con-
> structs as many in the material of the world. Therefore he would be
> proven mad who would deny that the soul, which in the arts and in
> governing competes with God, is divine.[127]

---

[124]*De dignitate et excellentia hominis* (1542/3), quoted in Trinkaus, *In Our Image*, 247.
[125]Quoted in Trinkaus, *In Our Image*, 250.
[126]Quoted in Trinkaus, *In Our Image*, 482.
[127]Quoted in Trinkaus, *In Our Image*, 484.

It is clear here that Ficino's aim is to envisage humanity in terms of the attributes traditionally restricted to God as creator and ruler of the world.[128] The human relationship to the world is therefore described in terms that, for all the magnificence of the vision, are ludicrously hyperbolic. All creaturely limitations are deliberately suppressed, as in the following passage which is worth quoting at length:

> In these industrial arts . . . man everywhere utilises all the materials of the universe as though all were subject to man. He makes use . . . of all the elements, the stones, metals, plants and animals, and he transforms them into many shapes and figures, which animals never do. Nor is he content with one element or few, as animals, but he uses all as though he were master of all. He tramps the earth, he sails the water, he ascends in the air by the highest towers. . . . He acts as the vicar of God, since he inhabits all the elements and cultivates all. . . . Indeed he employs not only the elements but all the animals of the elements, terrestrial, aquatic, and flying, for food, comfort and pleasure, and the supernal and celestial ones for learning and the miracles of magic. He not only uses the animals but he rules them. . . . He does not only use the animals cruelly, but he also governs, fosters and teaches them. Universal providence is proper to God who is the universal cause. Therefore man who universally provides for all things living is a certain god. He is the god without doubt of the animals since he uses all of them, rules them, and teaches some of them. He is established also as god of the elements since he inhabits and cultivates them all.[129]

If we understand Renaissance humanism as in some sense giving birth to the spirit of the modern project of unlimited domination of nature, then it is extremely instructive to see how explicit Ficino is in connecting a human aspiration to subjugate all things to human control with a human aspiration to divinity:

---

[128]Cf. J. Moltmann, *God in Creation*, trans. M. Kohl (London: SCM Press, 1985), 26–27; *God for a Secular Society*, trans. M. Kohl (London: SCM Press, 1999), 98–99. Moltmann sees the fundamental problem as a one-sided emphasis, in nominalism and the Renaissance, on God's absolute power. Human beings, as the image of such a God, are therefore bound to strive for power and sovereignty over the world. However, if this concept of God were, as Moltmann argues (as an alternative to Lynn White's thesis), the source of the modern project to subjugate nature, why did the latter not arise in Islamic societies? The problem posed for Christian theology by the Renaissance and the modern culture derived from it is not only a matter of getting the understanding of God right, but also of conceiving human likeness to God in a properly creaturely way, such that human self-understanding is formed by contrast as well as resemblance to God.

[129]Quoted in Trinkaus, *In Our Image*, 483–84.

> [Man] will not be satisfied with the empire of this world, if, having
> conquered this one, he learns that there remains another world which
> he has not yet subjugated. . . . Thus man wishes no superior and no
> equal and will not permit anything to be left out and excluded from
> his rule. This status belongs to God alone. Therefore he seeks a divine
> condition.[130]

The gap between such a view and the traditional Christian view of the human
dominion is vast. Anthropocentric as the latter was, it nevertheless understood
the human dominion in static and very limited terms and qualified it by a consciousness of humanity's creatureliness in common with the rest of creation.
In Ficino, on the other hand, human beings are godlike in their restless will to
power. Human dominion over the world has become a limitless aspiration.
The attitudes that have led to the contemporary ecological crisis can be traced
back to this source, but no further.

A final quotation, from the sixteenth-century Italian pantheist philosopher
Giordano Bruno, will illustrate just how far the idea of humanity's divine creativity could be taken:

> The gods have given man intelligence and hands, and have made him
> in their image, endowing him with a capacity superior to other animals.
> This capacity consists not only in the power to work in accordance with
> nature and the usual course of things, but beyond that and outside her
> laws, to the end that by fashioning, or having the power to fashion,
> other natures, other courses, other orders by means of his intelligence,
> with that freedom without which his resemblance to the deity would
> not exist, he might in the end make himself god of the earth.[131]

This idea of humanity's capacity to refashion the world at will into whatever
form of new creation we desire has provided, as it were, the ethos of much of
the modern project. It has been one of the myths by which modern Western
civilization has lived. But, of course, the scientific and technological means by
which modern society has attempted to put this myth into practice could not
relate to nature in quite the way Bruno (inspired by Renaissance magic) envisaged. Science and technology cannot act outside nature's laws. Much as they
might aspire to refashion nature, their ability to do so depends on their mastery of nature's laws. To find a version of the Renaissance humanist aspiration

---

[130]Quoted in Trinkaus, *In Our Image*, 491.
[131]*Spacio de la Bestia Trionfante*, quoted in B. Farrington, *The Philosophy of Francis Bacon:
An Essay on Its Development from 1603 to 1609 with New Translations of Fundamental Texts*
(Liverpool: Liverpool University Press, 1964), 27. It is ironical that Bruno is one of the
heroes of Matthew Fox's bizarre reading of Christian history: M. Fox, *Original Blessing*
(Santa Fe, N.M.: Bear, 1983), 10, 312.

that recognized this and thereby provided more precisely the ideology of the modern scientific movement in its attempt to subjugate nature to human use, we must turn to Bruno's English contemporary Francis Bacon.

Creating the modern tradition: (2) Francis Bacon

The extraordinary achievement of Francis Bacon (1561–1626) was to set out in advance a program for the modern scientific enterprise that can still stand as a classic statement of the ideology which has inspired and governed scientific research and technological innovation from the seventeenth to the twentieth centuries.[132] His contribution to the modern scientific method has been frequently discussed and debated, but methodology was not in reality his main contribution to modern science. This lay rather in his vision of organized scientific research with a utopian goal to be realized through scientific innovation and progress. It was this dream that inspired the pioneering scientists of seventeenth- and eighteenth-century England. Central to Bacon's vision of scientific progress is his understanding of the goal of science as the implementation of the God-given human dominion over nature, which Bacon himself presents as the meaning of Genesis 1:28.[133]

Taking entirely for granted the traditional view that the rest of creation exists for the sake of humanity, Bacon understands the human dominion as humanity's right and power to use nature for human benefit.[134] This human dominion was severely impaired at the fall, but it can be recovered: "Man by the fall fell at the same time from his state of innocency and from his dominion over creation. Both of these losses can in this life be in some part repaired; the former by religion and faith, the latter by arts and sciences."[135] The words

---

[132]Relevant studies of Bacon include Farrington, *The Philosophy of Francis Bacon*; P. Rossi, *Francis Bacon: From Magic to Science*, trans. S. Rabinovitch (London: Routledge & Kegan Paul, 1968); Leiss, *The Domination*, chap. 3; J. S. Preus, "Religion and Bacon's New Learning: From Legitimation to Object," in F. F. Church and T. George, eds., *Continuity and Discontinuity in Church History: Essays Presented to George Huntston Williams* (Leiden: Brill, 1979); J. Weinberger, *Science, Faith, and Politics: Francis Bacon and the Utopian Roots of the Modern Age* (Ithaca/London: Cornell University Press, 1985); R. K. Faulkner, *Francis Bacon and the Project of Progress* (Lanham: Rowman & Littleford, 1993). For a critique from a feminist and green theological perspective, see C. J. M. Halkes, *New Creation: Christian Feminism, and the Renewal of the Earth*, trans. C. Romanik (London: SPCK, 1991), 27–32, 56–58.

[133]For exegetical argument against Bacon's (and Baconians') interpretations of this and other texts in Genesis, see Wybrow, *The Bible*, chapter 5.

[134]Cf. Rossi, *Francis Bacon*, 102–3.

[135]Novum Organon 12.52, in F. Bacon, *The Works of Francis Bacon*, ed. J. Spedding, R. L. Ellis, D. D. Heath (London: Longman, 1857–1858), 4. 247–48.

of God to Adam after the fall—that "in the sweat of thy face shalt thou eat bread" (Gen. 3:19)—Bacon takes to mean that "by various labours" the earth can be "at length and in some measure subdued to the supplying of man with bread; that is, to the uses of human life."[136] These labors are primarily the intellectual labors of scientific research that make possible the technological exploitation of nature for human benefit.[137] The human task is to recover the dominion over the earth to its fullest extent.[138] This is "the real business and fortunes of the human race."[139] It is also the central goal of Bacon's own work, which is devoted to "my only earthly wish, namely to stretch the deplorably narrow limits of man's dominion over the universe to their promised bounds."[140] Hence the title of Bacon's projected masterpiece, which he never completed but which was to sum up all his work, was to be "The Great Instauration." By this term he means precisely the restoration of the human dominion over nature that was promised in Genesis 1: "that right over nature which belongs to [the human race] by divine bequest."[141] This restoration of dominion is a vast enterprise, not to be accomplished quickly. It is to be the work of dedicated scientific labor over many generations.[142]

Thus, much more clearly than in the Italian humanists, in Bacon the human dominion becomes a historical task, to be progressively accomplished. Indeed, it is the great task of the human race, to which all its best efforts should be directed. The restoration of the human dominion is not, as in the tradition of stories of saints and nature, given by God to those who live according to his will. It is not, in that sense, a concern of religion, though Bacon does expect the exercise of dominion to be "governed by sound reason and true religion."[143] He effectively drew a very firm distinction between the restoration of human innocence, which was the province of religion, and the restoration of human dominion, which would be accomplished by science and technology.

The task is very explicitly that of subjecting nature to human use. The language of domination comes readily to Bacon's pen: "I am come in very truth leading you to Nature with all her children to bind her to your service and make her your slave."[144] In a revealing passage, Bacon refers to three sorts of

---

136*Works* 4. 248.

137*Works* 3. 222–23.

138*New Atlantis*, quoted in Preus, "Religion," 269: "the enlargement of the bounds of Human Empire, to the effecting of all things possible."

139*Works* 4. 32.

140*The Masculine Birth of Time*, in Farrington, *The Philosophy of Francis Bacon*, 62.

141*Novum Organon* 1.129, in *Works* 4. 115.

142*Works* 4. 21.

143*Works* 4. 115.

144*The Masculine Birth of Time*, in Farrington, *The Philosophy of Francis Bacon*, 62.

ambition. Those who desire to increase their own power in their own country are not to be admired. The desire to increase one's own country's power over other nations is more admirable, but still culpable. By contrast, the endeavor "to extend the power and dominion of the human race itself over the universe" is wholly admirable, "a work truly divine."[145] This is because it is unselfishly directed to the benefit of all humanity. Bacon equates "the instigator [i.e., restorer] of man's domination of the universe" with "the champion of freedom" and "the conqueror of need."[146] This, appearing probably for the first time, is the modern vision of the scientific and technological enterprise as dedicated to the good of humanity by acquiring power over nature and using it to liberate humanity from all the ills of the human condition. It has a high ethical motivation and goal. But the ethical limit it places on human domination of nature is solely that of the love of humanity: the scientific enterprise should be governed not by desire for personal gain or glory but by love of humanity.[147] No limit is imposed by any sense that nature has intrinsic value for itself or for God. Because Bacon assumes that nature exists solely for human benefit, to exploit it for human benefit as far as possible is not only right but a prime human duty.

As well as an ethical limit, there is a practical limit to human power to dominate nature. This limit is imposed by the facts of nature. Nature has been constituted by its Creator in a certain way that human beings must understand if they are to be able to use nature to the fullest possible extent for human benefit.[148] This is the point at which Bacon so significantly does what the Italian humanists had not been able to do: he connects the vision of human dominion with the empirical science he advocates and inspires. Nature's laws cannot be ignored or set aside or breached. They must be understood if humanity is to exercise realistic power over nature.[149] This is Bacon's famous doctrine that "knowledge is power":[150]

> For man is but the servant and interpreter of nature: what he does and what he knows is only what he has observed of nature's order in fact or in thought. . . . For the chain of causes cannot by any force be loosed or broken, nor can nature be commanded except by being obeyed. And so those twin objects, human Knowledge and human Power, do

---

[145]*Valerius Terminus*, in *Works* 3. 223; cf. *Novum Organon* 1.129, in *Works* 4. 114.

[146]*De Interpretatione Naturae Prooemium*, in *Works* 3. 518, trans. in Rossi, *Francis Bacon*, 193.

[147]Cf. *Works* 3. 217–18; 4. 21.

[148]Cf. Rossi, *Francis Bacon*, 18.

[149]Cf. Rossi, *Francis Bacon*, 130.

[150]Farrington, *The Philosophy of Francis Bacon*, 51; Rossi, *Francis Bacon*, 21.

really meet in one: and it is from ignorance of causes that operation fails.[151]

In this sense, Bacon advocates a kind of humility,[152] which sounds a different note from the rather more promethean vision of some of the Italian humanists. It is the humility of the believing scientist, who respects the way God has made nature, studies its laws, and thereby gains the power over it that God intends humanity to have. In this sense, "nature cannot be conquered except by obeying her."[153] But the aim is certainly to conquer nature, and Bacon's vision of what it is possible for human power over nature to achieve is far from the limited medieval concept of imitating nature. He attacks the error "of looking upon art [i.e., technology] as a kind of supplement to nature; which has power enough to finish what nature has begun or correct her when going aside, but no power to make radical changes, and shake her in the foundations."[154] The language of conquering nature is not the least of Bacon's enduring bequests to modern Western culture—a metaphor that came to be used standardly and unreflectively until the quite recent development of ecological consciousness made it questionable. As a typical expression of the nineteenth-century view, the following quotation from Thomas Carlisle is plainly in direct descent from Bacon: "We war with rude nature; and, by our resistless engines, come off always victorious, and loaded with spoils."[155]

It is significant that Bacon does not speak, like the Italian humanists, of human deification or of humanity as a kind of god over the world. He accuses traditional natural philosophy of the sin of pride in wanting to be god, because in his view it constructed an idea of nature out of the philosopher's imagination. The traditional natural philosopher created the world as he would have liked it to be—thereby playing God—instead of humbly observing the world that God has actually made, as Bacon's empirical scientist does.[156] In this sense, Bacon sets the tone for the early modern scientific enterprise. Bacon's scientist is not a god who can recreate the world in any way he will, but he can by mastering the laws of nature subject it to the purpose for which God created it, human benefit. Bacon's achievement is to transfer the Renaissance vision of unlimited dominion away from its association with magic and alchemy, harnessing it instead to the practical pursuit of scientific knowledge

---

[151]*Works* 4. 32.

[152]*Valerius Terminus*, in *Works* 3. 224.

[153]*Thoughts and Conclusions*, in Farrington, *The Philosophy of Francis Bacon*, 93.

[154]*Sketches of the Intellectual World*, in *Works* 5. 506.

[155]Quoted in T. Blackwell and J. Seabrook, *The Revolt against Change* (London: Vintage, 1993), 24.

[156]*Historiae Naturalis*, in *Works* 5. 132–33.

and technological innovation, and to relate it to biblical and religious ideas in a way more congenial to Protestant England. But it is also significant that Bacon's formulation of the idea of human mastery of nature turned out to be easily secularized as the cultural impact of Christian belief steadily diminished in the centuries after his time. As Leiss puts it, "[Bacon's] contention that science shared with religion the burden of restoring man's lost excellence helped create the climate in which earthly hopes flourished at the expense of heavenly ones."[157]

By comparison with the tradition, there seems a total loss of any sense that human beings belong within creation alongside other creatures: Bacon's humanity simply stands above nature, mastering it by knowledge and power. As in the Italian humanists, the vertical relationship entirely replaces the horizontal. Also by comparison with the tradition, the value of nature has become purely utilitarian; the notion that all creatures exist for the glory of God and thereby assist humanity's contemplation of God has disappeared in favor of nature's usefulness for practical human needs. Despite the continued reference to God the Creator, this is the point at which Western attitudes to nature became exclusively anthropocentric rather than theocentric. Therefore it made little practical difference when atheistic scientists eventually took their place alongside believing scientists in the Baconian tradition.

The "Judeo-Christian tradition" has often been praised or blamed for the so-called de-sacralization of nature in the Western tradition. It has been praised for this by those who think the achievements of modern science were thereby made possible, and blamed by those who think the modern exploitation of nature—the root of the ecological crisis—was thereby made possible.[158] But we need to be clearer about the meaning of desacralization.[159] The Judeo-Christian tradition certainly dedivinized nature. Nature is not reverenced as divine in a pantheistic or animistic sense. But deeply rooted in the Judeo-Christian tradition is the sense that all creatures exist for the glory of God and reflect the glory of God. Human beings both praise God along with the rest of creation and praise God for the beauty and worth of the rest of creation in which they see the Creator's glory reflected. Only with the loss of this nonutilitarian sense of the value of creation for and in relation to God, in favor

---

[157]Leiss, *The Domination*, 53.

[158]White, "The Historical Roots," 25; Toynbee, "The Religious Background," 145–48, who ascribes the ecological crisis to "the monotheistic disrespect for nature" and recommends a return to pantheism as a remedy.

[159]Cf. Passmore, *Man's Responsibility*, 10–11; Wybrow, "The Old Testament," 80–83, who rightly argues that in the Old Testament nature is "De-divinized but not Deanimated."

of an exclusively utilitarian view of nature as given by God for human beings to exploit for human benefit, can we properly speak of a desacralization of nature. This happened in the Baconian understanding of the relation of humanity to the rest of creation. Significantly, it is in the seventeenth-century Christian scientist Robert Boyle that we find a call for the desacralization of nature, explicitly linked with a Baconian understanding of the human dominion: "The veneration wherewith men are imbued for what they call nature has been a discouraging impediment to the empire of man over the inferior creatures of God: for many have not only looked upon it, as an impossible thing to compass, but as something of impious to attempt."[160] Without the Baconian desacralization of nature, a scientific enterprise would have been possible, but not the actual scientific and technological enterprise of aggressive domination of nature that has been so significant a feature of modern Western history.

Reading Bacon is to experience frequent shocks of recognition as one finds all too familiar features of the modern scientific enterprise already clearly stated by him. For example, Bacon already expressed the conviction so often voiced by contemporary scientists that scientific work itself is value-free so that only its use can be right or wrong (with the implication, in contemporary discourse, that scientists are absolved of any responsibility for the use made of their discoveries[161]): "light is in itself pure and innocent; it may be wrongly used, but cannot in its nature be defiled."[162] Leiss comments: "This clear separation of natural knowledge and moral knowledge gradually became a cardinal principle of modern thought: it echoes in the fashionable contemporary distinction between 'facts' and 'values,' according to which questions of values constitute a unique discourse outside the scope of 'scientific' knowledge."[163] Another instance has only recently become observable. In his scientific utopia, the *New Atlantis*, Bacon anticipates scientific manipulation of animals such as has only now become possible through genetic engineering:

> By art, likewise, we make them greater or taller than their kind is; and contrariwise dwarf them, and stay their growth: we make them more fruitful and bearing than their kind is; and contrariwise barren

---

[160]Quoted in Passmore, *Man's Responsibility*, 11.

[161]This argument is a smoke screen disguising the fact that most scientific work is commercially driven and directed to specific ends that those funding and usually those doing the research judge desirable. The effort devoted to discovering and developing techniques of cloning animals, for example, would not have been exerted by the scientists involved had they been convinced that such techniques could never rightly be used.

[162]*Thoughts and Conclusions*, in Farrington, *The Philosophy of Francis Bacon*, 92, quoted in Leiss, *The Domination*, 50.

[163]Leiss, *The Domination*, 52.

and not generative. Also we make them differ in colour, shape, activity, many ways. We find means to make commixtures and copulations of different kinds, and them not barren, as the general opinion is. . . . Neither do we do this by chance, but we know beforehand of what matter and commixture what kind of those creatures will arise.[164]

Reading this one realizes that the *ideology* of the modern project, as already fully propounded by Bacon, *entailed* such results. Bacon had no notion of the means by which these results would be achieved four centuries later, but he could anticipate the results because he coined the ideology that still inspires the scientists in our twenty-first-century laboratories of biotechnology. In this chapter I am attaching huge importance for the historical transformation of ideas of human dominion to the work of this one man, but it seems that the scale and enduring impact of his influence really does justify this.

At this point it may be useful to summarize what the historical evidence we have examined implies with regard to Lynn White's thesis. I have argued that the ideological roots of the modern Western project of aggressive domination of nature are to be found in a traditional interpretation of the human dominion over nature that drew on Greek rather than biblical sources and was subsequently, in the Renaissance, removed from its broader context in a Christian understanding of creation. The dominant theological interpretation of the dominion in patristic and medieval times in some respects prepared the way for the modern scientific and technological project of conquering nature for human benefit, but it could not itself have provided the ideological support and motivation for that project. Only the significantly new interpretations given to the human dominion in Renaissance humanism and English Baconianism accomplished that. The crucial new elements were the understanding of the human dominion as a historical task, not a static condition of things but a mandate for progressive achievement of mastery over nature, to be accomplished by scientific discovery and technological innovation; the loss of an effective doctrine of creation, such that the human relationship to other creatures as fellow creatures gave way to an exclusively vertical relationship of humans to nature; and the reduction of the value of nature to the purely utilitarian, orientated only to practical human benefit.

---

[164]F. Bacon, *The Great Instauration and New Atlantis*, ed. J. Weinberger (Arlington Heights, Ill.: AHM Publishing, 1980), 73. On biotechnology as fulfilling Bacon's project, see D. F. Noble, *The Religion of Technology: The Divinity of Man and the Spirit of Invention* (New York: Penguin, 1999), chapter 11.

Domination of nature after Bacon

A history of the idea of mastery of nature after Bacon remains to be written.[165] It certainly passed through the Baconianism of seventeenth-century English scientists into general modern thinking about science, technology, and their place in the utopian idea of human progress that developed at the time of the European Enlightenment and became *the* ideology of the modern West. As we have already indicated, essentially Bacon's ideas prevailed. It was as though he had already expressed all that the modern age felt it necessary to be thought about this concept. According to Leiss,

> No outstanding thinker after Bacon devoted comparable attention to the concept of mastery over nature. In the ensuing period it undergoes little further development, even though it is more and more frequently employed. The measure of Bacon's achievement is that most of those who followed him have found the form in which he cast this concept to be sufficient for their own purposes. So definitive was his work that the history of all subsequent stages in the career of this idea down to the present can be arranged as a set of variations on a Baconian theme.[166]

There is, for example, a frequently quoted passage from Descartes's *Discourse on Method* (1637) in which he adopts a thoroughly Baconian approach to "practical philosophy," by which humans will "render ourselves masters and possessors of nature,"[167] but the passage is unique in Descartes's works. It was apparently an idea to which he felt no need to give more detailed attention, so thoroughly was he ready to take it over and to take it for granted.

However, one very important "variation on a Baconian theme" that has emerged more recently and could only have emerged much later than Bacon's own time, because it depends on the nineteenth- and twentieth-century idea of the evolution of life, is the notion that scientists are becoming masters of the evolutionary process (not least, human evolution), taking control of it and directing it. This idea has become especially plausible with the rapidly emerging possibilities of manipulating genes and changing the genetic basis of species. This particular variation of Baconianism makes sense in the context,

---

[165]Probably Leiss, *The Domination*, chapter 4, is the nearest we yet have to this, though he admits it is no more than a "fragmental biography of the idea" (95). The main concern of Leiss's book is the way in which the domination of nature developed the domination of other humans as a corollary. This is a very important aspect that cannot, unfortunately, be investigated in our present context.

[166]Leiss, *The Domination*, 71, cf. 79.

[167]*The Philosophical Works of Descartes*, trans. E. Haldane and G. Ross (New York: Dover Books, 1955), 1:119, quoted in Leiss, *The Domination*, 81.

as we have already noticed, of biotechnological research deeply imbued with and motivated by the Baconian ideology of dominion.

We have already noted that, despite its religious coloring, Bacon's vision could easily enough be secularized, and the same could be said for the explicitly more promethean Renaissance humanist one. For both, God enters into the human relationship with nature only in that he is believed to have granted humanity dominion. God sets no limits to the dominion, so that in effect humans play the role of God in relation to the world. The loss of truly divine transcendence left the human quasidivine transcendence over the world in place. Whether as creative gods or as conquerors through knowledge, human beings were already thought to have the destiny of subjecting nature wholly to their will. With the Enlightenment they merely took for themselves the destiny they had previously received from God. In doing so, however, they rejected altogether the Christian doctrine of creation, with its potential for a quite different perception of the human relationship to nature.

Leiss argues that the secularization of the notion of human dominion freed it from moral constraints:

> Lynn White's argument must be qualified to this extent, namely, that Christian doctrine sought to restrain man's earthly ambitions by holding him accountable for his conduct to a higher authority. So long as Christianity remained a vital social force in Western civilization, the notion of man as lord of the earth was interpreted in the context of a wider ethical framework. Religion's declining fortunes, however, led to the gradual secularization of this notion in imperceptible stages, and in contemporary usage it reveals few traces of its Judaeo-Christian background.[168]

This may not be entirely accurate. In Bacon's idea the achievement of human dominion is motivated, as we have seen, by an ethic of service to humanity, which has retained its force in scientific endeavor alongside other ideals and motivations. But the ethic in this case is purely humanistic, entirely subjecting nature to the good of humanity. There is no sense of the value of the natural world in itself or an ethical obligation to respect this value. This is what was lost with the loss of a doctrine of creation.

Moreover, in stepping outside a religious doctrine of creation, the Western project of dominating nature sidestepped not only the issue of ethical obligation to nature but also that of limits given in the created order of things. Both Bacon's recognition that nature's laws must be understood if nature is to be exploited (so that presumably nature's laws set limits to the kind of exploitation

---

[168]Leiss, *The Domination*, 34–35, cf. 54.

that is possible) and the Renaissance sense that humanity has unlimited creative power to unleash nature's potentialities have fed into the modern project, investing science with hugely utopian expectations and also inspiring the hubris that overreaches its capacities and brings unforeseen and disastrous consequences into being. In the late twentieth century it became more and more obvious that the Baconian dream had a powerful element of unreason hidden in its apparent rationality. This "cunning of unreason," as Leiss calls it, is revealed in the persistent illusion that the undertaking known as "the mastery of nature" is itself mastered.[169]

Finally, we should note that the secularization of the project of domination left it exposed to commercialization and consumerization. It is this that has fatally compromised the humanist ethical goal to be found in its more admirable versions. The satisfaction of human needs and the curing of human ills have proved too limited as goals for the exploitation of nature. Descartes envisaged "the invention of an infinity of arts and crafts which enable us to enjoy without any trouble the fruits of the earth and all the good things which are to be found there."[170] But he did not recognize how human desires would have to be manufactured to require the unlimited products of technology. Insatiable desires must match unlimited dominion in a spiral that makes the direction of causality quite obscure. This is where ethical as well as other limits fall away and where disregard of nature's own inherent limits finally makes them disastrously evident.

An alternative modern tradition: dominion as stewardship

The understanding of the human dominion over nature that has become most popular among Christians in the context of the contemporary ecological crisis, representing a new consciousness of ecological responsibilities in the churches, is the idea of stewardship. This is often thought to be more thoroughly rooted in the Christian tradition than it really is. A recognition that the world is God's creation and that this imposes ethical limits on human dominion over it (for example, inhibiting cruelty to animals) had, as we have seen, a place in the Christian tradition, however much in tension it might seem to be with the dominant view. But where the medieval and even Reformation commonplace that the rest of creation was created by God for human benefit held sway, we cannot speak of stewardship. The latter idea means, rather, that human beings have been entrusted by God with the care of creatures not pri-

---

[169]Leiss, *The Domination*, 23.
[170]*The Philosophical Works of Descartes*, trans. E. Haldane and G. Ross (New York: Dover Books, 1955), 1:119, quoted in Leiss, *The Domination*, 81.

marily existing for human benefit. This is not just a restraint on dominion but a different idea of dominion, which it is hard to find clearly expressed before the late seventeenth century.[171]

The stewardship concept seems to have been a response to the growing sense of human control over nature, which had also prompted the Italian humanist and Baconian interpretations of the dominion. Consciously or unconsciously, it provided an alternative, in the England of the Royal Society, to the excessively anthropocentric Baconian view. Those who espoused it shared the contemporary enthusiasm for the extension of human control over nature, but instead of thinking purely of a human right to use nature for human benefit, they maintained also a human responsibility to care for nature, since, as George Hughes put it, man's rule is "subordinate and stewardly, not absolutely to do as he list with God's creatures."[172] In other words, almost for the first time, the dominion was being interpreted in a way that acknowledged ethical obligations arising from nature's inherent value.

Although this idea seems to have been relatively popular in religious writers of the second half of the seventeenth century,[173] it was the eminent English lawyer Matthew Hale (1609–76) who gave it fullest expression. Hale, like some of his contemporaries, is clear that the world was created not solely for human benefit but for God's glory.[174] Humanity is "the Steward and Tenant of Almighty God,"[175] appointed to manage the earth on God's behalf, responsible to God for its treatment of it:

> In relation . . . to this inferior World of Brutes and Vegetables, the End of Man's Creation was, that he should be the Vice-Roy of the great God of heaven and earth in this inferior World; his Steward, Villicus, Bayliff or Farmer of this goodly Farm of the lower World, and reserved to himself the supreme Dominion, and the Tribute of Fidelity, Obedience, and Gratitude, as the greatest recognition or

---

[171]Cf. Passmore, *Man's Responsibility*, 28–31. Attfield, "Christian Attitudes," and *The Ethics*, chapter 3, argues against Passmore and claims to offer evidence for a strong tradition of stewardship through the patristic and medieval periods. But his definition of stewardship seems to me unhelpfully vague, and the fact that he can apparently include even Francis Bacon within a stewardship tradition seems to undermine his case considerably. Calvin's use of the image of stewardship for the way humans should treat all their possessions (quoted in L. Osborn, *Guardians of Creation* [Leicester: Apollos, 1993], 141–42) does not imply the inherent value of these things and does not contradict his belief that God created all things for human use and benefit; it merely limits the individual's use of what God intended for the benefit of all people.

[172]Quoted in Thomas, *Man*, 155.

[173]Cf. Thomas, *Man*, 154–55, 180, 359 n. 23.

[174]Glacken, *Traces*, 405.

[175]Quoted in Glacken, *Traces*, 405.

Rent for the same, making his Usufructuary of this inferior World to
husband and order it, and enjoy the Fruits thereof with sobriety, mod-
eration, and thankfulness.

And hereby Man was invested with power, authority, right, dominion, trust, and care, to correct and abridge the excesses and cruelties
of the fiercer Animals, to give protection and defence to the mansuete
and useful, to preserve the Species of divers Vegetables, to improve
them and others, to correct the redundance of unprofitable Vegetables, to preserve the face of the Earth in beauty, usefulness, and fruit-
fulness.[176]

Hale presupposes that nature left to itself would be chaotic: fierce animals
would render the gentler and more useful animals extinct, the earth would be
submerged in marsh and overgrown with trees and weeds. The earth needs a
superior creature to keep it in order. Humanity's duty is therefore to keep
things in balance, to prevent the wilder aspects of nature from creating chaos.
Human beings are to control the earth for the earth's sake as well as for their
own sake.[177] The prejudice that nature controlled and managed by humanity
is preferable to wilderness, a prejudice from which since classical times few
except the hermits had been free, is still dominant here. Human control
improves nature. Technology is justified as an instrument of humanity's benef-
icent stewarding of the world. As yet there is no admission that human control of nature might be destructive, that wilderness might be better left alone,
that nature might have its own order that human interference turns to chaos
and its own balance that technology might upset.

The value of the notion of stewardship was that it formally introduced the
notion of justice into the human relationship to nature. It is no accident that
Hale was a lawyer. As steward responsible to the divine King, humanity has
legal obligations to administer the earth justly and without cruelty.[178] If the
concept of stewardship did nothing to preserve wild nature from human interference, it was significantly linked with an apparently growing Christian sen-
sitivity about cruelty to animals.[179] Matthew Hale himself was one of those
who thought it unjustified to chase and kill animals for mere sport.[180] He
decided to put his aged horses out to graze, rather than selling them to the
knackers.[181] Other living creatures have a value in themselves and a right to
life that human beings, as their responsible superintendents, must respect and

---

[176]Quoted in Glacken, *Traces*, 481.

[177]Glacken, *Traces*, 480–82.

[178]Glacken, *Traces*, 481.

[179]Thomas, *Man*, 173–81.

[180]Thomas, *Man*, 162.

[181]Thomas, *Man*, 190.

protect.[182] Even the right of human beings to kill animals for food was being doubted by the late seventeenth century, and Hale, though he maintained that right, admitted that the sight of sheep grazing always made him feel God must have intended "a more innocent kind of food for man."[183]

The appeal of the notion of stewardship is that it recognizes value in the nonhuman creation other than its usefulness to humanity and gives humanity obligations to treat the nonhuman creation accordingly, while at the same time recognizing the unique degree of power over the rest of creation that human beings wield in modern times. However, it should be noticed that it sets human beings over nature just as emphatically as Italian humanism and Baconianism did. In that sense it shares not only the early modern period's exclusively positive evaluation of human control over nature but also its concentration on the vertical relationship of "superior" humanity to "inferior" nature at the expense of the horizontal relationship of human beings to their fellow creatures.

In the recent Christian revival of the notion of stewardship,[184] it seems to be a rather flexible term. It is, for example, employed on all sides of the debate about biotechnology. For some, deeply involved in the recent developments in genetic science and technology, such as Francis Collins, director of the Human Genome Project, Donald Munro, and V. Elving Anderson, stewardship seems to be the Christian notion that authorizes an uninhibitedly Baconian project.[185] It mandates the scientific task of unlimited improvement of creation. On the other hand, in the recent *Evangelical Declaration on the Care of Creation*[186] the role of human stewards is portrayed not as improving nature but as preserving and protecting it. (The stress therefore comes close to Lawrence Osborn's preferred image of "guardians" of creation,[187] Loren Wilkinson's "earthkeeping,"[188] or even Andrew Linzey's "servants" of creation.[189]) Here the emphasis is more on the givenness of the created order than on human intervention to change nature. It is not that nature needs human

---

[182]Thomas, *Man,* 279.

[183]Thomas, *Man,* 293.

[184]See, e.g., D. J. Hall, *Imaging God: Dominion as Stewardship* (Grand Rapids: Eerdmans, 1987); Cooper, *Green Christianity,* chapter. 2; L. Wilkinson, ed., *Earthkeeping in the Nineties: Stewardship of Creation* (Grand Rapids: Eerdmans, 1991; revised edition of *Earthkeeping: Christian Stewardship of Natural Resources,* 1980); Osborn, *Guardians,* chap. 8; C. A. Russell, *The Earth, Humanity, and God* (London: UCL Press, 1994), 146–48.

[185]Noble, *The Religion,* 194–200.

[186]Berry, *The Care,* 18–22.

[187]Osborn, *Guardians.* The image comes from Heidegger.

[188]Wilkinson, *Earthkeeping.*

[189]A. Linzey, *Animal Theology* (London: SCM Press, 1994), chapter 3.

protection from its own destructiveness, but that it needs protection and healing from human abuse of it. Stewardship here has acquired a late-twentieth-century content, along with somewhat chastened and humbled aims by comparison with the technological confidence it expressed in the seventeenth century. But because, in the words of others, it retains precisely that original force, the idea of stewardship itself without further definition, involving relationship to other biblical and Christian themes, may not be very helpful.

One problem with the concept of stewardship[190] today may be highlighted by referring to the now widespread agreement that we urgently need to protect wilderness, nature free from human interference, insofar as any part of nature still remains that. Wilderness can now survive only if humans protect it from human interference. But, unlike nature farmed and modified by humans, the value of wilderness is wholly independent of any human part in it. Protecting the last great wildernesses—Antarctica and the depths of the oceans, not to speak of the moon—is a challenge humans have scarcely faced before in history. Until recently wildernesses were just always there outside the sphere of human habitation, feared by most, loved by the remarkable few, the hermits and the monks, who chose to live with wild nature. The question now is whether, now that humans have the power to interfere everywhere on earth (and even beyond), we can learn to care without interfering, simply to keep away and to keep our hands off, and to do so not so that we still have wildernesses to visit as eco-friendly tourists, but actually because God's other creatures have their own value for God and for themselves, quite independently of us. For this purpose it may be that the image of stewardship is still too freighted with the baggage of the modern project of technological domination of nature. Can we entirely free it of the implication that nature is always better off when managed by us, that nature needs our benevolent intrusions, that it is our job to turn the whole world into a well-tended garden inhabited by well-cared-for pets? The problem is in part that stewardship remains, like most interpretations of the Genesis dominion and as we have already suggested, an image that depicts the human relationship to the rest of creation in an entirely vertical way. It sets humans above the rest of creation, sharply differentiated from it, in God-given charge of it. As far as the resources of Christian history go, it needs at least to be supplemented by the medieval Christian awareness—vividly expressed in many of the stories of saints and animals and never more fully realized than by Francis of Assisi—of mutuality, interdependence, friendliness, and confraternity between human beings and the other creatures of God.

---

[190]For criticisms of the idea of stewardship, cf. Northcott, *The Environment*, 129; Worster, *The Wealth*, 187–88; H. Spanner, "Tyrants, Stewards—or Just Kings?" in Linzey and Yamamoto, *Animals*, 222–23.

Dominion in biblical context

Our historical study brings us into substantial agreement with Wybrow's conclusion: "[T]he modern idea of mastery was, from its inception, expressed in Biblical language. And . . . the correct conclusion to be drawn from this fact is, not that the Bible taught modern mastery, but that the language of the Bible was adopted in order to legitimate ideas of human dominion which were not themselves Biblical in origin or spirit."[191] To a large extent the problem has been that Genesis 1:28 and a few other texts have been interpreted without the aid of their larger biblical context but with the aid of ideas drawn from other sources and traditions of thought. We conclude therefore by placing the idea of human dominion in its biblical context, indicating both the ways in which it is interpreted by other biblical texts and also that it is only one of at least two other major themes by which the Bible understands the human relationship to nature. These other themes need to be restored to their proper place alongside the theme of dominion, and this will be easier to do when we have also explored the interpretations and limitations that the Bible itself places on the dominion.

(1) Human dominion in creation (Gen. 1:26–28; Pss. 8:6–8; 115:16)

There is little disagreement on the fundamental meaning: by virtue of their creation in the divine image, humans represent within creation God's rule over his creation. To object that any such ascription to humanity of a special status and role within creation is unacceptably anthropocentric, as some environmentalists do, is unrealistic. Factually humans do have unique power to affect most of the rest of creation on this planet. We cannot but exercise it, even if we do so by restraining our use of it. We cannot but affect other creatures, even if we do so by sparing them the harm we could do them. What the Genesis mandate does is to recognize this power and to situate it within a framework of God's creative intention, so that humans exercise it responsibly.

That the rest of creation was made for the use and benefit of humans is not the point or the presupposition of the dominion. The Genesis creation narrative is not anthropocentric, but theocentric. The goal of God's creative work is not the creation of humanity on the sixth day, but God's Sabbath rest, God's enjoyment of God's completed work on the seventh day (Gen. 2:1–3). Creation exists for God's glory. Moreover, the image of rule does not imply that the subjects exist for the use and benefit of the ruler. The Bible is consistently critical of exploitative despotism. If the dominion is a sacred trust in which

---

[191]Wybrow, *The Bible*, 163.

God delegates some aspect of God's own rule over creation, then it is of course the Bible's portrayal of God's rule that should be the model for humanity's. God's rule is undoubtedly for the good of all God's creatures. "The LORD is good to all, and his compassion is over all that he has made" (Ps. 145:9); God saves "humans and animals alike" (Ps. 36:6). God's rule is God's compassionate and salvific care for all creatures.

However, because the model of God's rule has proved so dangerous in the history of the reading of Genesis 1:28, tempting humans to put themselves in a purely vertical relationship to the rest of creation, transcendent over the world on the model of God's creative and sovereign transcendence, it is wise also to consider the only kind of human rule over other humans that the Old Testament approves.[192] Deuteronomy interprets the kingship it allows Israel in a way designed to subvert all ordinary notions of rule (17:14–20). If Israel must have a king, then the king must be a brother. He is a brother set over his brothers and sisters, but still a brother, and forbidden any of the ways in which rulers exalt themselves over and entrench their power over their subjects. His rule becomes tyranny the moment he forgets that the horizontal relationship of brother/sisterhood is primary, and kingship secondary. In the case of the Genesis dominion, the horizontal relationship is that of fellow creatures. It is worth observing that, in the careful schema of the six days of creation, humanity is created on the same day as the other land animals (Gen. 1:24–31). Even though in other respects the creation of humans is distinguished, in this respect humans are classified firmly within the scheme of created animals. The dominion is therefore best understood as authority within creation, not over it. The cure for the hubris that has so often in the modern period distorted the human dominion into tyranny and destruction is a recovery of the biblical understanding of creation and the sense of creaturely limits and restraints that comes with a recognition that everything human, not excluding the special human role and responsibility in relation to other creatures, is creaturely. The aspiration to divinity, the dream of liberation from created limits, the illusion of unlimited freedom like God's, still perpetuated both in theological talk of cocreation with God and in biotechnological utopianism, has proved disastrous for both humanity and the rest of creation. Creation in the image of God both assigns a certain likeness to God and at the same time makes clear that this is precisely a likeness in created form. It no more makes humanity divine than the likeness of a painted portrait to its human subject makes the painting human.

---

[192]Cf. Spanner, "Tyrants," 222–24.

Reading Genesis 1:28 in its context within Genesis[193] itself provides interpretation of the human dominion; it is illustrated by Adam's role of serving and preserving the garden (Gen. 2:15, where the Hebrew verbs usually translated "till" and "keep" could also be translated "serve" and "preserve"[194]) and by Noah's conservation of all species (Gen. 6–8). The paradox of identifying rule (Gen. 1:28) and service (Gen. 2:15)[195] can be justified even by an Old Testament understanding of kingship (1 Kgs. 12:7), even more so by the New Testament representation of the divine lordship as service and authority in God's kingdom as service. The same paradox informs the beatitude: "the meek . . . will inherit the earth" (Matt. 5:5). Not those who aspire to mastery and control, but those who take their human place in creation, with respect for other creatures and recognition of fellow-creatureliness in relation to the one Creator, can legitimately exercise the dominion.

Another aspect of the way the Genesis dominion is interpreted by other material in its canonical context is the limits that legislation in the Torah clearly sets to the exercise of dominion (Exod. 20:10; 23:11; Lev. 25:7; Deut. 5:14; 25:4). The sabbatical laws restrain the use of nature for human benefit, recognizing, of course, that humans, like all animals, must make use of their environment in order to live, but denying that the peculiar human power to exploit the environment excessively should in fact be used in this way. In other words, the dominion is exercised as much in restraint as in use. The periodical allowance of freedom from human interference to wild nature, even within the sphere of Israelite farming (Exod. 23:11; Lev. 25:7), is a kind of symbol of respect for wilderness, reminding both ancient Israel and later readers of Scripture that dominion includes letting nature be itself. Even more of a dissuasive to exaggeration and overinterpretation of the Genesis dominion is God's speech to Job in Job 38–39, which so graphically and incisively draws Job's attention to the creatures over which he plainly does not exercise dominion. The point is precisely that he has no bearing on the value and purpose of their existence for their own sake and for God's sake. Job is not the unique reference point for all God's purposes in God's earthly creation. The lesson is to teach Job his place as one creature among others.[196] That

---

[193]I am not concerned to deny the existence of Pentateuchal sources, but I do not think distinguishing a Yahwist from a Priestly theology of the human place in creation, as Hiebert, *The Yahwist's Landscape*, does, while it may be historically justified, is hermeneutically appropriate in the reading of Genesis as Christian Scripture.

[194]See, e.g., Wilkinson, *Earthkeeping*, 287; Hiebert, *The Yahwist's Landscape*, 157.

[195]In a nevertheless insightful discussion, Hiebert, *The Yahwist's Landscape*, 155–62, makes this contrast the key to his construction of two different Pentateuchal views of the human role in creation.

[196]Cf. McKibben, *The Comforting Whirlwind*, 35–42; D. Strong, "The Promise of Technology Versus God's Promise in Job," *Theology Today* 48 (1991–92): 170–81.

lesson is taught by other biblical themes too (see sections 2 and 3 below), but I mention Job at this point because the lack precisely of human dominion is there so clearly implied (especially 39:9–12).

Even with all these forms of input from other parts of Scripture, we have not yet fully put dominion in its place. The vertical relationship in which dominion places humans to the rest of creation on earth is, as we have seen, biblically understood only in the closest connection with the horizontal relationship of humans to other creatures. But the latter relationship also comes into its own, without reference to hierarchical relationship at all, in two other major biblical themes that are as important as that of dominion in defining the place of humanity in creation.

(2) Humanity within the community of creation

The Bible fully recognizes the extent to which nature is a living whole to which human beings along with other creatures belong, sharing the earth with other creatures of God, participating, for good or ill, in the interconnectedness of the whole. In Genesis 9:8–17, the covenant God makes after the flood is not only with Noah and his descendants but also with every living creature; it is for the sake of them all that God promises there will never again be a universal deluge. Psalm 104 treats humans (v. 23) simply as one of the many kinds of living creatures for whom God provides. It depicts the world as a shared home for the many kinds of living creatures, each with its God-given place. In passages which state that God provides for all living creatures (Ps. 147:9, 14–16; Job 38:19–41; Matt. 6:26) there is the implication that the resources of the earth are sufficient for all, provided they live within created limits. When Jesus compares humanity with the birds and the wild flowers (Matt. 6:25–34), the effect is to discourage the excessive desires and unrestrained consumption by humans that are presently destroying the earth as a habitat for all creatures.

(3) The praise of God by all creation

Most important among the Bible's ways of placing us among the creatures, not over them, is the theme of creation's worship of God,[197] portrayed in the Psalms (e.g., Pss. 19:1–3; 97:6; 98:7–9; and especially 148)[198] and, with christological and eschatological character, in the New Testament (Phil. 2:10; Rev. 5:13). All creatures, animate and inanimate, worship God. This is not, as modern biblical interpreters so readily suppose, merely a poetic fancy or some

---

[197]On this subject, see my article "Joining Creation's Praise of God," forthcoming in *Ecotheology* (2002).
[198]See T. E. Fretheim, "Nature's Praise of God in the Psalms," *Ex Auditu* 3 (1987): 16–30; S. Hoezee, *Remember Creation* (Grand Rapids: Eerdmans, 1998), 50–52.

kind of primitive animism. The creation worships God just by being itself, as God made it, existing for God's glory. Only humans desist from worshiping God; other creatures, without having to think about it, worship God all the time. There is no indication in the Bible of the notion that the other creatures need us to voice their praise for them. This idea, that we are called to act as priests to nature, mediating, as it were, between nature and God, is quite often found in recent Christian writing,[199] but it intrudes our inveterate sense of superiority exactly where the Bible will not allow it. If creation needs priests, they are the four living creatures around God's throne (Rev. 4:6–8), only one of which has a human face, acting as our representative worshiper in heaven, whereas the others represent the animal creation with no need of human help. If anything, we should think of the rest of creation assisting our worship (in Ps. 148, the human praise follows the worship by all other creatures, from the angels downwards). But the key point is that implicit in these depictions of the worship of creation is the intrinsic value of all creatures, in the theocentric sense of the value given them by their Creator and offered back to God in praise. In this context, our place is beside our fellow creatures as fellow worshipers. In the praise in which we gratefully confess ourselves creatures of God, there is no place for hierarchy. Creatureliness levels us all before the otherness of the Creator. As we have noticed in our historical survey, Christians in the premodern period were probably more aware of this, because they more often consciously placed their own praise of God in the context of all creation's worship.

---

[199]See Northcott, *The Environment*, 131–34, for summary of the arguments of Philip Sherrard and Paulos Gregorios, with critique.

8

Freedom in the
Crisis of Modernity

Centrally at issue in the widely perceived crisis of modernity that character-izes the beginning of the twenty-first century are the value and meaning of human freedom. So essential has freedom been to the metanarrative moder-nity told about itself that it has become impossible to think about freedom without engaging with that metanarrative of progressive emancipation. Whether modernity has in fact delivered the emancipation it saw as its goal, whether it has proved a movement of liberation or a project of domination, whether the freedom it has delivered is a boon or a burden, whether the kind of freedom it envisaged was the authentic goal of human fulfillment or a defor-mation of human freedom—that such questions are now inescapable consti-tutes the crisis of modernity. That they must be questions for public theology in the twenty-first century hardly needs arguing. For modernity itself the question of human freedom was a theological question, even when its answer entailed atheism. In the crisis of modernity the question of the death of God still lurks behind every discussion of human liberation in which it is not explicit.

Duncan Forrester has recently reminded us that R. H. Tawney claimed, "In order to believe in human equality it is necessary to believe in God."[1] In view of the close connection he correctly saw between equality and freedom, he might well have said the same of freedom. In a straightforward sense it would obviously not be true; not all atheists are determinists, though many are. The

---

[1] D. B. Forrester, *On Human Worth* (London: SCM Press, 2001), 137, quoting J. M. Winter and D. M. Joslin, *R. H. Tawney's Commonplace Book* (Cambridge: Cambridge University Press, 1972), 53.

question as it will arise in this chapter is rather whether freedom is sustainable, whether it does not become a kind of slavery, demeaning human life and destroying human community, without a context of other values and practices of life in which human life is related to God. We shall call in evidence two secular thinkers, a novelist and a political theorist, and two Christian theologians.

Freedom at the end of history:
Michel Houellebecq and Francis Fukuyama

According to Michel Houellebecq's extraordinary novel *Les Particules élémentaires*[2] (in English translation *Atomised*), winner of the *Prix novembre* and something of a literary sensation in France, the idea of personal freedom was, by the end of the twentieth century, "a concept which had already been much devalued. . . . and which everyone agreed, at least tacitly, could not form the basis for any kind of human progress" (383).[3] Individual autonomy is the central feature of late twentieth-century Western society as Houellebecq portrays it, with Jonathan Swift–like disgust, in this savage satire. The modern age, as he sees it, has reached its nadir in the egotistical and especially sexual hedonism by which most individuals are now driven, dominated as they are by the ideals of personal freedom projected by the entertainment industry and commerce generally (63). The breakdown of community through the excesses of modern individualism entered its final phase with the sexual revolution, which, by destroying the traditional couple and the family, removed the last social factor protecting the individual from the market (28, 135–36). Most people loath the "atomised society" (185) that is the result (the book's title plays on this sense, along with a reference to particle physics and molecular biology, which form the scientific strand of the plot; cf. 358–59) but are condemned to the lonely lives it creates.

Against a background of violence and beggars on the urban streets, the banality of commercially regulated culture, and the mindless triviality and delusions of New Age alternatives, Houellebecq's characters live loveless and meaningless lives. Three of the four main characters kill themselves, the other passes the latter part of his life in a psychiatric clinic, drugged beyond the possibility of unhappiness. Most people in this culture, the novel claims, are terrified, not of death itself, but of aging, the loss of sexual attractiveness and capacities, and the indignity of dependence on others: "Each individual has a simple view of the future: a time will come when the sum of the pleasures that life has to offer

---

[2]Paris: Flammarion, 1999.
[3]Page references to the novel are to the English translation: *Atomised*, trans. F. Wynne (London: Heinemann, 2000).

is outweighed by the sum of pain (one can actually hear the meter ticking, and it ticks inevitably towards the end). This weighing up of pleasure and pain which, sooner or later, everyone is forced to make, leads logically, at a certain age, to suicide" (297). This is the logic of a society in which most people have no other aim than the pursuit of physical pleasure. One reviewer complains of the "long and arid tracts of anti-erotic pornography":[4] the wearisome detail conveys the joyless obsession with sex for mere sexual pleasure's sake in a society whose "remaining myth was that sex was something to do" (155).

The story aspires to the status of metanarrative. It centers on the lives of two half-brothers: Bruno, who typifies his generation, and Michel,[5] who becomes one of the architects of the future. Emotionally crippled by parental neglect (especially by their mother, a precursor of the me-generation)—and in this respect, of course, paradigmatic—neither is capable of love. Bruno's life is completely driven by the pursuit of sexual pleasure, while Michel, a brilliant molecular biologist, leads an almost purely intellectual life, devoid of emotion, but sadly aware of his own incapacity to love and of the near impossibility of love in the world he observes. Discussing the work of Aldous and Julian Huxley with his brother, Michel enunciates the novel's theory of the modern age: "Metaphysical mutation, having given rise to materialism and modern science, in turn spawned two great trends: rationalism and individualism" (191). A metaphysical mutation is a global transformation in the values by which most people live (4). The rise of Christianity was one such mutation; modern science was responsible for the next; and Michel and Bruno live in the generation when the implications of this modern mutation are pressing relentlessly to their logical and destructive conclusion, stoppable only by another metaphysical mutation.

Michel reads Huxley's *Brave New World* not as a satire, but as a utopia. (For Huxley, of course, it is precisely the loss of individual freedom that qualifies the society he imagines in that book as a dystopia. Michel's contrary evaluation of it is highly significant and revealing.) According to Michel, *Brave New World* is "our idea of heaven: genetic manipulation, sexual liberation, the war against age, the leisure society. This is precisely the world that we have tried—and failed—to create" (187). Why then has the metaphysical mutation of scientific modernity not led to such a utopia? Michel continues:

---

[4]Andrew Marr in *The Observer*. He continues, "Anyone who thinks book-reviewing is an easy trade should try getting through a hundred pages or so about unattractive middle-aged Frenchmen getting blow-jobs."

[5]It cannot be accidental that the author gives this character his own name. Houellebecq finds both half-brothers in himself (he is no stranger to Bruno's sexual appetites), but his chosen identification is with Michel.

[Aldous] Huxley's mistake was in not being able to predict the power struggle between rationalism and individualism—he crucially underestimated the power of the individual faced with his own death. Individualism gives rise to the idea of freedom, the sense of self, the need to feel that one is superior to others. A rational society like the one he describes in *Brave New World* defuses the struggle. Economic rivalry—a metaphor for animals competing for territory[6]—should not exist in a society of plenty, where the economy is strictly regulated. Sexual rivalry—genes competing over time—is meaningless in a society where the link between sex and procreation has been broken. But Huxley forgets about individualism. He doesn't seem to understand that, stripped of their link with reproduction, lust and greed still exist—not as pleasure principles, but as forms of egotism. . . . [T]he metaphysical mutation brought about by modern science depends on individuation, narcissism, malice and desire. Any philosopher, not just Buddhist or Christian, but any philosopher worthy of the name knows that, in itself, desire—unlike pleasure—is a source of suffering, pain and hatred. The Utopian solution—from Plato to Huxley by way of Fourier[7]—is to do away with desire and the suffering it causes by satisfying it immediately. The opposite is true of the sex-and-shopping society we live in, where desire is marshalled and organised and blown up out of all proportion. For society to function, for competition to continue, people have to want more and more until it fills their lives and finally devours them. (191–92)

Thus, in Michel's view, the rationalism of the modern age seeks a society of utopian happiness but is prevented from achieving it by the competitive individualism also characteristic of the modern age. Consumerism is both the product of this individualism and ensures that its desires can never be satisfied.

Why has the modern metaphysical mutation produced this egotistical individualism? Michel's answer seems to be simply that it has replaced religion and its otherworldly hope with materialism and the inevitable finality of death. Scientific awareness of mortality makes it impossible to return to the religious worldview that curbed egotism and fostered community. So Michel's problem becomes: "How could society function without religion?" (193). His lifework—scientific and quasiphilosophical—is to solve this problem and thereby enable

---

[6]In his youth, from watching nature programs on television, Michel had become convinced "that, taken as a whole, nature was not only savage, it was a repulsive cesspit" (38).

[7]Charles Fourier (1772–1837); see the account of his utopia in J. Carey, ed., *The Faber Book of Utopias* (London: Faber & Faber, 1999), 208–19. The parallel Fourier draws between the behavior of particles of matter in Newton's theory of gravitation and the behavior of human individuals must surely have suggested Houellebecq's updated scientific equivalent: the parallel between the behavior of subatomic particles in contemporary physics and the behavior of individuals of the new posthuman species.

the next metaphysical mutation, which takes place after his death during the twenty-first century. The solution is purely biological: the production, through genetic engineering of a new, posthuman species. The new species is asexual, in that it does not reproduce sexually, though it has the means of experiencing much greater sexual pleasure than humans have. A perfected process of cloning makes possible exact reproduction, such that all members of the species, including all future members of the species, are related as identical human twins are, individuated by experience but "maintaining a mysterious fraternity" by virtue of their genetic identity (375). Love now comes naturally: it is rooted in the posthuman DNA. Although Houellebecq does not expressly say so, humanity has overcome the biological competitiveness of Darwinian evolution by creating a new species with a radically new biological constitution. As the posthumans, revealed at the end to be the putative writers of the narrative, observe how relatively peacefully the extinction of the old species has occurred, they comment, "It has been surprising to note the meekness, the resignation, perhaps even the relief of humans at their own passing away" (378).

As science fiction goes, this is a modest speculation. But Houellebecq surely means it seriously at least in this sense: he does not think the problem of the contradiction between individual freedom and community is soluble while humans remain humans. This is a profoundly misanthropic form of the long tradition of thought about posthistory (*posthistoire*), stemming in France especially from Auguste Comte and more recently expressed in Hegelian form by Alexandre Kojève, the main inspiration[8] of Francis Fukuyama's now famous American version.[9] Throughout this tradition runs the vision of transcending the historical condition of humanity that is characterized by dissatisfaction, aspiration, suffering, struggle, and conflict: history itself will lead to a posthistorical condition that has a finality about it at least in its transcendence of the conflictual character of history. If the human is defined as the historical, then humans in attaining their posthistorical goal will cease to be human. Thus Kojève, whose work has almost certainly had some influence on Houellebecq and who can also be construed as misanthropic, understands the end of history as humanity's rational self-destruction.[10] Houellebecq also sees it in this way but introduces genetic engineering to solve the problem his radically pessimistic view of modernity produces for the notion of human history's self-

---

[8]There is a racy account of Kojève's influence on Fukuyama in P. Berman, *A Tale of Two Utopias: The Political Journey of the Generation of 1968* (New York: Norton, 1996), 298–337.

[9]F. Fukuyama, *The End of History and the Last Man* (London: Penguin, 1992).

[10]P. A. Lawler, "Fukuyama versus the End of History," in T. Burns, ed., *After History? Francis Fukuyama and His Critics* (Lanham, Md.: Rowman and Littlefield, 1994), 70.

transcendence into posthistory. Humans, in his novel, finally realize the impossibility of attaining the human dream of happiness beyond conflict and suffering through the pursuit of freedom, just at the moment when the achievements of scientific rationality make the creation of a posthuman species, liberated from human individualism, possible. The struggle between rationalism and individualism in the modern era, a notion not unknown in the tradition of thinking about posthistory, Houellebecq is able to perceive as an irreconcilable one, without abandoning the dream of a posthistorical solution of it, because he also envisages a scientific means of ensuring a complete triumph of rationalism over individualistic freedom.

Freedom is almost inescapably a central theme in theories of posthistory, just as it is in virtually all forms of the modern metanarrative of progress. This makes it illuminating for our theme to compare and to contrast Houellebecq and Fukuyama. There are significant similarities that reflect their common ideological background in the tradition of posthistorical thought. They are both Hegelian in their conviction that ultimately it is consciousness and ideas, rather than material factors, that determine history, and that in the long run ideological principles will work themselves out to their logical conclusion in the course of historical events. They also both see the goal of history as the achievement of the rational but differ crucially in their understanding of the relationship of individual freedom to the rational ordering of life in the interests of happiness. For Houellebecq these are fundamentally antithetical, whereas for Fukuyama, the liberal optimist, they are not only compatible but indispensable to each other. These judgments are integral to their evaluation of the modern age as one of progress (Fukuyama) or decline (Houellebecq). But we should also note that their concerns about freedom focus on quite different forms of freedom. Houellebecq seems not at all concerned with the fundamental freedoms guaranteed by liberal democracies for their citizens, except insofar perhaps as the violence on the streets of suburban Paris implicitly suggests their declining efficacy. For Fukuyama, of course, it is in the irreversible recognition of the ideal of liberal democracy as the final political ideology that the end of history is achieved.

However, there are elements in Fukuyama that suggest that the two perspectives are not as clearly incompatible as at first appears. Fukuyama has his own criticism of excessive individualism. He dissociates himself somewhat from the Anglo-Saxon liberal tradition stemming from Hobbes and Locke, in which liberal democracy is founded on the selfish interests of the individual, and embraces a more Hegelian emphasis on the social being of humanity, such that democratic societies must be held together by shared democratic values.[11]

---

[11]Fukuyama, *The End of History*, 145, 160–61.

Moreover, he allows that liberal democracy only provides a framework for the good life, rather than defining or ensuring it.[12] But he comes much closer to Houellebecq in a chapter one suspects Houellebecq himself has pondered, the penultimate chapter of *The End of History*, where Fukuyama himself speaks of "the tendency of democratic societies toward social atomization"[13] and the tendency of "liberal economic principles . . . to atomize and separate people."[14]

The Anglo-Saxon version of liberal theory, on which the United States was founded, bases society solely on the enlightened self-interest of individuals. As this liberal theory has permeated all aspects of American society, it has inevitably, according to Fukuyama, weakened or destroyed community at every level, including now the family ("families don't really work if they are based on liberal principles, that is, if their members regard them as a joint stock company, formed for their utility rather than being based on ties of duty and love"[15]). Fukuyama also observes that "the pressures of the capitalist marketplace" also destroy community because they require of individuals constant shifts both in locality and in the nature of their work.[16] What really support and strengthen community, he continues, are shared religious values, which the "Lockean liberals who made the American Revolution" did to some extent presuppose: they "did not hesitate to assert that liberty required belief in God.[17] This religious support for liberty has necessarily, with the onset of greater pluralism in American society, given way to "a purer form of liberalism," in which the basic liberal theory of the right of individuals to pursue enlightened self-interest has had to survive in, as it were, naked form. In this naked form it was bound to destroy community.[18]

Thus Fukuyama, who considers secularization essential to liberal democracy,[19] is obliged to argue that liberalism itself creates a gaping whole at the heart of liberal societies:

> Liberal democracies, in other words, are not self-sufficient: the community life on which they depend must ultimately come from a source different from liberalism itself. The men and women who made up

---

[12]Cf. H. Williams, D. Sullivan, and G. Matthews, *Francis Fukuyama and the End of History* (Cardiff: University of Wales Press, 1997), 81, citing F. Fukuyama, "A Reply to My Critics," *The National Interest* 18 (Winter 1989–90): 26–28.

[13]Fukuyama, *The End of History*, 324.

[14]Fukuyama, *The End of History*, 325.

[15]Fukuyama, *The End of History*, 324.

[16]Fukuyama, *The End of History*, 325.

[17]Fukuyama, *The End of History*, 326.

[18]For a fuller account, see F. Fukuyama, *Trust: The Social Virtues and the Creation of Prosperity* (London: Hamish Hamilton, 1995), part 4.

[19]Fukuyama, *The End of History*, 216–17.

American society at the time of the founding of the United States were not isolated, rational individuals calculating their self-interest. Rather, they were for the most part members of religious communities held together by a common moral code and belief in God. The rational liberalism that they eventually came to embrace was not a projection of that pre-existing culture. It existed in some tension with it. "Self-interest rightly understood" came to be a broadly understandable principle that laid a low but solid ground for public virtue in the United States, in many cases a firmer ground than was possible through appeal to religious or pre-modern values alone. But in the long run those liberal principles had a corrosive effect on the values predating liberalism necessary to sustain strong communities, and therefore on a liberal society's ability to be self-sustaining.[20]

This is a remarkable qualification of Fukuyama's overall thesis that "liberal democracy in reality constitutes the best possible solution to the human problem"[21] and therefore represents the end of history. If liberal democracy both depends on and itself tends to corrode "pre-liberal traditions,[22] if it cannot survive without values that it cannot itself produce and even tends to debilitate, it would appear to be much more radically unstable even than Fukuyama admits in his last chapter, and quite incapable by itself of constituting "the best possible solution to the human problem." The search for such a solution and with it the continuing history of humanity would seem rather to shift to a concern for what might promote human solidarity and community in the face of the atomizing power of triumphant liberalism.[23]

At this point it seems that Fukuyama's argument, despite his resolute optimism, could easily come to meet Houellebecq's; he too perceives a very serious contradiction between freedom and community at the heart of the liberal society that he, unlike Houellebecq, lauds. But there is also a key point at which Houellebecq connects liberalism and egotistical individualism, but which Fukuyama, for understandable ideological reasons, does not perceive or ignores. This is the economic power and culture of consumerism. For

---

[20]Fukuyama, *The End of History*, 326–27. On the assumption of the Founding Fathers that liberty required virtue, see G. Himmelfarb, *On Looking into the Abyss* (New York: Random House, 1995), 98–99.

[21]Fukuyama, *The End of History*, 338.

[22]Fukuyama, *The End of History*, 335.

[23]Fukuyama's subsequent book, *Trust*, is an attempt to pursue this issue, though in fact it does little more than observe at length what he has already stated concisely in *The End of History*: that modern liberal democracy and capitalism depend on the survival of premodern "cultural habits." He does not follow any further the more threatening notion of an actual contradiction between liberal politics and economics, on the one hand, and the social virtues, on the other, such that the former inevitably tends to undermine the latter.

Fukuyama, free-market capitalism is part and parcel of the ideal of liberal democracy. The spread of Western consumerist culture throughout the world is an index of and agent in the spread of liberal values. Fukuyama does, as we have seen, admit that capitalism tends to social atomization through mobility. But he does not see that consumerism is destructive of social values. Houellebecq, on the other hand, while he does not comment on the connection between democracy and consumerism, clearly sees consumerism as part and parcel of the egotistical individualism that is reducing life in Western society to banal hedonism and threatening the survival of society. Moreover, in the passage quoted above from Michel in the novel, he puts his finger on a significant flaw in Fukuyama's position. The consumerist "sex-and-shopping society" depends on keeping human desire endlessly unsatisfied, in constant and competitive pursuit of more and new, whereas a posthistorical society, a rational utopia such as Michel helps to achieve, depends for its stability on the immediate satisfaction of desire. Fukuyama's end of history is inherently unstable and insecure because it requires the endless prolongation of exponential economic growth. (That the resources of the planet cannot sustain this is an argument recognized by neither author.)

It is not my intention to endorse either Fukuyama's or Houellebecq's diagnosis of the contemporary world as such. Partly because the posthistory thesis requires of both a particularly strong form of the typically modern desire for a metanarrative of modernity and its future, their accounts are undoubtedly selective and exaggerated. For this reason we can find both illuminating in different ways. But the point of most interest for our present purpose is the surprising one that, despite their apparently opposite evaluations of freedom in contemporary Western society, both perceive a serious contradiction between the kind of freedom nurtured by the liberal values of that society and the requirements of human community. Both think that the decline of religion in Western society has left a void that liberal individualism cannot fill. Neither considers a lasting resurgence of religion in Western society either possible or desirable. Michel's problem, "How could society function without religion?"[24] is taken with extreme seriousness by Houellebecq and answered only with the extreme solution: the biological creation of a new species. Fukuyama, despite his enthusiasm for technology, indulges in no such futurology and does not have the luxury of the genre of the novel to provide an ironic distance from such extreme solutions. Moreover, to recognize the full seriousness of the dilemma would endanger his whole argument.

---

[24]Houellebecq, *Atomised*, 193.

An uncharacteristically theological passage, from a response Fukuyama wrote to a volume of essays on his thesis about the end of history, is revealing in its incoherence. In a highly perceptive essay in the volume,[25] Peter Lawler compared Fukuyama unfavorably with the work of Kojève on which he is heavily dependent. According to Lawler, Kojève is a consistent atheist, Fukuyama not. Kojève recognized that belief in God sustains human freedom because it cannot allow that there can be a historical resolution of the irrationality of human history. Within a historical framework human aspirations can never be finally satisfied. Kojève, on the other hand, is the consistent atheist who sees the implications of Enlightenment rationalism to their logical conclusion. There can be an end of history in a finally rational satisfaction of human desires, and this will be the end of human freedom. (This is essentially also Houellebecq's view, though he substitutes biotechnological for Kojève's political means of bringing history to an end.) God, history, and humanity, entailing human dignity and freedom, stand or fall together. Fukuyama, on the other hand, envisages an end of history in which human beings remain human beings, with the conditions for their dignity and freedom established, paradoxically, by this end of history. Lawler writes:

> The most misleading incoherence of Fukuyama's book is his combination of a seemingly moderate defense of human dignity and liberal democracy with comprehensive atheism. He seems to hold that human liberty can be perpetuated in the absence of the distinction between man and God. With this suggestion, he departs from the rigor of the comprehensive atheism of his mentor, Kojève, as well as from that of Nietzsche, whom he regards as Kojève's most thoughtful antagonist. Kojève and Nietzsche agree that the death of God, or, as Fukuyama puts it, the banishing of religion from the West by liberalism,[26] signals the end of human liberty or distinctiveness.[27]

Fukuyama's response to Lawler's essay, which he understands to be posing the question whether it is possible to have a sense of human dignity without God, is this:

> My answer to Lawler's question is: if the question of man's dependence on God is meant in a practical sense, that is, if he is asking whether a liberal society is sustainable without religion and other pre-modern sources of constraint and community, the answer is probably *no*. If his question is meant in a theoretical sense (i.e., are there other sources of cognition [of human dignity] besides God?), the answer is, *I don't*

---

[25]Lawler, "Fukuyama," 63–79.
[26]Fukuyama, *The End of History*, 217.
[27]Lawler, "Fukuyama," 64.

know. It may be that God is the only possible source for such knowledge; if so, and if God has indeed died, then we are in a lot of trouble and need desperately to find another source on which to base our belief that human beings have dignity. Enlightenment rationalism is not the solution but part of the problem.[28]

The incoherence of the penultimate sentence here is breathtaking. If God is "the only possible source" for knowledge of human dignity, then we cannot find "another source." The trouble is terminal. Fukuyama here escapes only by blatant self-contradiction from agreeing with Kojève and Lawler (as well as with Houellebecq) that the death of God entails an end of history that is also the end of humanity's distinctively human being: human dignity and freedom. Moreover, the desperate search Fukuyama invokes, beyond Enlightenment rationalism, for "another source on which to base our belief that human beings have dignity" must mean the continuance of history.

Fukuyama's thesis about the end of history cannot but raise the question of God, and the ludicrous inadequacy of his response to it reveals that the question of God is the most serious flaw in his whole argument. Is the freedom Fukuyama values, and for the sake of which he values liberal democratic and liberal economic principles, a consequence of the death of God or undermined by it? Fukuyama appears to say both. We must at least conclude that the question of human freedom in the crisis of modernity is inescapably also the question of God.

The crisis of modernity in theological Perspective: Jürgen Moltmann and Ellen Charry

In recent years Jürgen Moltmann has devoted a number of lectures and essays to reflecting on the crisis of modernity that he with so many others identifies.[29] Indeed, one could say that this theme has recently become the most prominent aspect of his "public theology."[30] Moltmann's reflections on this theme are of particular interest in that he is not willing, with some theologians, to

---

[28]F. Fukuyama, "Reflections on *The End of History*, Five Years Later," in Burns, ed., *After History?* 254.

[29]I am referring especially to the essays collected in English in *God for a Secular Society: The Public Relevance of Theology*, trans. M. Kohl (London: SCM Press, 1999). Page numbers in the text that follows refer to this book. Most of these essays were delivered as lectures or first published earlier in the 1990s. Three of the same essays also appear in J. Moltmann, N. Wolterstorff, and E. T. Charry, *A Passion for God's Reign: Theology, Christian Learning, and the Christian Self*, ed. M. Volf (Grand Rapids: Eerdmans, 1998), 1–64.

[30]By this I mean those parts of his work in which he explicitly addresses the relevance of theology to the public life of the contemporary world; cf. J. Moltmann, *Experiences*

accept a complete, postmodern repudiation of the values of modernity, but, on the other hand, he is very far from sharing Fukuyama's optimism about the spread of Western liberal values in the contemporary world. He recognizes the individualism and atomization of Western society, and goes further than Houellebecq is able (given the limitations of the genre in which he writes) in implicating economic liberalism in the destruction of community. Communities are threatened from one side by increasing individualism and from the other by "the global marketing of everything," which, he points out,

> is much more than pure economics. It has become the all-embracing law of life. We have become customers and consumers, whatever else we may be. The market has become the philosophy of life, the world religion, for some people even "the end of history." The marketing of everything destroys community at all levels, because people are weighed up only according to their market value. They are judged by what they can perform or by what they can afford. (153)

What could perhaps be clearer in Moltmann's treatment (though it is not absent: 161) is the intimate connection between the global free market and individualism. Not only does the market destroy community by reducing people to their economic value and subjecting their lives to its imperious needs, which are not those of community. It also, insofar as it treats people as subjects, treats them as acquisitive individuals who must be seduced into wanting more and more. Though these connections cannot be reduced to simple one-way causative relationships, consumerism constitutes a deeply interconnected relationship between increasing individualism and the global free market and, highly significantly for our subject, enables the oppression of the latter to be perceived as liberating. Of course, the most important aspect of this, which we shall notice shortly in Moltmann's treatment, is that it is liberating for the affluent who enjoy consumer choice, while oppressing others whose conditions of life and work make that possible, but even for those who enjoy consumer choice—the vast majority of people in Western societies—the perception of this as liberating masks the way in which the market oppresses also them by its destruction of community.

---

in Theology: Ways and Forms of Christian Theology, trans. M. Kohl (London: SCM Press, 2000), 14–15, 65, 79: "If Christian theology sees itself solely as a function of the church (as, in modern times, Schleiermacher and Barth demanded it should), it must withdraw to its own circle of believers, and can present itself to the public forum of its own society or the world-wide community of the nations only through the church's proclamation and mission. . . . But if Christian theology sees itself as a function of *the kingdom of God*, for which Christ came and for which the church itself is, after all, there, then it must develop as a public theology (*theologia publica*) in public life" (79).

It is characteristic of Moltmann's analysis of modernity and its crisis that he speaks not only, like Houellebecq and Fukuyama, of freedom and individualism but also of domination. The modern period has produced not only modernity and its "progress" but also submodernity, the condition of the victims at whose expense modern "progress" has occurred. For the modern project has been a project of exploitative domination—both the domination of the third world by the West and the domination of nature by humanity. When he asks, "What interests and concerns, and what values, rule our scientific and technological civilization?" the simple answer is "the boundless will towards domination" (97; cf. 15). Both forms of domination create a world situation that cannot be stable; the growing impoverishment of the third world cannot but react in some way against the prosperity of the rich countries, while the finite resources of nature cannot be exploited to meet the ever accelerating standard of living of the affluent without catastrophe (cf. 12–15). This conviction of unstable contradictions within the global economic system grounds Moltmann's dissent from Fukuyama's thesis about the end of history. Even if it is true, as Fukuyama holds, that there are no longer any alternatives to liberal democracy and the global free market, this does not indicate the end of history, so long as there are "challenging contradictions" that "thrust forward to a new solution." If new solutions are not found, the consequence will be, not only the end of history, but the end of humanity (154–55).

Domination is a means of securing the freedom of some at the expense of the freedom of others. As Moltmann has it, domination is one definition of freedom.[31] It connects freedom with the struggle for power and therefore sees it as competitive. Freedom is that of the master who makes others his slaves. But in this way Moltmann not only represents the dark side of modernity, its domination of others, as the correlative of its freedom. He also sees the individualism of European and American democratic societies as stemming from this idea of competitive freedom. In the democratic revolutions the freedom of the feudal lord was democratized. Each one's freedom is his (and, later, her) independence of others; each is related to others only insofar as they are limits on his freedom and he may not encroach on theirs. The result is "individuals in an atomized world" (155–56).[32] Moltmann's next move is not unusual

---

[31]Cf. also N. Lash, *The Beginning and the End of "Religion"* (Cambridge: Cambridge University Press, 1996), 230, on this kind of freedom as "the unquiet individualism that sustains the will to power." Like Moltmann, Lash sees it as the driving force behind the ecological crisis.
[32]Cf. also J. Moltmann, *The Spirit of Life*, trans. M. Kohl (London: SCM Press, 1992), 117–18.

in late twentieth-century theology:[33] in contrast to this notion of freedom as domination or individualism, he commends another definition of freedom: "communicative freedom" or "freedom as free community," according to which mutual respect and friendliness create free relationships between community members. In a shared life, the freedom of each is not bounded by the freedom of others, but is extended in the mutual sharing of love or solidarity (158).[34] Moltmann's distinction here between two types of freedom—individualistic and communicative—is valuable, and a major advantage over the much less discriminating talk of freedom and individualism in both Houellebecq and Fukuyama.

At first sight it may seem that Moltmann is contrasting the typically modern concept of freedom as individual autonomy with an alternative that is less typically modern. But there is an important element in his argument that shows that the notion of communicative freedom as he understands it retains a typically modern character in a basic respect. Moltmann asks how people can resist increasing individualism and live in a more communitarian way. He immediately states that "we cannot revert to the predetermined affiliations of traditional societies." Rather, the way forward is through committing ourselves and keeping promises, such as to engender trust between people (157). In other words, it seems that *freedom of choice* remains basic. Unlike premodern communities, modern or postmodern communities will be formed as people choose relationships and freely commit themselves to them: "The paradigm of a free society is not predetermined membership. The paradigm is the covenant. A free society rests on social consensus" (88). Elsewhere Moltmann has spoken of friendship as in this sense the paradigm of free relationships, in that it is a chosen rather than given relationship. He has also used this model of friendship to characterize the church as a society to which one does not passively belong but actively joins.[35] This model also corresponds with major social trends in urban life, where the given ties of family and neighborhood have been increasingly eroded, while instead people form networks of friends (cf. 85–86).

Whether such a model of free relationships is adequate, however, can be questioned by the observation that it is very easy for people to be left out of

---

[33]Cf., e.g., C. E. Gunton, *Intellect and Action* (Edinburgh: T. & T. Clark, 2000), 101–4, 177–78. But Gunton draws a stronger contrast between the individualistic freedom of Enlightenment liberalism and the relational freedom of Christian theology than, as we shall see, Moltmann does.

[34]Also J. Moltmann, *The Trinity and the Kingdom of God*, trans. M. Kohl (London: SCM Press, 1981), 214–16; Moltmann, *The Spirit*, 118–19.

[35]J. Moltmann, *The Open Church*, trans. M. D. Meeks (London: SCM Press, 1978), chapter 4; J. Moltmann, *The Church in the Power of the Spirit*, trans. M. Kohl (London: SCM Press, 1977), 314–17.

such freely chosen associations. Cases where people have been found dead in their homes weeks after they died illustrate what can happen when no one relates to neighbors, but only to friends. Moltmann seems to accept as axiomatic the modern sense that what is given, predetermined by history or circumstances, is necessarily a constraint on freedom, even when the given is not oppressive in any sense other than that one has not selected it from a choice of options. But this excessive revolt against the given may well, in fact, be a factor in the crisis of modernity, closely allied to egotistical individualism. Recovery of community may require a rediscovery of the ability to find freedom within given relationships and circumstances—to choose, for example, to befriend a person people find hard to like but for whom one accepts a responsibility simply because circumstances put one in the position to do so, or to put up with difficult relatives because they are relatives. While the freedom and commitments of friendship are one important model of relationships, perhaps the parent-child relationship (including the responsibility of adult children for their parents) should remain another model, in which givenness rather than chosenness is constitutive of the relationship without detriment to freedom properly understood. Is it really slavery to recognize obligations to people to whom we have not freely made even implicit promises of commitment? To insist that a person is only truly free when every aspect of life becomes a matter of choice between available alternatives is really to understand freedom as a rejection of finiteness. Arguably this is indeed a strong tendency in the modern ideal of individual freedom. It is revealing to observe Moltmann's thought tending in the same direction.

Aside from this final issue, on which Moltmann aligns himself with a typically modern perception of freedom, his account of modernity as we have so far reported it has been strongly critical. But there is a profound ambiguity in Moltmann's evaluation of modernity. A tension that goes to the heart of his understanding of modernity becomes apparent when we place alongside his claim, already quoted, that the ruling principle of the modern age is "the boundless will towards domination" (97; cf. 15), the following claim: "The first principles and supreme values of the modern world are to be found in *the self-determination of the determining human subject.* . . . [H]uman dignity lies in individual self-determination" (212). These two claims are not simply contradictory, for according to the definition of freedom as domination, "the boundless will towards domination" is the corollary of individual self-determination. They can be seen as two sides of the one coin. From the Enlightenment principle of individual self-determination derive both "the humanitarian ideas of human dignity and the universality of human rights," to which Moltmann passionately asserts there is no alternative except barbarism (17), and the rampant individualism that is destroying community (212–13). It is the apparent tension between individual self-determination and community that, as we have just noticed, Moltmann attempts to overcome by a notion of community formed by individual self-determination in promise and dependability. He evidently treats individual self-determination as an absolute not to be compromised by any concession to a notion of community that might qualify it. In this sense Moltmann remains profoundly modern in his thinking about the self and community.

The ambiguity of the modern principle of individual self-determination appears even more emphatically in an essay entitled "Protestantism: 'The Religion of Freedom'" (191–208).[36] Here Moltmann attributes the origins of modern concepts of freedom to the Protestant Christian tradition: first to the Reformation—whose message of justification by faith alone was a liberating message of freedom from the compulsion to evil, from the law of self-justification, and from fear of death—and then to the German and American Enlightenments (which, unlike the anticlerical and atheistic French Enlightenment, were Protestant in character). While the Reformation produced a relational concept of freedom in relation to the gracious God, the Enlightenment added a subjective concept of freedom of individual choice. Principles of individual freedom concerned in the first place with religion—religious liberty over against the state, liberty of conscience over against the church, and liberty of belief over against the authority of Bible, tradition, or church—became the foundations of liberal democracy. Of course, so bald a sketch of the history of ideas can easily be contested. It ignores, for example, not only the pre-Enlightenment origins of English democracy in the seventeenth century, but also the contributions of English and French deism to American democracy.

However, what is notable is Moltmann's apparent contentment, in this context, with describing the whole development of modernity's understanding of freedom as an authentically Christian one. Here, rather surprisingly, Moltmann seems at home in the nineteenth-century German liberal Protestant view of nineteenth-century German culture as the logical and authentic development of the Reformation. His abstention from critical theological assessment of the theology of the German Enlightenment is apparent in the following: "Protestant subjectivism has led religiously and culturally to all possible kinds of individualism, pluralism and egoism. But it has also brought into modern culture the dignity of every human person, and individual human rights, so that these can never be forgotten" (202–3). But why has it had such mixed consequences? Was there some flaw at the heart of modernity in its origins? Were there more ideological factors at work than "Protestant subjectivism"? By what

---

[36]Cf. also, more briefly, Moltmann, *The Spirit*, 115–16.

theological or other principles can we justify applauding and retaining part of this modern heritage while resisting other aspects?

Most remarkably, in attributing to the Christian tradition both the credit and the blame for the modern notion of individual freedom, with its positive and negative consequences, Moltmann never seems to ask whether an idea such as the dignity and freedom of the individual, originating within a framework of Christian belief, can be expected to remain the same notion when removed from that context and divorced even from belief in God. What, we might ask, becomes of the freedoms of the Enlightenment when they no longer supplement but replace the essentially God-related freedom proclaimed by the Reformers? Moltmann does recognize the loss of God as an aspect of the crisis of modernity (16–17) but never explores the relationship of this to other aspects of that crisis. Arguably Moltmann shares a kind of theological prejudice common to theologians and to opponents of the Christian tradition, that is, a propensity to seek the origins of key features of modernity deep in the Christian tradition rather than in modernity's increasingly self-conscious detachment of itself from that tradition. Another very striking example in this same collection of Moltmann's essays is an argument that traces modern individualism all the way back to Augustine (82–84). So why was community so strong and why is individualism in the modern sense so difficult to discern in precisely the many centuries in which Augustine's influence over Western Christendom was at its height? Such an argument seems entirely to ignore the obvious fact that the individualism of contemporary atomized society emerges just in the period when Christianity's influence in Western society has spectacularly waned. Houellebecq draws the obvious conclusion: atomization is the consequence of the demise of religion. It is extraordinary that Moltmann never seems to notice this possible explanation. This may have something to do with the continuing influence of Bonhoeffer's appraisal of secularity and a determination not to confuse public theology with apologetics. It almost certainly reflects Moltmann's strong consciousness of the fact that often in the modern period an authoritarian church opposed movements of freedom and lent its ideological support to authoritarian political regimes.[37] A Christian critique of the modern understanding of freedom may seem altogether too much like a reversion to this ecclesiastical suppression of freedom.

At this point we may usefully refer to the critique of Moltmann offered by American theologian Ellen Charry.[38] Her essay responds only to one of Moltmann's several essays on this theme, but nevertheless her criticisms and her

---

[37]See Moltmann, *The Spirit*, 107–8.
[38]E. T. Charry, "The Crisis of Modernity and the Christian Self," in Moltmann, Wolterstorff, and Charry, *A Passion*, 88–112. For the background to Charry's argument

alternative approach are significant. Charry understands Moltmann to accept the modern understanding of the self, which she sees as decisively different from the Christian understanding. In its fundamental notion of individual autonomy, the modern understanding of the self does not derive from Christian tradition but is a departure from Christian tradition: "The modern values of individuality, autonomy and freedom that define the modern self may have some distant links to Christian themes, but they now have a life of their own. The secular self is grounded in itself, while the Christian self is grounded in God."[39] The roots of the crisis of modernity lie in this decisive difference: "a certain secular understanding of the self that disagrees with the Christian tradition on just one small point: that we (really) need God."[40] Instead of stressing the Christian tradition's responsibility for the crisis of modernity, as Moltmann does,[41] Christians need to gain a critical distance from modernity by recovering a key insight of their own tradition, precisely the key insight that modernity lost: "we need God."[42]

At stake is a decisively different notion of freedom. The modern understanding of the self assumed that the individual self inherently has all it needs for its own happiness and requires only to be set free from external constraints. It is this supposed self-sufficiency of the modern self that sets it in opposition both to socialization in human community and to dependence on God. These are restrictions from which the self must be free in order to flourish. Charry sums up her narrative of the way this has led to the problems of hyperindividualism in contemporary American society in this way:

> [By] turning from confidence in God to confidence in itself alone, the secular self proves to be quite alone. It is thrown on the world to seek its fortune, without history, without guidance, with scant moral boundaries, and without a framework of meaning within which to interpret failure and suffering. The modern self is discouraged from supporting social and political life, for these necessarily place limits on the self and demand compromise, self-restraint, and even self-sacrifice

---

in this essay, see not only her book, *By the Renewing of Your Minds: The Pastoral Function of Christian Doctrine* (New York/Oxford: Oxford University Press, 1997) but also her article "Reviving Theology in a Time of Change," in M. Volf, C. Krieg, and T. Kucharz, eds., *The Future of Theology*, FS J. Moltmann (Grand Rapids: Eerdmans, 1996), 114–26.

[39]Charry, "The Crisis," 95.

[40]Charry, "The Crisis," 95–96.

[41]Cf. Charry, "The Crisis," 93–94: "Complicity narratives that blame Christianity for modernity's crisis are important, but, I submit, no longer sufficient. . . . Christian self-criticism, wanting to show its strength, is tempted to take responsibility for more than its share of problems."

[42]Charry, "The Crisis," 93.

that are no longer supported by the culture. Freedom, self-sufficiency and an expectation of happiness render it anomic, amoral, asocial, and alone. Having no access to God, sin, and grace, it has only itself to confide in or worry about. Families and bonds of community cannot be sustained on this highly individualistic and morally vacuous basis. This asociality and amorality are, I suggest, the source of the crisis of modern values.[43]

In place of this modern idea of the liberation of the self as mere release from all constraint, Charry proposes "a Christian theological understanding of emancipation that is keyed to transformation," a critical retrieval of the tradition's insights that emancipation is needed "from the unlovely side of the self" and "that the way to emancipation is through self-mastery achieved by attending to God."[44] While the secular self is on its own, the Christian self is formed by intimacy with God within the Christian community with its helps to finding identity in God. Charry is well aware that much of the traditional language of Christian formation—self-denial, humility, self-control, submission to God—is easily associated with the repressive authoritarianism against which Western society is still in reaction and of which the church certainly has been guilty all too often. But her argument that the hyperindividualism of the contemporary West is now in serious overreaction against such authoritarianism coheres with much observation from many quarters, including Houellebecq's satire, exaggerated though it is and as satire must be. The intrinsic tendency to amorality and asociality in contemporary individualism surely does suggest that Moltmann's attempt to accommodate the modern self within a form of community that does not require any qualification of its absolute autonomy is quite insufficient to meet the need. The elements of oppression and repression in the Christian tradition need not prevent a retrieval of the tradition's realistic recognition of the neediness and dependence of the self, its need of ordered and intentional growth and formation, supremely its need of God.

If Charry knew more of Moltmann's work than the essay she discusses, she might find some support for her perspectives. In the chapter on freedom in *The Spirit of Life*,[45] where many of the themes we have already noticed in Moltmann's essays also appear, though without orientation to the current crisis of modernity, Moltmann deplores the false alternative "God or freedom" that has characterized modern thought, propagated by the church's opposition to modern freedoms as well as by the movements of liberation. He asks, "Must belief in God go together with authority, while freedom is made over to athe-

---

[43]Charry, "The Crisis," 104.
[44]Charry, "The Crisis," 93.
[45]Chapter 5: The Liberation for Life.

ism? If these are turned into opposing positions, faith in God is corrupted, because it loses its biblical and messianic foundation; and so is human freedom, because it loses its most vital driving power."[46] However, it is quite unclear whether this means that without God human freedom is distorted in its very nature. He also writes, referring to the exodus and God's continuing presence with the people of Israel in the wilderness, that "God does not merely deliver people from slavery. He remains present among the people, as the foundation of their freedom. In the limited opportunities for developing one's own freedom, to trust in the sustaining foundation of freedom that accompanies us means believing."[47] But here too Moltmann seems to stop short of distinguishing the kind of freedom the Christian self finds in dependence on God from the wholly self-determining autonomy of the modern self. This is also the case even when he devotes the last section of the chapter to "The Experience of Freedom as Experience of God: The Lord Is the Spirit."

Interim conclusions

What is quite clear is that the history of freedom in the modern period is double-edged. On the one hand, there is the affirmation of individual human dignity, the foundation of democracy in the equal right to freedom of all individuals, and the fundamental freedoms of individuals over against the powers of state and church. Moltmann is correct that the struggles for such freedoms are far from complete and that in fact the growing economic domination of the third world by the first requires a new chapter in the history of the liberation of all from oppressive rule and oppressive circumstance.

On the other hand, the Enlightenment belief in the wholly self-sufficient and self-determining self has led to the asocial, amoral, and isolated individual of contemporary atomized society in the West, portrayed so contemptuously by Houellebecq and characterized more analytically by Charry. It is striking that all four of the authors we have discussed converge on the contradiction between this hyperindividualism and community, while all except Moltmann also connect it with the demise of religion or the rejection of God. It is also noteworthy that this individualism itself threatens the positive values of modern freedom. Consumerism is one, if not the only vehicle of egotistical individualism, as well as being integral to the global economic system of domination.

We can usefully relate Charry's argument to Moltmann's by seeing it as bringing to light a further implication of the false understanding of freedom

---

[46]Moltmann, *The Spirit*, 109.
[47]Moltmann, *The Spirit*, 113.

as domination. In Moltmann's argument this is exemplified in the two major contemporary forms: the West's economic domination of the third world and humanity's technological domination of nature. Charry adds that the modern understanding of the self as wholly self-determining has led to the postmodern reduction of the self to the will to power. Freedom as self-liberation from every last vestige of constraint and as the freedom to construct one's life and one's self wholly according to choice is another form of freedom as domination.

How is it that the modern age has bequeathed both the idea of the inherent dignity of the human individual, entailing the right to freedom *from* domination, and also its contradiction, freedom *as* domination? It must be that respect for the dignity and freedom of the individual requires a context of other convictions and beliefs without which the right to self-determination degenerates into the banal pursuit of self-gratification or the cynical pursuit of power. It may be as simple as Charry puts it: human beings need God. If it is adequately to address the problematic of freedom in the twenty-first century, the church in its conversation with the secular world certainly must not be hesitant at the same time to address the question of God. That means, of course, not only whether there is God, but what sort of God there is.

Freedom in the Trinitarian love of God

Is God the problem or the solution, the enemy or the source of truly human freedom? We have suggested that without a transcendent source and ground, human freedom degenerates into egotistical hedonism and the will to power, new forms of servitude and domination. But much of the modern world has proceeded on the opposite conviction, that true freedom entails emancipation from God. The atheist philosopher Bertrand Russell said that the idea of God is "a conception derived from ancient Oriental despotisms . . . , quite unworthy of free men,"[48] while according to Ernst Bloch, also an atheist but much more sympathetic to biblical religion, "[W]here the great lord of the world reigns, there is no room for liberty, not even the liberty of the children of God."[49] These quotations make it obvious enough where the problem has been held to lie: in the political analogy. The modern age has characteristically sought liberation from absolute rulers and totalitarian regimes. God as the absolute ruler of the whole creation could easily seem the greatest oppressor of all. Moreover, earthly rulers had often enough legitimated their abso-

---

[48]Quoted in J. McLelland, *Prometheus Rebound: The Irony of Atheism* (Waterloo, Ont.: Wilfrid Laurier University Press, 1988), 5.
[49]Quoted in Moltmann, *The Spirit*, 105.

lutism by claiming divine right to rule: theirs was the earthly reflection and form of the cosmic monarchy of God. For full realization of human freedom, therefore, the yoke of God must be once and for all thrown off. Yet, as the writers we have called in evidence in this chapter testify, in some respects at least the expected liberation of humanity has turned out to be a degradation of humanity. Perhaps it is now not God but the death of God that threatens human freedom.

Emancipation from God has been to a large extent achieved in the secular West, and it is now freedom that is the problem—the problem for community, the problem for any kind of human good other than sheer self-determination. The right of every individual to absolute self-determination is becoming the idol for which all else may be sacrificed and, like all idols, a form of enslavement. It may be time to seek once again a freedom grounded in God and formed in relationship to God rather than a freedom won from rejection of God and impelled by the desire to replace God. But then we must confront again the issue raised by our quotations from Russell and Bloch: what of the parallel between the divine rule and human autocracy? If the latter contradicts human freedom, why should the former not also do so and on a greater scale? Theologians sensitive to this issue, including Moltmann,[50] Leonardo Boff[51] and Paul Fiddes,[52] have sought to address it by distinguishing sharply between monarchical images of the one God, on the one hand, and the Christian understanding of God as Trinity, on the other.

The former is what Moltmann calls simply "monotheism" and Boff "a-trinitarian monotheism" (English in fact has a more satisfactory term: unitarianism). Whether this is pure unitarianism or, as in much of the Christian tradition, a prioritization of divine unity over Trinitarian differentiation in God, it is said to be closely allied with the monarchical image of God as the single supreme ruler of all things. In this view, as Boff summarizes it, God

> is the supreme authority of the universe, from whom all other religious and civil authorities derive, in descending order of hierarchy. As there is only one eternal authority, so the tendency to have only one authority in each sphere of the world is confirmed: a single political

---

[50]Moltmann, *The Trinity*, chapter 6.

[51]L. Boff, *Trinity and Society*, trans. P. Burns (Tunbridge Wells: Burns & Oates/New York: Orbis, 1988).

[52]P. Fiddes, *Participating in God: A Pastoral Doctrine of the Trinity* (London: Darton, Longman & Todd, 2000), chaps. 2–3. His understanding of the Trinity differs from the "social Trinity" of Moltmann and Boff, in that, whereas for the latter the Trinitarian persons are subjects or agents constituted by their mutual relationships, for Fiddes they simply are the relationships. But in many other respects his argument about God and domination runs parallel to theirs.

leader, a single military chief, a single social leader, a single religious head, a single guardian of the truth, and so on. God is presented as the great universal Superego, alone and unique. Much of the atheism of developed societies today is no more than a denial of this sort of authoritarian God and of the patriarchal sort of religion that follows from it and obstructs the development of human freedoms.[53]

The freedom of this God is evidently the individualistic freedom of the master who is free at the expense of his slaves. By contrast, when the understanding of God as Trinity is taken fully seriously, God is seen as a nonhierarchical fellowship or community of interdependent Persons, whose freedom is constituted by their loving relationships. Here there is no rule or subordination, only freedom in mutuality. Plainly this differs not only from the model of monarchical domination, against which it is alleged the modern age revolted, but also from the hyperindividualism into which freedom has degenerated in the contemporary crisis of modernity. It points beyond the incompatibility of freedom and community that has been a major focus of this chapter.

These theologians largely banish all talk of rule, sovereignty, lordship, obedience, and service from their accounts of the relationship between God and humans, with scant recognition of the profusion of such terms in both Old and New Testaments. But Moltmann (as the title of his book indicates: *The Trinity and the Kingdom of God*) takes seriously the need to relate the Trinity to the biblical notion of God's rule. He sees it as an issue of which serves to define the other. In the doctrine of divine monarchy, the kingdom of God is given priority over the Trinity. God is defined as lordship rather than, as the social Trinity requires, as love. Taking the Trinity fully seriously means that, because God's being is an open fellowship of love, God also relates to the world in love, both acting and suffering in love for the world. It is not, after all, just a matter of numbers:[54] a divine oligarchy of three could presumably be as oppressive as the solitary one of monotheism. Rather, the loving fellowship of the Trinity is who God is and therefore defines the way God relates to the world. Thus, if the Trinity is given priority over the notion of God's kingdom, God's rule must be defined as the rule of love, which is compatible with freedom, indeed—as it is within God—constitutive of freedom.

Precisely how the Trinity relates to human freedom is somewhat confused in Moltmann and Boff, since they speak both of the Trinity as a model for the kind of society human society should be and also of the Trinity as an interpersonal fellowship into which humans are drawn by grace and in which they

---

[53]Boff, *Trinity*, 169.
[54]It is not clear to me why God as "one person" *must* be "a dominating subject" (Fiddes, *Participating*, 78).

participate. I have criticized elsewhere Moltmann's attempt to combine these two notions, suggesting that the former, the Trinity as an external model to which human society should conform itself, should be dropped.[55] This is now also Fiddes's view: "the point of trinitarian language is not to provide us an example to copy, but to draw us into participation in God, out of which human life can be transformed."[56] Probably the main reason Moltmann and Boff use the concept of model in this connection is that they feel the need to replace one model, the monarchical God whose domination is replicated by his earthly deputy, with another model.[57] They also appeal to the creation of humanity "in the image and likeness" of God, arguing that in the light of the Trinity this image is not individualistic but social.

The argument assumes that God does and should provide a model for human society. Differing concepts of God correspond to different political and social forms in human society, either oppressive or liberating. (It is unclear whether, according to Moltmann and others who follow this argument, the concepts of God cause or reflect different forms of society. Perhaps this differs between the two models.) But this is certainly too simple a view. It is worth observing that the two models are not strictly parallel in this sense: it is only the human ruler, not his or her subjects, who copies the monarchical God. But, although this has undoubtedly happened in many historical instances, it is not a necessary consequence of the monarchical image of God. As we noticed in some detail in chapter 6, there is an important strand in the biblical traditions, not without its impact in Christian history, that draws quite a different consequence: that under God's rule all are equally God's subjects and none should claim privilege or hierarchical status above others. Because absolute rule belongs to God alone, it is precisely not a model for human imitation. Acknowledging it can indeed be significantly liberating in that it relativizes all human authority. Those who acknowledge only the one lordship of God are inwardly free of the claims of human tyrannies, recognizing them as the idolatrous, self-deifying projects they are.[58]

The simple contrast between "a-trinitarian monotheism" as crushing human freedom and Trinitarian faith as fostering human freedom cannot do justice to the Old Testament (not to mention Judaism, Islam, and other monotheistic faiths). There is a sense in which Moltmann is correct to argue

---

[55]R. Bauckham, *The Theology of Jürgen Moltmann* (Edinburgh: T. & T. Clark, 1995), 176–79.
[56]Fiddes, *Participating*, 66.
[57]Cf. Boff, *Trinity*, 120: "The domination model is replaced by the communion model: production by invitation, conquest by participation."
[58]Cf. Moltmann, *The Trinity*, 219.

that the rule of God should be defined in the light of the Trinity, rather than vice versa, since in the latter case the image of God's rule all too easily becomes a projection and justification of human aspirations to autocratic empire. But it would be better to say that the meaning of God's rule is defined by the biblical story of it, which from a Christian theological perspective is, in Moltmann's terms, "the trinitarian history of God," but not yet explicitly so in the Old Testament. But already in the exodus it is clear that God's rule is qualitatively quite different from Pharaoh's. As Moltmann himself says of Israel in Egypt on the eve of the exodus, "The expression 'the Lord' is none other than the assurance of freedom for the enslaved people. It has nothing to do with the lords who are enslaving them, and nothing to do with male domination either."[59] The exodus was liberating, even though (or we might say on further reflection, actually because) it was not a liberation of Israel from any rule at all, but liberation from Pharaoh's oppression to the service of YHWH. The New Testament makes the same kind of point more explicitly when it speaks of Jesus Christ as the one who redeems people from slavery to sin and treats their resulting condition paradoxically both as freedom from slavery and as enslavement to the new master who has bought them, the Lord Jesus. The divine lordship, unlike any human lordship, is the condition of true freedom.

This paradox should make us aware that *transcendence* is of more importance in the use of this kind of language about God than the simple talk of divine monarchy as a model for human rule recognizes. The paradox that "God's service is perfect freedom" (*Book of Common Prayer*, cf. 1 Pet. 2:16) can be true only because there are ways in which the relation of God to humans is not really comparable at all with any relations between humans. This paradox belongs with the claim that God's rule is unique and *rules out* anything comparable among people. God's rule is different precisely because it coincides with human freedom, and human obedience to God is unlike obedience to any human authority precisely because it is fully compatible with human freedom. Both sides of these paradoxes are necessary to prevent us from imagining that truly human freedom is attainable in pursuit of our own will rather than God's.

It is a happy accident that in contemporary English the use of the word *Lord* for God or Christ has virtually lost any direct association with human lordship. In Britain nonreligious use of the word is virtually confined to the lords who until recently composed the House of Lords, but it is unlikely that anyone who uses the word *Lord* in prayer supposes that they are comparing God or Christ with this antiquated aspect of English social structures. Despite (or because of?) its lack of nonreligious reference, *Lord* remains very popular as an

---

[59]J. Moltmann, *Experiences in Theology*, trans. M. Kohl (London: SCM Press, 2000), 34.

address to God in the extemporary prayers of ordinary Christians, as well as in liturgy that has not been deliberately purged of the word. It has become a purely religious term, whose meaning people learn, not from the world, but solely from the Bible and liturgy. As such, it is not in the least likely to promote or support hierarchical relationships between humans. It has become a term that evokes just that uniqueness of the relationship between God and humans that makes obedience and service to *this* Lord uniquely liberating. In contexts where address to God as *Father* evokes human patriarchal oppression for some, we might well use *Abba* to similar effect, as a word whose meaning we only know from the way Jesus portrays his Abba and his relationship to his Abba in the Gospels.

We must return to the argument of Moltmann and others that the monarchical image of God must be replaced by the social Trinitarian image as the divine model for human society. The argument seems to depend on a kind of narrative of the origins of the modern rejection of God as inimical to human freedom: (1) there was a mistaken view of God in the Christian tradition: an effectively non-Trinitarian God whose freedom is domination; (2) this was the model for a corresponding domination in human society: the monarch is free at the expense of his subjects; (3) for the sake of human freedom not only human autocracy but also God had to be rejected. One may add that (4) the concept of freedom as domination was democratized in modern individualism, which makes each individual his or her own master in independence of others, like the monarchical God. The argument is then for reconceiving God, in a Trinitarian way, such that this view of divine freedom in nonhierarchical mutuality of relationships provides a better model for human freedom. However, what the argument crucially misses is that there was a mistake involved in the very idea of modeling human freedom on divine freedom. This (as we have seen in chapters 2 and 7) occurred at the Renaissance, when the humanists for the first time claimed for humanity the unlimited freedom of God. Instead of the view that truly human freedom is *unlike* God's in being finite, it came to be thought that humanity should aspire to the unrestricted freedom of God, the freedom of the one who is not created but self-constituting, who is not dependent but self-subsistent, whose freedom is his inherent nature, not received or conditioned by others or by circumstances. It was not necessarily mistaken to think of God's freedom in this way (though it would be if this divine freedom were abstracted from God's love); it was mistaken to model human freedom on it. The mistake was perpetuated, perhaps exacerbated, as Western humanity steadily replaced God in the prevalent worldview. The understanding of properly human limitation as a created good for human creatures, which within the tradition of Christian belief was readily accessible in the acknowledgment of the *contrast* between the Creator and the creature, waned as consciousness of God truly as God waned in the Western cultural tradition.

Treating God as a model for human freedom runs the alternative risks either of promoting an aspiration to unlimited freedom that has proved ultimately destructive and dehumanizing or of reducing the transcendent otherness of the divine freedom to something humanly imitable. The way to respect the difference between the unrestricted, sovereign (!) freedom of God and the limited, creaturely freedom that is properly human is to realize that humans become truly free, in an appropriately human way, not by copying God but in relationship to God. Of the two ideas that Moltmann and Boff combine, the means really to break out of the modern problematic of God and freedom is to be found, not in the modeling of human freedom on the Trinity, but in the participation of humans in the life of the Trinity. This is the truly Christian alternative to modernity's metanarrative of freedom. The biblical narrative, from the incarnation onwards an unambiguously Trinitarian one, is the context in which Christian freedom is constituted and formed, as Christians, within the human community of the church, are drawn into the field of Trinitarian relationships. They do so as the Spirit enables them to share Jesus' relationship to the one he called Abba. They experience God in a threefold way, in a highly differentiated relationship to the three divine Persons: to Jesus as God become our fellow human, brother, and friend; to God the Father as the one on whom Jesus was wholly dependent and whom he obeyed in love; and to the Holy Spirit as indwelling life and the power of God-related personhood. We cannot stand outside these specific and differentiated relationships in which we know the Trinitarian God and view the Trinity as a model of community to imitate. We become a truly human community not in copying but in relationship to the divine persons, as the Spirit makes us like Jesus in his community with the Father and with others. We gain and grow in freedom within this specific field of relationships that form the Christian relationship to God the Trinity.

This means we need to think about our freedom, given and formed in relationship to God, as constituted by three poles, which are the way we relate to each of the divine persons. Each of these three necessarily interconnected relationships is a facet of our freedom, and, just as our relationship to God requires the differentiated threefold structure of relationship to each person, so an adequate understanding of our freedom requires account to be taken of all three facets. But before proceeding to these, it is worth noticing something about the properly limited and human nature of the freedom we find in this way. We can observe in human life, without making reference to God, that genuine freedom—as opposed to the freedom imagined by hyperindividualism—is not self-constituting and independent of anything outside itself but is constituted and formed in human relationships and in concrete situations.[60] Similarly, in our account of the profounder level of the formation of freedom in relation to God, human freedom is relational and is situated within the narrative of God's Trinitarian love for the world. It is not an inherent property but an experience of growing into freedom in relationship to God. It is not a matter of mere emancipation from external constraints, like the degenerate freedom of the contemporary West, but a process of formation of the self in relationship. And while this freedom is limited, its limitation is not experienced as an evil but as the creaturely condition for relationship with the infinite God.

Moltmann, developing in his own way the Trinitarian schema of history advanced by Joachim of Fiore, offers a way of thinking of three dimensions of freedom in relation to each of the divine persons.[61] I have explained elsewhere why I find this scheme inadequate. It corresponds very poorly to the ways the New Testament speaks of relationship to each of the three persons.[62] Boff has three chapters of much more detailed and nuanced discussion: on the Father as "Origin and Goal of All Liberation," the Son as "Mediator of Integral Liberation," and the Spirit as "Driving Force of Integral Liberation."[63] My own comments here are necessarily much briefer. Their starting point is the set of metaphors that portray our threefold relationship to God as knowing God in three spatial directions: God above us (the Father), God alongside us (Jesus, the Son) and God within us (the Spirit).[64] In briefest summary, the dynamic of freedom in this threefold relationship to God is this: In relation to God the Father, we know God as authority to command in a relationship of loving belonging. In relation to God the Son, Jesus Christ, we know God as loving solidarity, the fellow human who befriends us. In relation to God the Spirit, we know God as the spontaneity of love in which we make God's will our own. These are the three poles of Christian freedom, which develops in all three dimensions at once. Only such a Trinitarian unfolding of the Christian experience and practice of freedom in relation to God is sufficiently complex to avoid the false problematics of contradiction between God and human freedom and to show, on the contrary, that it is relationship with God that enables truly human freedom. The fact that the threefold structure is both the structure of human freedom in God and also the structure of God's love for us

---

[60]On "situated freedom" see J. Webster, *Barth's Moral Theology* (Edinburgh: T. & T. Clark, 1998), 122–23, following Charles Taylor.
[61]Moltmann, *The Trinity*, 219–22.
[62]Bauckham, *The Theology*, 179–81.
[63]Boff, *Trinity*, chapters 9–11.
[64]Cf. Boff, *Trinity*, 149, where he describes the directions as (1) backwards and upwards, (2) outwards, (3) inwards.

excludes the domination that eliminates freedom. ("For love means a union which does not absorb the other but sets him free to be himself and thus brings him to fulfillment."[65]) But the fact that God's love has *this* structure excludes also the merely paternalistic care that inhibits freedom.

God the Father is the Abba of Jesus, the one Christians know only through entering Jesus' own relationship with his divine Father: "God has sent the Spirit of his Son into our hearts, crying, 'Abba! Father!' So you are no longer a slave but a child" (Gal. 4:6–7; cf. Rom. 8:15–16). Thus the Christian meaning of God's fatherhood is defined by the Gospel accounts of Jesus' relationship to God his Father, not by any other source. Jesus' own freedom in relation to his Father combines (1) obedience to the Father's authority ("I have come . . . not to do my own will, but the will of him who sent me" [John 6:38]) to the point of radical self-abnegation ("yet, not what I want, but what you want" [Mark 14:36]); (2) radical dependence on the Father, who authorizes his unique mission ("I do nothing on my own, but I speak these things as the Father instructed me" [John 8:28]); (3) the highest degree of loving intimacy ("you, Father, are in me and I am in you" [John 17:21]). We shall elaborate a little on each of these three: obedience, dependence, and intimacy:

(1) Throughout Jesus' teaching it is clear that God is the one who commands (Jesus takes the Torah with complete seriousness) with the authority of grace[66] and that human fulfillment lies in the loving devotion of the whole self to the service of God (e.g., Luke 10:27–28). This is liberation from the idols (including the false human self) whose claim to human devotion demeans and distorts human life because they do not provide an adequate object of human devotion. (2) Throughout Jesus' teaching it is clear that God is the Creator of all things, the loving source of all and the loving provider for all (e.g., Matt. 5:45; 6:25–34; 7:7–11). The correlative is human dependence on God the Father, acknowledged and appropriated in prayerful and confident trust. This is liberation from the unrealizable and destructive compulsion to total control over one's life and the impossible and dehumanizing dream of being the self-constituting creator of oneself. Dependence on God is not acquiescence in being dominated,[67] because it is the ultimately total dependence of all created things on the Creator, in which all creaturely activity is grounded and properly creaturely independence rooted. The grace of creation and the grace of redemption are not the subjection of the creature, but the liberation and empowerment of the creature. (3) Finally, the loving intimacy with the Father

---

[65]W. Kasper, *The God of Jesus Christ*, trans. M. J. O'Connell (London: SCM Press, 1984), 45.
[66]On God's authority as the authority of grace, see chapter 3.
[67]On this, see Fiddes, *Participating*, 106–8.

that Jesus shares with his disciples is the source of freedom with belonging, the fulfillment of the two human needs, to be free and to belong, that the false freedom of contemporary hyperindividualism has forced into opposition. This is what takes the relationship with God the Father beyond the image of servants to a king or master and into the figuring of family relationships: "The slave does not have a permanent place in the household; the son has a place there forever. So if the Son makes you free, you will be free indeed" (John 8:35–36). This is the freedom of security in belonging, not an image of childishness but of the adult appropriation of lasting and binding ties. It is liberation from the adolescent quest to secure one's independence from everything and everyone that might tie one down.

In a common New Testament metaphor Jesus is the Lord whom Christians serve as his servants or slaves. He is Lord because he exercises the divine lordship over the world and because he has brought his people from slavery to sin so that they may serve him as his own. Yet, in the paradox we have already discussed above, it is "for freedom" that "he has set us free" (Gal. 5:1). Moreover, just as, in relation to God the Father, mere servanthood is subsumed into the relationship of son or daughter, so, in relationship to Jesus, mere servanthood is subsumed into friendship: "I do not call you servants any longer, because the servant does not know what the master is doing; but I have called you friends, because I have made known to you everything that I have heard from my Father" (John 15:15). Only here and in the accusation that Jesus was "a friend of tax collectors and sinners" (Matt. 11:19) does the New Testament speak of the friendship of Jesus, but it is an apt image for the loving solidarity with humans, carried to the furthest possible extreme (John 15:13), that God expresses and enacts in the incarnation of the Son.[68] Friendship is not a relationship given by birth but must be freely entered. It cannot be coerced but only given and received in freedom. It is a relationship of unconditional acceptance that enables freedom. In Jesus who comes alongside us as one of us, who espouses the cause and opts to share the plight even of the most wretched, and who takes his disciples into his confidence, sharing with them his intimate knowledge of the Father, there is a kenosis in which God transcends his otherness in order to be befriend us.

"[W]here the Spirit of the Lord is, there is freedom," writes Paul (2 Cor. 3:17). To God the Holy Spirit we relate in ways for which human interpersonal relationships do not provide helpful analogies, as they do for our relationships to God the Father and to Jesus Christ. The Spirit therefore has a

---

[68]On Jesus as friend, see J. Moltmann, *The Church in the Power of the Spirit*, trans. M. Kohl (London: SCM Press, 1977), 114–21.

special relevance to the issue of human freedom in relationship with God, suggesting that even the analogies that the experience of freedom in human personal relationships provide are not adequate to the unique case of freedom in
relation to the God who is the source of all freedom. The Spirit in us is God's
transformative involvement in human volition and action, thought and feeling, enlightening and enabling, liberating from inner compulsions and making possible the growth in freedom that takes place in the constant
appropriation and practice of freedom in concrete relationships and circumstances. The mystery of the Spirit's activity is that this divine presence at the
center of human personhood does not reduce personal freedom but enables
the free spontaneity of those who embrace God's will as their own. As Thomas
Aquinas put it:

> The free man is the one who belongs to himself; the slave, however,
> belongs to his master. Whoever acts spontaneously therefore acts
> freely, but whoever receives his impulse from another does not act
> freely. The man who avoids evil, not because it is an evil, but because
> of a law of the Lord's, is therefore not free. On the other hand, the
> man who avoids evil because it is an evil is free. It is here that the Holy
> Spirit works, inwardly perfecting our spirit by communicating to it a
> new dynamism, and this functions so well that man refrains from evil
> through love, as though divine law were ordering him to do this. He
> is therefore free not because he is not subject to divine law, but because
> his inner dynamism leads him to do what divine law prescribes.[69]

It is the activity of the Spirit that transcends the alternative of autonomy and
heteronomy by actualizing in our personal existence the truth that God's law
is not the will of another, in the ordinary sense in which this would be true of
the will of another creature, but, as the law of the Creator and his creation,
also the law of our own being, in conforming to which we become most truly
ourselves.[70]

This account of Christian freedom in relationship to the three divine Persons is not intended to be read individualistically, as though it were a matter
only of the individual in relation to God. On the contrary, it is of the greatest
importance that these three forms of relationship are experienced by the indi-

---

[69]Thomas Aquinas, In 2 Cor. c.3, lect. 3, quoted in Y. M. J. Congar, *I Believe in the Holy
Spirit*, trans. D. Smith (New York: Seabury/London: G. Chapman, 1983), 2:125.
[70]On autonomy, heteronomy, and theonomy, see P. Tillich, *Systematic Theology* (London: SCM Press, 1978), 1:83–86. When she claims that relationship to the Christian
God is necessarily purely heteronomous, Daphne Hampson neglects both the doctrine
of the Holy Spirit and the possibility of theonomy as a category transcending the
dichotomy between autonomy and heteronomy: "On Autonomy and Heteronomy," in
D. Hampson, ed., *Swallowing a Fishbone* (London: SPCK, 1996), 1–16.

vidual not only in direct relationship to God but also as mediated by others and in mediating them to others. When freedom is given us by others in liberating relationships, this is not a source of freedom additional to or independent of God's giving of freedom, but a mediation of God's own giving of freedom. But this is not true of the three relationships in the same way. Humans cannot, as it were, stand in for God the Father or for God the Holy Spirit, but they can in a certain sense "be Christ" to others.[71] Liberated in the relationship to God that is characterized by the three distinctive facets of knowing the Father, the Son, and the Holy Spirit, Christians mediate this freedom to each other and to others not by way of the commanding authority that is the uniquely divine prerogative (Matt. 23:9), nor by way of the indwelling presence in the personhood of others that is a uniquely divine possibility, but by way of the loving solidarity or open friendship that is God's incarnate way of enabling freedom. If the freedom for which Jesus Christ has set us free is to prove itself the way forward in the crisis of modernity, there must be Christian communities that live within the field of freedom created by the Trinitarian love of God and who practice this freedom in the world.

---

[71]Cf. Martin Luther, *Christian Liberty*, ed. H. J. Grimm (Philadelphia: Fortress, 1957), 30–31: "Hence, as our heavenly Father has in Christ freely come to our aid, we also ought freely to help our neighbor through our body and its works, and each one should become as it were a Christ to the other that we may be Christs to one another and Christ may be the same in all, that is, that we may be truly Christians."

Epilogue

Freedom in Fragments

The human race is not yet free.
Ben Okri[1]

⊸⊷⊷⊷⊷⊶

The Christian Gospel is an offer of freedom which is often accused of being the opposite.
Colin Gunton[2]

⊸⊷⊷⊷⊷⊶

Work brings freedom.
Sign over the entrance to Auschwitz

⊸⊷⊷⊷⊷⊶

Genuine freedom is not subjective arbitrariness, but freedom from the motivation of the moment.
Rudolf Bultmann[3]

⊸⊷⊷⊷⊷⊶

We too easily assume that we *are* our real selves, and that our choices are really the ones we want to make when, in fact, our acts of

---

[1]B. Okri, *A Way of Being Free* (London: Phoenix, 1998), 61.
[2]C. E. Gunton, *Intellect and Action* (Edinburgh: T. & T. Clark, 2000), viii.
[3]Quoted in C. E. Gunton, *Enlightenment and Alienation* (Basingstoke: Marshall, Morgan & Scott, 1985), 92.

210

free choice are . . . largely dictated by psychological compulsions,
flowing from our inordinate ideas of our own importance. Our
choices are too often dictated by our false selves.
  Thomas Merton[4]

❦❦❦❦❦

"Autonomy" should not mean freedom to choose (and so to obtain?)
whatever one wills, but responsibility for what one chooses.
  Joseph McLelland[5]

❦❦❦❦❦

A free will is the same thing as a will that conforms to moral law.
  Immanuel Kant[6]

❦❦❦❦❦

Autonomy implies the interiority of the law, a condition which, for
human agents at least, is not native, but has to be achieved through
arduous progress. Rebels hate the sacrifice that the interiorization of
the law requires.
  Yves Simon[7]

❦❦❦❦❦

The double fight against an empty autonomy and a destructive heteronomy makes the quest for a new theonomy as urgent today as it
was at the end of the ancient world. The catastrophe of autonomous
reason is complete. Neither autonomy nor heteronomy, isolated and
in conflict, can give the answer.
  Paul Tillich[8]

❦❦❦❦❦

The opposite of freedom is not necessity, but guilt.
  Søren Kierkegaard[9]

❦❦❦❦❦

---

[4]T. Merton, *No Man Is an Island* (London: Hollis & Carter, 1955), 20–21.
[5]J. McLelland, *Prometheus Rebound: The Irony of Atheism* (Waterloo: Wilfrid Laurier
University Press, 1988), 279.
[6]Quoted in McLelland, *Prometheus*, 102.
[7]Y. R. Simon, *A General Theory of Authority* (Notre Dame/London: University of Notre
Dame Press, 1962), 79.
[8]P. Tillich, *Systematic Theology* (London: SCM Press, 1978 [first published 1951]), 1:86.
[9]C. E. Moore, ed., *Provocations: Spiritual Writings of Kierkegaard* (Farmington/Roberts-
bridge: Plough Publishing House, 1999), 291.

It is the central attribute and paradox of the classic that its commandments are liberating. The core of response, of reaction, is one
of compelled freedom.
  George Steiner[10]

❧❧❧❧❧

Human freedom is the God-given freedom to obey.
  Karl Barth[11]

❧❧❧❧❧

Freedom without opportunity is a devil's gift.
  Noam Chomsky[12]

❧❧❧❧❧

Freedom is a distinctively Western concept. In Japanese, for example, the best translation of the word "freedom" is *jiyu* which had previously meant licentiousness.
  Geoff Mulgan[13]

❧❧❧❧❧

I have become entangled in my own data and my conclusions
directly contradict my original premises. I started out with the idea
of unrestricted freedom and I have arrived at unrestricted despotism.
  Shigalov in Fyodor Dostoevsky's The Possessed[14]

❧❧❧❧❧

Marx has laid his finger on the sore spot of modern industrial society . . . that is the growth of economic institutions into a power of
such overwhelming influence on the life of every single man, that
in the face of such power all talk about human freedom becomes
futile.
  Eric Voegelin[15]

❧❧❧❧❧

---

[10]G. Steiner, *Errata: An Examined Life* (London: Weidenfeld & Nicolson, 1997), 25.
[11]K. Barth, *The Humanity of God*, trans. J. N. Thomas and T. Wieser (London: Collins, 1961), 82.
[12]Quoted in N. Klein, *No Logo* (London: Flamingo, 2000), 185.
[13]G. Mulgan, *Connexity: Responsibility, Freedom, Business and Power in the New Century* (London: Vintage, 1998), 53.
[14]Quoted in O. Guinness, *The Dust of Death* (London: InterVarsity Press, 1973), 23.
[15]Quoted in D. Walsh, *After Ideology: Recovering the Spiritual Foundations of Freedom* (San Francisco: HarperCollins, 1990), 57.

Only through discipline may a man learn to be free.
   Dietrich Bonhoeffer[16]

⥽⋅⥽⋅⥽⋅⥽⋅⥽

Nothing's free when it is explained.
   Les Murray[17]

⥽⋅⥽⋅⥽⋅⥽⋅⥽

Seeking to "free" sexual love from its old communal restraints, we
have "freed" it also from its meaning, its responsibility, and its exaltation. And we have made it more dangerous. . . . We are now living
in a sexual atmosphere so polluted and embittered that women must
look on virtually any man as a potential assailant, and a man must
look on virtually any woman as a potential accuser.
   Wendell Berry[18]

⥽⋅⥽⋅⥽⋅⥽⋅⥽

We philosophers and "free spirits" in fact feel at the news that the "old
God is dead" as if illumined by a new dawn; our heart overflows with
gratitude, astonishment, presentiment, expectation—at last the hori-
zon seems to us again free, even if it is not bright, at last our ships can
put out again, no matter what the danger. . . , the sea, *our* sea again lies
open before us, perhaps there has never yet been such an "open sea."
   Friedrich Nietzsche[19]

⥽⋅⥽⋅⥽⋅⥽⋅⥽

Your God is only your faith in him, your values are only your commitment to them. That is liberation. You're free.
   Don Cupitt[20]

⥽⋅⥽⋅⥽⋅⥽⋅⥽

The ordinary person does not, unless corrupted by philosophy,
believe that he creates values by his choices.
   Iris Murdoch[21]

---

[16]D. Bonhoeffer, *Letters and Papers from Prison*, trans. R. Fuller, F. Clarke, J. Bowden,
et al., revised ed. (London: SCM Press, 1971), 371. The quotation is from Bonhoeffer's poem "Stations on the Road to Freedom," in which the four stations are discipline,
action, suffering, and death.
[17]"Ariel," in L. Murray, *Collected Poems* (Manchester: Carcanet, 1988), 342.
[18]W. Berry, *Sex, Economy, Freedom and Community* (New York: Random House, 1993),
142.
[19]R. J. Hollingdale, ed., *A Nietzsche Reader* (London: Penguin, 1977), 209–10.
[20]Quoted in G. Loughlin, *Telling God's Story: Bible, Church and Narrative Theology*
(Cambridge: Cambridge University Press, 1996), 25.
[21]I. Murdoch, *The Sovereignty of the Good* (London: Routledge, 1991 [first published
1970]), 97.

There are any number of signs showing that the men of our age
have now for a long time been starved of obedience. But advantage
has been taken of the fact to give them slavery.
  Simone Weil[22]

At the opposite pole of being compelled by destiny or nature or men
there does not stand being free of destiny or nature or men but to
commune and to covenant with them. To do this, it is true that one
must first have become independent; but this independence is a
foot-bridge, not a dwelling-place. Freedom is the vibrating needle,
the fruitful zero.
  Martin Buber[23]

I have not brought my being into being. Nor was I thrown into
being. My being is obeying the saying "Let there be!" Commandment and expectation lie dormant in the recesses of being and come
to light in the consciousness of being human. What Adam hears first
is a command.
  Abraham Heschel[24]

Faith is free. But its freedom does not consist in its being the unco-
erced choice of a neutral will (i.e., one standing apart from God),
which it could have made otherwise. Faith is free because it is joy in
God, which enlarges and intensifies who one really is and can be, in
relation to the dynamics through which God is who God is. Freedom is being freed for God through the spirit of faith which drives
to worship.
  Alistair McFadyen[25]

Freedom for the pike is death for the minnows.
  R. H. Tawney[26]

---

[22]S. Weil, *The Need for Roots*, trans. A. F. Wills (London: Routledge, 1987), 14.
[23]M. Buber, *Between Man and Man*, trans. R. Gregor Smith (London: Fontana, 1961),
117–18.
[24]A. J. Heschel, *Who Is Man?* (Stanford, Calif.: Stanford University Press, 1965), 97.
[25]A. McFadyen, *Bound to Sin: Abuse, Holocaust and the Christian Doctrine of Sin* (Cambridge: Cambridge University Press, 2000), 220.
[26]Quoted in D. B. Forrester, *On Human Worth* (London: SCM Press, 2001), 144.

Your freedom and mine cannot be separated.
   Nelson Mandela[27]

∾∾∾∾∾

One section of the community cannot be truly free while another is
denied a share in that freedom.
   Desmond Tutu[28]

∾∾∾∾∾

When apologists for market freedom complain that measures taken
in the name of equality restrict individual liberty they do not say
whose liberty they are talking about. It is probable that they are not
thinking about the liberty of shanty-town dwellers.
   Timothy Gorringe[29]

∾∾∾∾∾

What appears as globalization for some means localization for others; signalling a new freedom for some, upon many others it
descends as an uninvited and cruel fate. Mobility climbs to the rank
of the uppermost among coveted values—and the freedom to
move . . . fast becomes the main stratifying factor of our late-modern
or postmodern times.
   Zigmunt Bauman[30]

∾∾∾∾∾

Those of us who have to live on the side of the perpetrators, not on
the side of the victims, perceive another dimension of the history of
freedom. In this dimension freedom is not liberation from poverty,
suffering and death; it is liberation from historical guilt and its consequences, which are the urge for justification and the compulsion
towards repetition.
   Jürgen Moltmann[31]

---

[27]Quoted in M. Benson, *Nelson Mandela* (Harmondsworth: Penguin, 1986), 237. Mandela, addressing the people, is explaining why he rejected President Botha's offer to
release him, subject to the condition of dissociating himself from the policies of the
ANC.
[28]Quoted in J. de Gruchy, *Cry Justice!* (London: Collins, 1986), 190.
[29]T. J. Gorringe, *Capitalism and the Kingdom* (New York: Orbis/London: SPCK, 1994),
53.
[30]Z. Bauman, *Globalization: The Human Consequences* (New York: Columbia University
Press, 1998), 2.
[31]J. Moltmann, *Experiences in Theology*, trans. M. Kohl (London: SCM Press, 2000),
241.

❧❧❧❧❧

Gratuitous, beyond our fathom, both binding and freeing,
this love re-invades us, shifts the boundaries of our being.
  Micheal O'Siadhail[32]

❧❧❧❧❧

[The Christian] ought to think: "Although I am an unworthy and
condemned man, my God has given me in Christ all the riches of
righteousness and salvation without any merit on my part, out of
pure, free mercy, so that from now on I need nothing except faith
which believes that this is true. Why should I not therefore freely,
joyfully, with all my heart, and with an eager will do all things which
I know are pleasing and acceptable to such a Father who has over-
whelmed me with his inestimable riches? I will therefore give myself
as a Christ to my neighbor, just as Christ offered himself to me; I
will do nothing in this life except what I see is necessary, profitable,
and salutary to my neighbor, since through faith I have an abun-
dance of all good things in Christ."
  Martin Luther[33]

---

[32]From the love sonnet "Out of the Blue," in M. O'Siadhail, *Poems 1975–1995* (Newcastle upon Tyne: Bloodaxe, 1999), 124.
[33]M. Luther, *Christian Liberty*, ed. H. J. Grimm (Philadelphia: Fortress, 1957), 30.

Index of Authors